Teach Yourself
VISUALLY™
Word 2010

Visual

by Elaine Marmel

WILEY

Wiley Publishing, Inc.

Teach Yourself VISUALLY™ Word 2010

Published by
Wiley Publishing, Inc.
10475 Crosspoint Boulevard
Indianapolis, IN 46256
www.wiley.com

Published simultaneously in Canada

Library of Congress Control Number: 2010922561

ISBN: 978-0-470-56680-0

Manufactured in the United States of America

10 9 8 7 6 5 4

Trademark Acknowledgments

Disclaimer

In order to get this information to you in a timely manner, this book was based on a pre-release version of Microsoft Office 2010. There may be some minor changes between the screenshots in this book and what you see on your desktop. As always, Microsoft has the final word on how programs look and function; if you have any questions or see any discrepancies, consult the online help for further information about the software.

Contact Us

For general information on our other products and services please contact our Customer Care Department within the U.S. at 877-762-2974, outside the U.S. at 317-572-3993 or fax 317-572-4002.

For technical support please visit www.wiley.com/techsupport.

Wiley Publishing, Inc.

Sales

Contact Wiley
at (877) 762-2974 or
fax (317) 572-4002.

Credits

Executive Editor
Jody Lefevere

Project Editor
Jade L. Williams

Technical Editor
Vince Averello

Copy Editor
Kim Heusel

Editorial Director
Robyn Siesky

Editorial Manager
Cricket Krengel

Business Manager
Amy Knies

Senior Marketing Manager
Sandy Smith

Vice President and Executive Group Publisher
Richard Swadley

Vice President and Executive Publisher
Barry Pruett

Project Coordinator
Sheree Montgomery

Graphics and Production Specialists
Jennifer Henry
Andrea Hornberger
Jennifer Mayberry

Quality Control Technician
Jessica Kramer

Proofreading and Indexing
Cindy Ballew
Potomac Indexing, LLC

Screen Artist
Jill A. Proll
Ronald Terry

Illustrators
Ronda David-Burroughs
Cheryl Grubbs
Mark Pinto

About the Author

Elaine Marmel is President of Marmel Enterprises, LLC, an organization which specializes in technical writing and software training. Elaine spends most of her time writing; she has authored and coauthored over 50 books about *Microsoft Project, Microsoft Excel, QuickBooks, Peachtree, Quicken for Windows, Quicken for DOS, Microsoft Word for Windows, Microsoft Word for the Mac, Windows 98, 1-2-3 for Windows,* and *Lotus Notes.* From 1994 to 2006, she also was the contributing editor to monthly publications *Peachtree Extra* and *QuickBooks Extra.*

Elaine left her native Chicago for the warmer climes of Arizona (by way of Cincinnati, OH; Jerusalem, Israel; Ithaca, NY; Washington, D.C. and Tampa, FL) where she basks in the sun with her dog Josh, and her cats, Watson and Buddy.

Dedication

To Cato, a sweet and loyal friend for 17 years. You are sorely missed by all of us, little girl.

Author's Acknowledgments

A book is far more than the work of the author; many other people contribute. I'd like to thank Jody Lefevere for once again giving me this opportunity. Sarah Cisco, it is a pleasure to work with you and I hope you'll get in touch with me the next time you visit your sister. My thanks to Kim Heusel for making me look good and to Vince Averello for helping to ensure that this book is technically accurate. Finally, my thanks to the graphics and production teams who labor tirelessly behind the scenes to create the elegant appearance of this book.

How to Use This Book

Who This Book Is For

This book is for the reader who has never used this particular technology or software application. It is also for readers who want to expand their knowledge.

The Conventions in This Book

❶ Steps

This book uses a step-by-step format to guide you easily through each task. Numbered steps are actions you must do; bulleted steps clarify a point, step, or optional feature; and indented steps give you the result.

❷ Notes

Notes give additional information — special conditions that may occur during an operation, a situation that you want to avoid, or a cross reference to a related area of the book.

❸ Icons and Buttons

Icons and buttons show you exactly what you need to click to perform a step.

❹ Tips

Tips offer additional information, including warnings and shortcuts.

❺ Bold

Bold type shows command names, options, and text or numbers you must type.

❻ Italics

Italic type introduces and defines a new term.

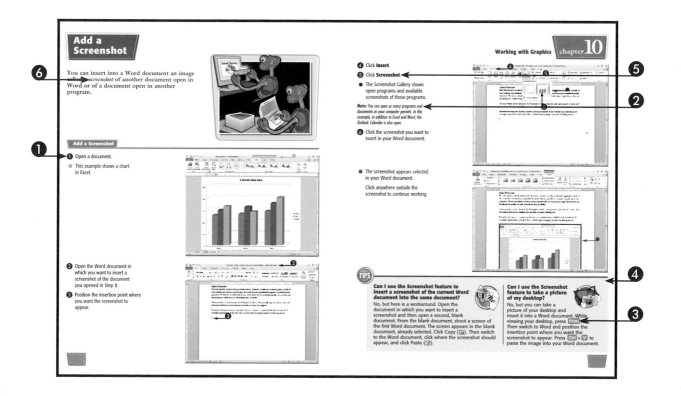

Table of Contents

chapter 3 Editing Text

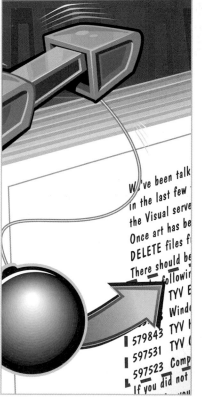

Table of Contents

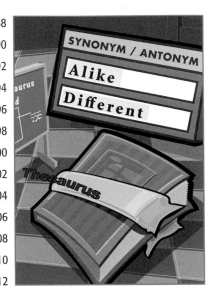

chapter 6 Formatting Paragraphs

Table of Contents

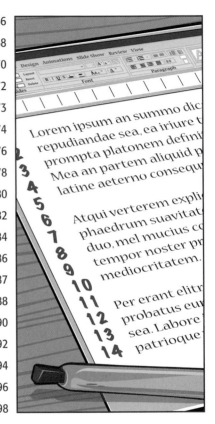

chapter 8   **Printing Documents**

chapter 9 Creating Tables and Charts

Table of Contents

chapter 11   Customizing Word

chapter 12   Work with Mass Mailing Tools

chapter 13   Using Word to Interact Over the Internet

CHAPTER 1

Getting Familiar with Word

Are you ready to get started in Word? In this first chapter, you become familiar with the Word working environment and you learn basic ways to navigate and to enter text.

You can open Microsoft Word a number of ways. This section demonstrates how to open Word from the All Programs menu. Once Word opens, a blank document, ready for you to type text, appears.

❶ Click **Start**.

❷ Click **All Programs**.

● All Programs changes to Back once you click it.

❸ Click **Microsoft Office**.

❹ Click **Microsoft Word 2010**.

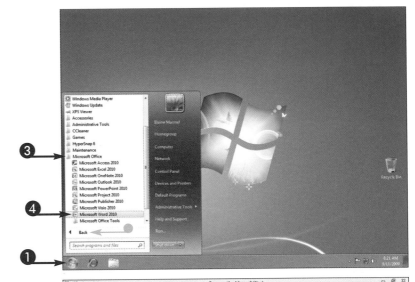

● A blank document appears in the Word window.

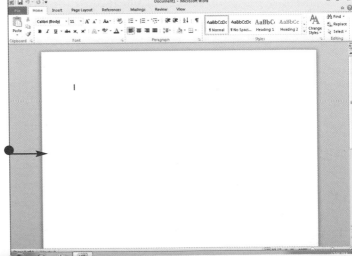

Explore the Word Window

The Word window contains tools you can use to work quickly and efficiently while you create documents.

Title Bar

Shows the program and document titles.

Document Area

The area where you type. The flashing vertical bar, called the *insertion point,* represents the location where text will appear when you type.

Scroll Bar

Enables you to reposition the document window vertically. Drag the scroll box within the scroll bar or click the scroll bar arrows (and).

Dialog Box Launcher

Appears in the lower-right corner of many groups on the Ribbon. Clicking this button opens a dialog box or task pane that provides more options.

Quick Access Toolbar (QAT)

Contains buttons that perform common actions: saving a document, undoing your last action, or repeating your last action. To customize the QAT, see Chapter 11.

Status Bar

Displays document information as well as the insertion point location. From left to right, this bar contains the number of the page on which the insertion point currently appears, the total number of pages and words in the document, the proofing errors button ( ), the macro recording status button, the View buttons, and the Zoom Slider. To customize the Status Bar, see Chapter 11.

Ribbon

Contains commands organized in three components: tabs, groups, and commands. **Tabs** represent common actions you take in Word. They appear across the top of the Ribbon and contain groups of related commands. **Groups** organize related commands with each group name appearing below the group on the Ribbon. **Commands** appear within each group. To customize the Ribbon, see Chapter 11.

Work with Backstage View

Clicking the File tab opens Backstage view, which resembles a menu. In Backstage view, you find a list of actions — commands — you can use to manage files and program options. For example, from Backstage view you can open, save, print, remove sensitive information, and distribute documents as well as set Word program behavior options.

① Click the **File** tab.

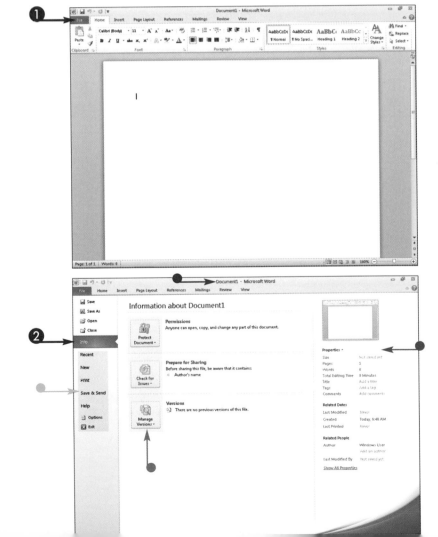

● In the Backstage view, commonly used file and program management commands appear here.

② Click Info.

● The title of the open document appears here.

● Information about the currently open document appears here.

● Buttons appear that you can click.

❸ Click an option in the left column; this example shows the results of clicking Save & Send, which contains commands that help you share Word documents.

● As you click a button in the Save & Send column, the information shown to the right changes.

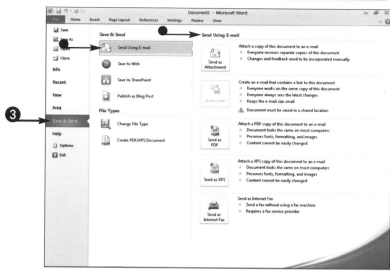

❹ Repeat Step **3** until you find the command you want to use; this example shows the results of clicking **Recent**, which displays up to the last 20 documents opened, plus folders you have recently opened. You can select a document or a folder to open it; see Chapter 2.

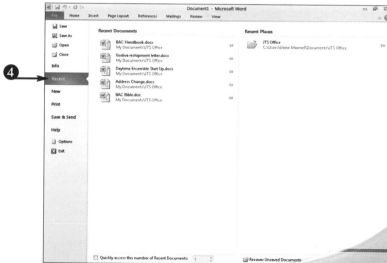

TIP

Is there a way to return to working in Word without making any selections in Backstage view?
Yes. You can click the File button or press the Esc key on the keyboard. Although you might be tempted to click Exit, resist the temptation, because clicking Exit closes Word completely.

Select Commands with the Keyboard

To keep your hands on the keyboard and work efficiently, you can use your keyboard to select commands from the Ribbon or the Quick Access Toolbar.

Select Commands with the Keyboard

① If appropriate for the command you intend to use, place the insertion point in the proper word or paragraph.

② Press **Alt** on the keyboard.

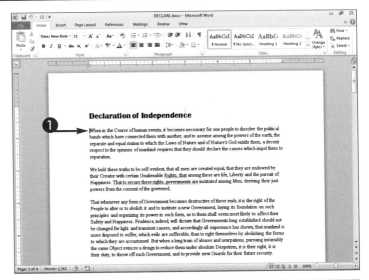

● Shortcut letters and numbers appear on the Ribbon.

Note: *The numbers control commands on the Quick Access Toolbar.*

③ Press a letter to select a tab on the Ribbon.

This example uses **P**.

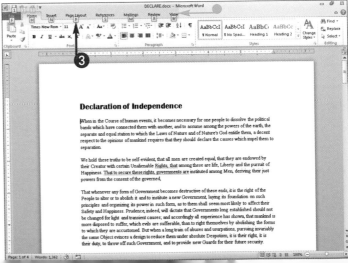

- Word displays the appropriate tab and letters for each command on that tab.

4 Press a letter or letters to select a command.

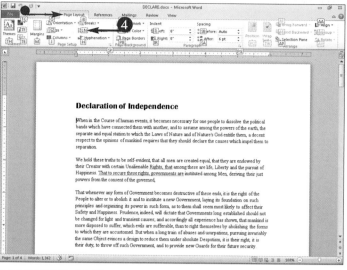

- Word displays options for the command you selected.

5 Press a letter or use the arrow keys on the keyboard to select an option.

Word performs the command you selected, applying the option you chose.

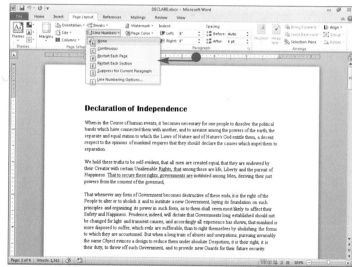

TIPS

Is there a way to toggle between the document and the Ribbon using the keyboard?

Yes. Each time you press F6, Word changes focus of the program, switching between the document, the Status bar, and the Ribbon.

What should I do if I accidentally press the wrong key?

You can press Esc to back up to your preceding action. For example, if you complete Steps **1** to **3** and, in Step **3**, you press S when you meant to press W, press Esc to redisplay the letters associated with tabs and then press W.

Select Commands with the Mouse

You can use the mouse to navigate the Ribbon or select a command from the Quick Access Toolbar (QAT) at the top of the window. The Ribbon organizes tasks using tabs. On any particular tab, you find groups of commands related to that task.

The QAT appears on the left side of the title bar, immediately above the File and Home tabs and contains three commonly used commands: Save, Undo, and Redo. Click a button to perform that command. To customize the QAT, see Chapter 11.

Select Commands with the Mouse

① Click the tab containing the command you want to use.

② Click in the text or paragraph you want to modify.

③ Point to the command you want to use.

● Word displays a ScreenTip describing the function of the button at which the mouse points.

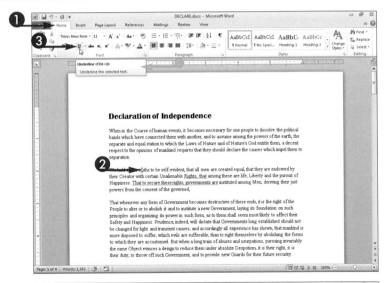

④ Click the command.

● Word performs the command you selected.

Work with the Mini Toolbar

You can use the Mini toolbar to format text without switching to the Home tab. The Mini toolbar contains a combination of commands available primarily in the Font group and the Paragraph group on the Home tab.

Work with the Mini Toolbar

① Select text.

● The Mini toolbar appears transparently in the background.

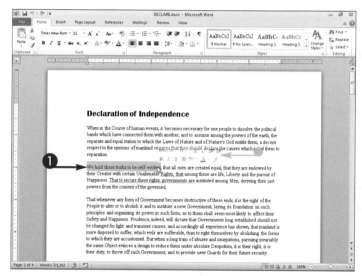

② Position the mouse pointer close to or over the Mini toolbar.

● The Mini toolbar appears solidly.

③ Click any command or button.

Word performs the actions associated with the command or button.

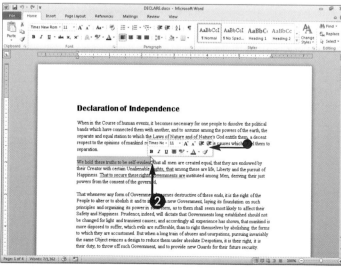

Work with Context Menus

You can use context menus to format text without switching to the Home tab. The context menu contains the Mini toolbar and a combination of commands available primarily in the Font group and the Paragraph group on the Home tab.

Work with Context Menus

1 Select text.

● The Mini toolbar appears in the background.

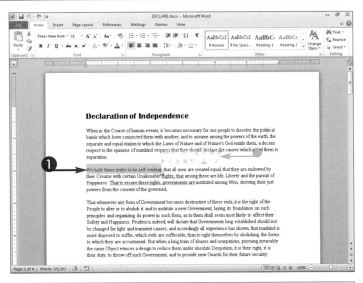

2 Right-click the selected text.

● The context menu appears along with the Mini toolbar.

Note: *You can right-click anywhere, not just on selected text, to display the Mini Toolbar and the context menu.*

3 Click any command or button.

Word performs the actions associated with the command or button.

Launch a Dialog Box

Although the Ribbon contains most of the commands you use on a regular basis, you still need dialog boxes occasionally to select a command or refine a choice.

Launch a Dialog Box

① Position the mouse pointer over a Dialog Box launcher button (📭).

● Word displays a ScreenTip that describes what will happen when you click.

This example uses the Paragraph dialog box.

② Click 📭.

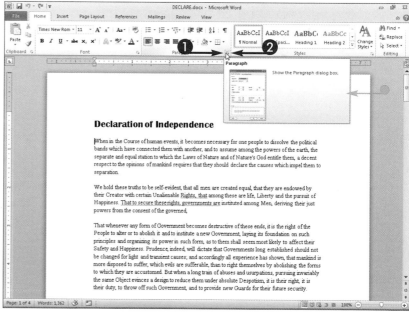

● The Paragraph dialog box appears.

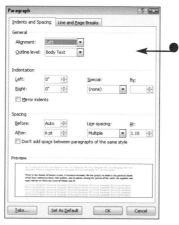

Work with Commands

You can use the galleries Word often provides to view the choices for a particular command.

In many cases, Word 2010 previews the effects of a command choice before you select it. Think of this behavior as an opportunity to try before you buy.

Work with Galleries

1 In galleries containing the More button (⊽), click 🔼 and 🔽 to scroll through command choices.

2 Click ⊽ to open the gallery and view additional choices.

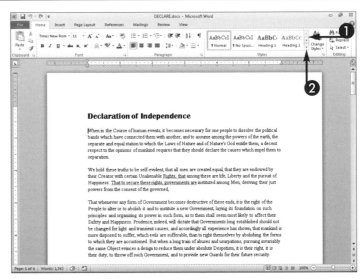

● Word hides ⊽ to display the gallery.

3 Scroll over choices to see a live preview.

4 Click a choice from the gallery to apply it.

To close the gallery without choosing a command, click anywhere outside the gallery.

Watch a Live Preview

① Click in the word or paragraph you want to modify.

② Click the tab containing the command you are considering performing.

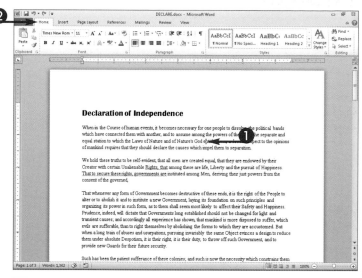

③ Position the mouse pointer above the choice you are considering applying.

● Word displays the effects of the choice without performing the command.

In this example, the paragraph containing the insertion point appears in the Heading 1 style.

You can click to select your choice.

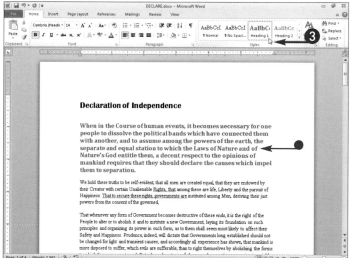

TIP

What do the small down arrows below or beside buttons mean?

When you see a small list box arrow (⬟) on a button, there are several choices available for the button. If you click the button directly, Word applies a default choice. However, if you click ⬟, Word displays additional options as either lists or galleries. As you move the mouse pointer over the two parts of the button, Word highlights one or the other to alert you that you have more choices.

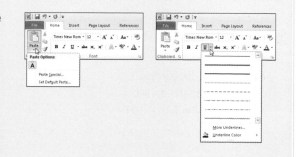

Enter Text

Word makes typing easy: you do not need to press Enter to start a new line. Word calculates when a new line should begin and automatically starts it for you.

To add more than one space between words, use the Tab key instead of the spacebar. See Chapter 6 for details on setting tabs.

Type Text

1 Type the text that you want to appear in your document.

● The text appears to the left of the insertion point as you type.

● As the insertion point reaches the end of the line, Word automatically starts a new one.

Press **Enter** only to start a new paragraph.

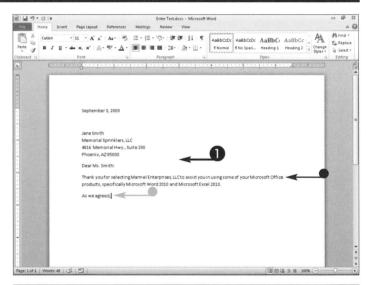

Separate Information

1 Type a word or phrase.

2 Press **Tab**.

To align text properly, you press **Tab** to include more than one space between words.

Several spaces appear between the last letter you typed and the insertion point.

3 Type another word or phrase.

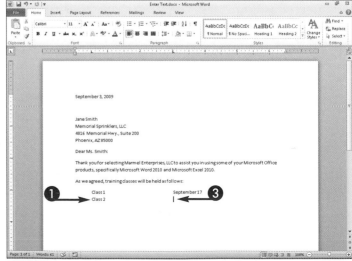

Enter Text Automatically

1 Begin typing a common word, phrase, or date.

The AutoComplete feature suggests common words and phrases based on what you type.

● Word suggests the rest of the word, phrase, or month.

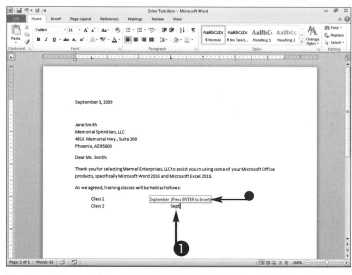

● You can press **Enter** to let Word finish typing the word, phrase, or month for you.

You can keep typing to ignore Word's suggestion.

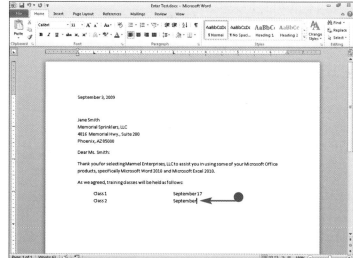

TIP

Why should I use **Tab** instead of **Spacebar** to include more than one space between words?

Typically, when you include more than one space between words or phrases, you do so to align text in a columnar fashion. Most fonts are proportional, meaning each character of a font takes up a different amount of space on a line. Therefore, you cannot calculate the number of spaces needed to align words beneath each other. Tabs, however, are set at specific locations on a line, such as 3 inches. When you press **Tab**, you know exactly where words or phrases appear on a line. Word sets default tabs every .5 inches. To avoid pressing **Tab** multiple times to separate text, change the tab settings. See Chapter 6 for details.

Move Around in a Document

You can use many techniques to move to a different location in a document; the technique you select depends on the location to which you want to move.

Move One Character

1 Note the location of the insertion point.

2 Press ➡.

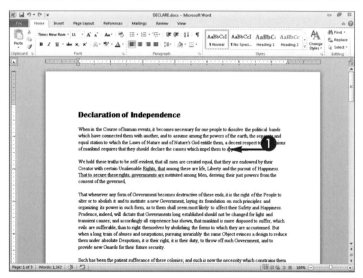

● Word moves the insertion point one character to the right.

You can press ⬅, ⬆, or ⬇ to move the insertion point one character left, up, or down.

Holding any arrow key moves the insertion point repeatedly in the direction of the arrow key.

You can press Ctrl + ➡ or Ctrl + ⬅ to move the insertion point one word at a time to the right or left.

Move One Screen

1 Note the last visible line on-screen.

2 Press `Page down`.

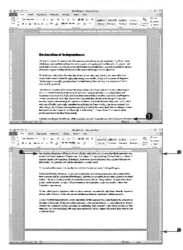

● Word moves the insertion point down one screen.

You can press `Page up` to move the insertion point up one screen.

● You can click ▧ to scroll up or ▨ to scroll down one line at a time in a document.

TIPS

How do I quickly move the insertion point to the beginning or the end of a document?

Press `Ctrl` + `Home` to move the insertion point to the beginning of a document or `Ctrl` + `End` to move the insertion point to the bottom of a document. You can press `Shift` + `F5` to move the insertion point to the last place you changed in your document.

Is there a way to move the insertion point to a specific location?

Yes. You can use bookmarks to mark a particular place and then return to it. See Chapter 3 for details on creating a bookmark and returning to the bookmark's location. See Chapter 4 for details on searching for a specific word and, if necessary, replacing that word with a different one.

Get Help

You can search for help with the Word tasks you perform. By default, Word searches the Help file on your computer as well as the Internet.

① Click the **Help** button (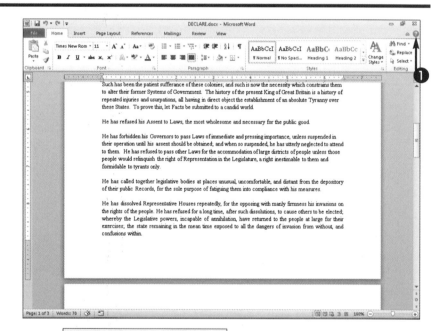).

The Word Help window appears.

② Type a word or phrase related to the help topic you want to view.

③ Click **Search** or press Enter.

● Help topics related to the word or phrase you typed appear in the task pane.

④ Click the topic most closely related to the subject on which you want help.

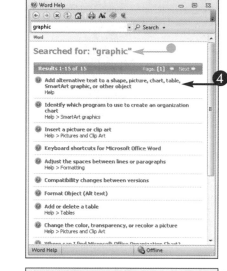

● The help topic information appears in the Word Help window.

⑤ To close the Help window, click .

The Word window reappears.

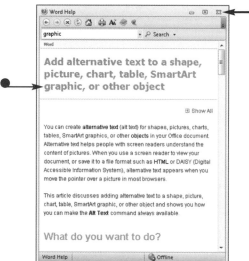

TIPS

Can I leave the Word Help window open while I work in Word?

Yes. Simply do not perform Step **5**. By default, the Word Help window remains on top of the Word window. You can move the Word Help window by dragging its title bar. You can resize the window by positioning the mouse pointer over any edge of the window; when the mouse pointer changes to a two-headed arrow, drag in to make the window smaller and out to make the window larger.

I want to keep the Help window open, but not in front of the Word window. Is there a way to make it drop down to the Windows task bar?

Yes. Click the **pushpin** button ( ). When you subsequently click in the Word window, Word Help drops down to the Windows task bar. You can redisplay Word Help by clicking its task bar button.

Managing Documents

Now that you know the basics, it is time to discover how to navigate among Word documents efficiently. In this chapter, you learn how to manage the Word documents you create.

Save a Document

You can save a document so that you can use it at another time in Microsoft Word. Word 2010 uses the same XML-based file format that Word 2007 uses, reducing the size of a Word document, and improving the likelihood of recovering information from a corrupt file.

After you save a document for the first time, you can click the Save icon on the Quick Access Toolbar (QAT) to save it again.

Save a Document

- Before you save a document, Word displays a generic name in the title bar.

1 Click the **File** tab.

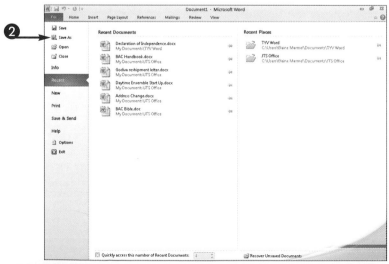

The Backstage view appears.

2 Click **Save As**.

The Save As dialog box appears.

③ Type a name for the document here.

● You can click here to select a location on your computer in which to save the document.

● You can click the **New Folder** button to create a new folder in which to store the document.

④ Click **Save**.

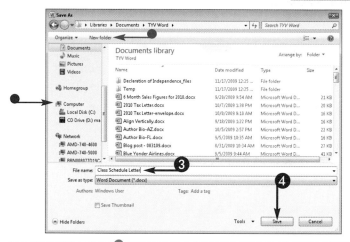

● Word saves the document and displays the name you supplied in the title bar.

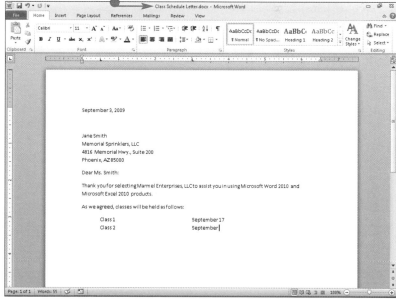

Will my associate, who uses Word 2003, be able to open a document I save in Word 2010?

To make it easier for your associate, you can create the document in Word 2010 but save it in Word 2003 format. See the section "Save a Document to Word 97-2003 Format" for more information.

How can I tell if I am working on a document saved in Word 2010 as opposed to one saved in Word 2003?

Word 2010 uses the file name extension .docx to designate its file format, while the file name extension for a Word 2003 document is .doc. If you set your computer's folder options to display extensions of known file types, the full file name of the document appears in the title bar of the program. If you do not display extensions for known file types, a document created in Word 2003 name with appear in the program title bar.

Reopen an Unsaved Document

You can open documents you created within the last seven days but did not save because, as you work, Word automatically saves your document even if you take no action to save it.

Reopen an Unsaved Document

1 Click the **File** tab.

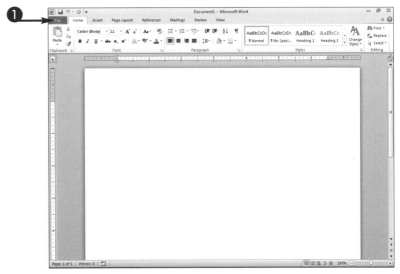

The Backstage view appears.

2 Click **Info.**

3 Click **Manage Versions.**

4 Click **Recover Draft Versions.**

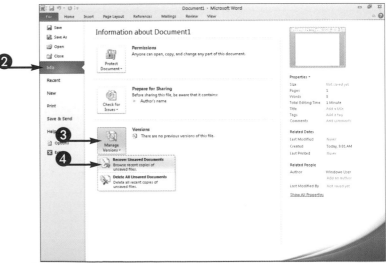

The Open dialog box appears, showing you available draft files that were auto-saved by Word but not saved as documents by you.

⑤ Click the unsaved file you want to open.

⑥ Click **Open.**

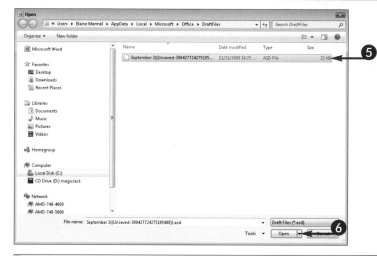

The draft version appears on-screen as a read-only file to which you cannot save changes.

● This gold bar identifies the number of days before Word automatically deletes the file.

⑦ Click **Save As** to save the file as a Word document and work with it.

Note: See the section "Save a Document" for details.

After you save the document, the gold bar disappears.

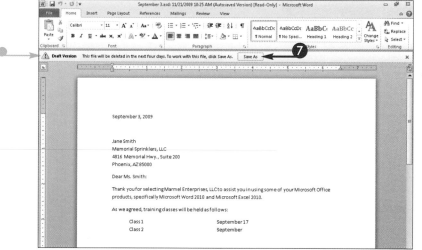

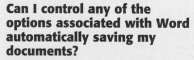

Is it possible to open documents that I closed without saving?

Yes, if you open them fairly soon after closing without saving. These documents appear in the Recent Documents list and remain there until you open 20 other documents. You can compare the unsaved version with the saved version or replace the saved version with the unsaved version. See the section "Open a Document" for details on using the Recent Documents list. See Chapter 4 for details on combining versions of a document.

Can I control any of the options associated with Word automatically saving my documents?

Yes. You can specify how often Word automatically saves your document and where Word stores the files it uses to help you recover lost work. You also can control some other settings associated with saving documents; see the section "Set Options for Saving Documents" later in this chapter for details.

Save a Document to Word 97-2003 Format

You can save documents you create in Microsoft Word in a variety of other formats, such as Word templates, Microsoft Works files, text files, or Word 97-2003 format to share them with people who do not use Microsoft Word 2010.

Although the steps in this section focus on saving a document to Word 97-2003 format, you can use these steps to save a document to any file format Word supports.

Save a Document to Word 97-2003 Format

1 Click the **File** tab.

The Backstage view appears.

2 Click **Save As**.

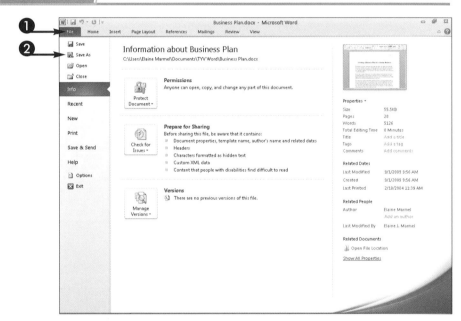

The Save As dialog box appears.

3 Type a name for the document.

4 Click here to display the formats available for the document and click **Word 97-2003 Document (*.doc)**.

5 Click **Save**.

Word saves the document in the format that you select.

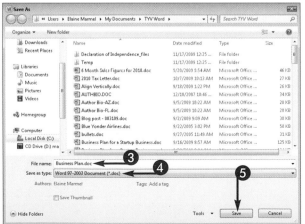

You can save Word documents in PDF or XPS formats. Anyone using Adobe Corporation's free Adobe Reader can open a PDF file. XPS is Microsoft's alternative to a PDF file.

Windows Vista and Windows 7 come with an XPS viewer; users of other versions of Windows can view XPS documents using Internet Explorer 7 or higher.

Save a Document in PDF or XPS Format

1 Click the **File** tab.

The Backstage view appears.

2 Click **Save As**.

The Save As dialog box appears.

3 Click here to type a name for your document.

4 Click here to select either **PDF (*.pdf)** or **XPS Document (*.xps)**.

Note: If you choose XPS format, you can opt to save and then open the document.

5 Click **Save**.

Word saves the document in the selected format.

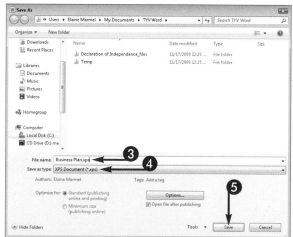

Set Options for Saving Documents

You can set a variety of options for saving documents, like whether Word creates a backup copy of your document and the location Word suggests when you save your documents.

Choose a save option ...

Option 1

Option 3

Option 2

Set File Saving Options

1 Click the **File** tab.

The Backstage view appears.

2 Click **Options**.

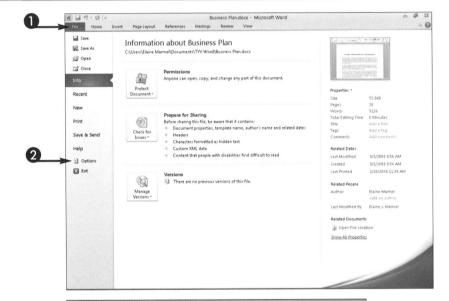

The Word Options dialog box appears.

3 Click **Save**.

● Select the Save AutoRecover information every option (☐ changes to ☑) and specify an interval for saving recovery information.

● You can select the Keep the last AutoRecovered file if I close without saving option (☐ changes to ☑) to make sure Word saves unsaved documents.

4 Click **OK** to save your changes.

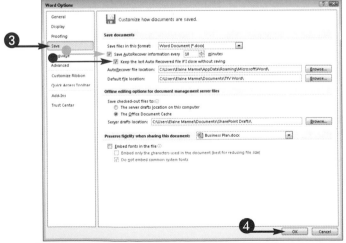

Set File Saving Locations

① Complete Steps **1** to **3** in the subsection "Set File Saving Options" on the preceding page.

② Click **Browse** next to Default file location.

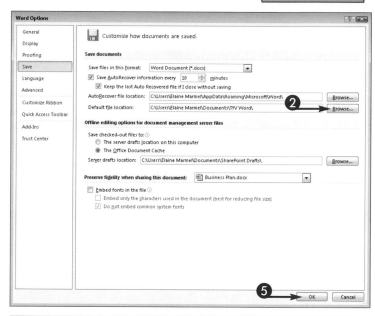

The Modify Location dialog box appears.

③ Click here to navigate to the folder where you want to save Word documents.

④ Click **OK** to redisplay the Word Options dialog box.

You can repeat Steps **3** and **4** to set the AutoRecover File and the Server drafts locations.

⑤ Click **OK** to save your changes.

Word saves your changes.

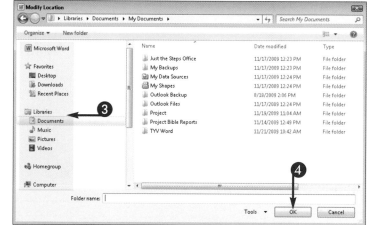

Can I make Word automatically save a backup copy of my document?

Yes. Follow these steps:

① Complete Steps **1** and **2** in the subsection "Set File Saving Options" on the previous page.

② Click **Advanced** and scroll down to the Save section.

③ Select the **Always create backup copy** option.

④ Click **OK**.

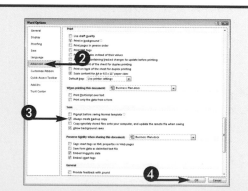

Open a Word Document

You can display documents you previously saved on-screen. When you open a document, you can make changes to it.

Open a Word Document

1 Click the **File** tab.

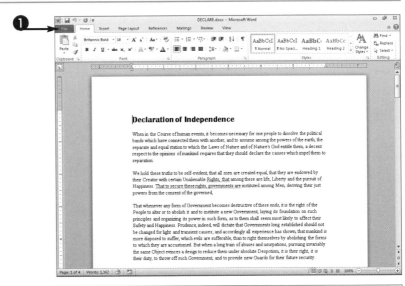

The Backstage view appears.

2 Click **Open**.

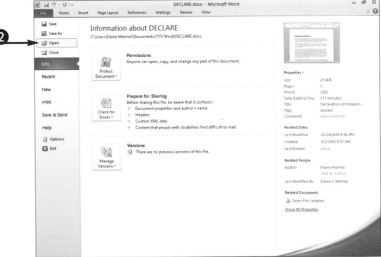

The Open dialog box appears.

③ Click here to navigate to the folder containing the document you want to open.

● Documents in a folder appear here.

④ Click the document you want to open.

⑤ Click **Open**.

The document appears on-screen.

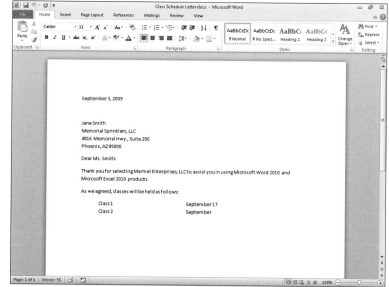

Are there other ways to open a document?
Yes. By default, the 25 most recently opened documents appear in Backstage view. You can click any of these documents to open them.

① Click the **File** tab to display Backstage view.

② Click **Recent**.

③ Click a document to open it.

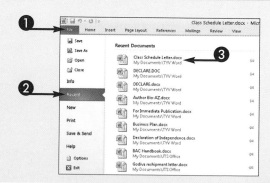

Open a Document of Another Format

You can open documents created by colleagues using several other word-processing programs besides Word.

1 Click the **File** tab.

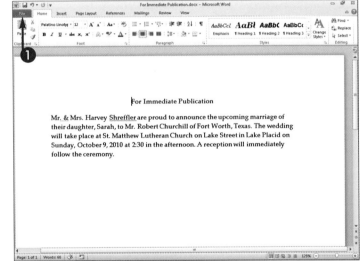

The Backstage view appears.

2 Click **Open**.

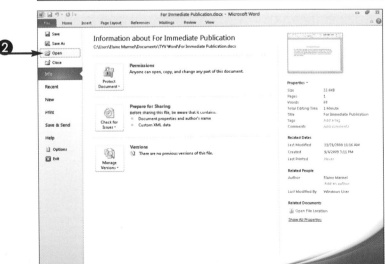

The Open dialog box appears.

③ Click here to navigate to the folder containing the document you want to open.

● Documents in a folder appear here.

④ Click here to select the type of document you want to open.

⑤ Click the file you want to open.

⑥ Click **Open**.

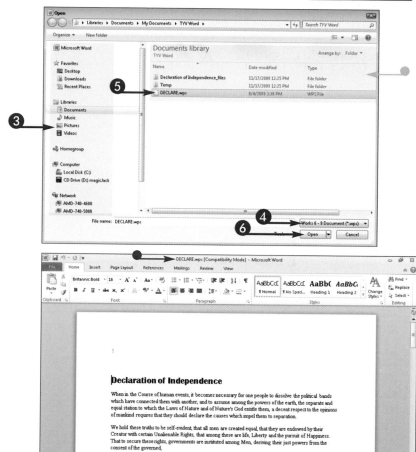

Note: *You may be prompted to install a converter to open the file; click **Yes** or **OK** to install the converter and open the file.*

● Word opens the file in Compatibility Mode.

TIP

How do I open a backup copy?
① Follow Steps **1** to **3** in this section.
② Click here and click **All Files**.
③ Select the document. "Backup of" precedes the original document file name. The document's extension is .wbk.
④ Click **Open**.

Start a New Document

Although a new, blank document appears when Word opens, you do not need to close and reopen Word to start a new, blank document.

You can use a variety of templates — documents containing predefined settings that save you the effort of creating the settings yourself — as the foundation for your documents.

Start a New Document

1 Click the **File** tab.

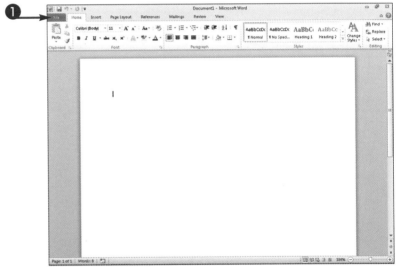

The Backstage view appears.

2 Click **New**.

● Templates available on your computer appear here.

● Templates available online appear here.

3 Click an available type of template.

④ Select a template to use for your document.

● A preview of the template appears here.

⑤ Click **Create**.

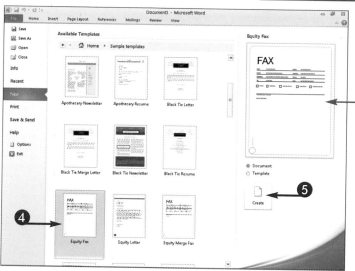

The new document appears.

You can edit this document any way you choose.

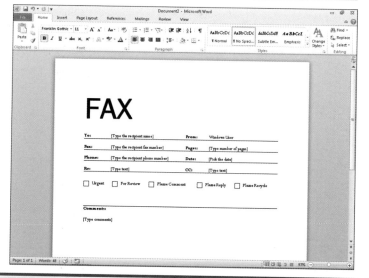

TIP

What is a template?

A template provides a foundation for a Word document. All documents are built on some template; blank documents are built on the Normal template. Using templates, your company can create documents with consistent appearances because templates contain a specific set of fonts and styles and use the same formatting. Some Word templates, like the FAX cover sheets or the forms, also contain text that helps you quickly and easily create a document. Many of the available templates come from the Office Online Web site; when you select one, you download it.

Switch Between Open Documents

If you have two or more documents open, you can switch between them from within Word or by using the Windows taskbar.

If buttons representing each open document do not appear on the Windows taskbar, you can set options to display them.

Switch Documents Using Word

1 Click the **View** tab.

2 Click **Switch Windows**.

● A list of all open documents appears at the bottom of the menu.

3 Click the document you want to view.

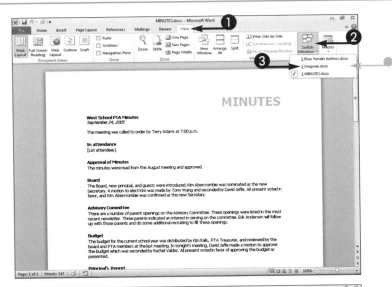

The selected document appears.

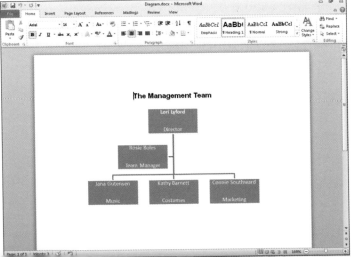

Switch Documents Using the Windows Taskbar

① Open all the documents you need.

Note: To open a document, see the section "Open Documents."

② Click the Word button in the Windows taskbar.

● An entry appears for each open document.

● You can point at an entry and click the red X (⊠) to close the document.

③ To view a document, click its taskbar button or its name in the list.

The document appears.

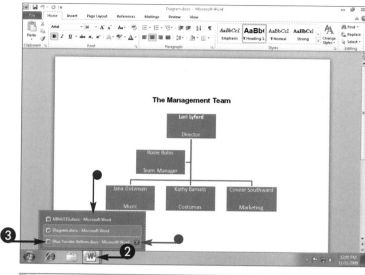

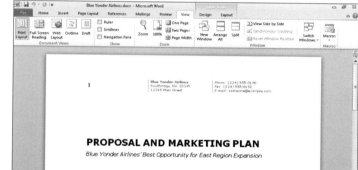

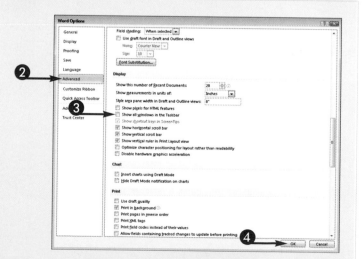

How do I deselect the feature that enables a button to appear in the Windows taskbar?

Follow these steps to turn the feature off:

① Open the Word Options dialog box.

Note: See the section "Set Options for Saving Documents" to open this dialog box.

② Click **Advanced**.

③ In the Display section, select the **Show all windows in the Taskbar** option (☑ changes to ☐).

④ Click **OK**.

Compare Documents Side By Side

You can view two open documents side by side to compare their similarities and differences.

Using the technique described in this section, you can scroll through both documents simultaneously.

Compare Documents Side By Side

Compare Documents

1 Open the two documents you want to compare.

Note: See the section "Open Documents" for details on opening a document.

2 Click the **View** tab.

3 Click **View Side by Side**.

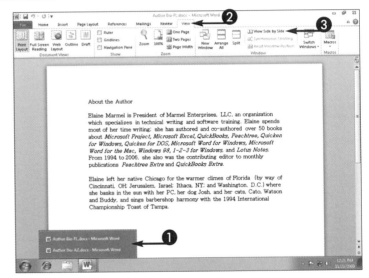

Word displays the documents in two panes beside each other.

4 Drag either documents' scroll bar.

Word scrolls both documents simultaneously.

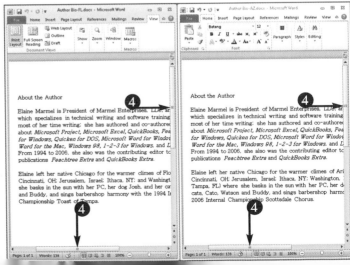

chapter 2

Stop Comparing Documents

5 Click **Window** in the document on the left.

Options drop down from the Window button.

6 Click **View Side by Side**.

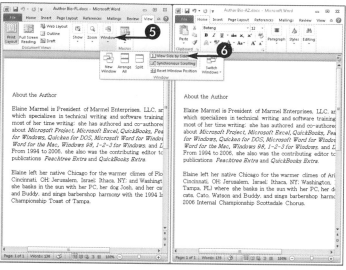

Word redisplays the document in a full screen.

● The second document is still open. You can see buttons for both documents in the Windows taskbar and you can click a button to switch to the other document.

Note: For more on this technique, see the section "Switch Between Open Documents" earlier in this chapter.

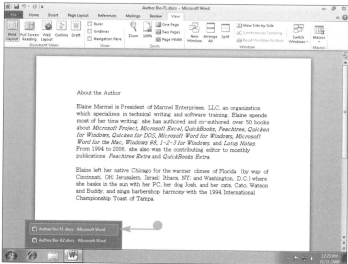

Is there a way to compare two documents with their differences highlighted?

Yes. You can compare different document versions to see their differences. See Chapter 4 for details.

What does the Reset Window Position button do?

You can use **Arrange All** to place one window above the other, each in its own separate pane. To return to side-by-side viewing, click **Reset Window Position**.

Work with Document Properties

You can supply information about a document that you can then use when you search for documents.

Windows XP users can search for files using document properties by downloading Windows Desktop Search from the Microsoft Web site. Windows Vista and Windows 7 users can use each operating system's built-in search engine.

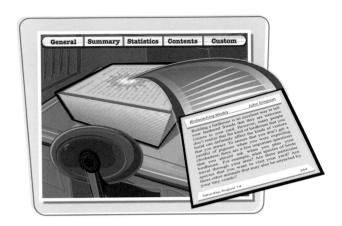

Work with Document Properties

1 Click the **File** tab.

The Backstage view appears.

2 Click **Info**.

● The Information panel appears.

3 Click **Properties**.

4 Click **Show Document Panel** to display the properties you can fill in above the document.

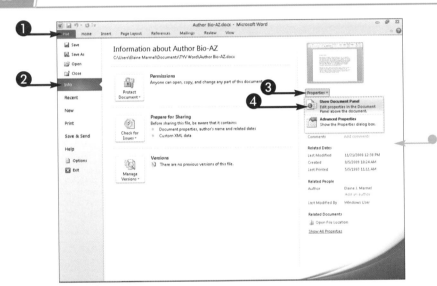

● The Document Properties panel appears above the document.

5 Click in a box and type information.

6 Repeat Step **5** as needed.

7 Click the **X** in the Document Properties panel to save your changes and return to editing the document.

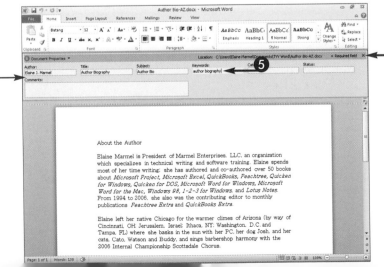

Close a Document

When you finish working with a document, you close it. If you made any changes that you did not save, Word prompts you to save them before closing the document.

Close a Document

① Click the **File** tab.

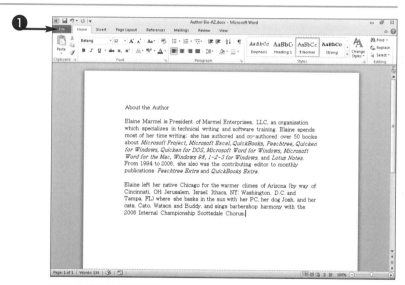

The Backstage view appears.

② Click **Close.**

Word removes the document from your screen.

If you had other documents open, Word displays the last document you used; otherwise, you see a blank Word window.

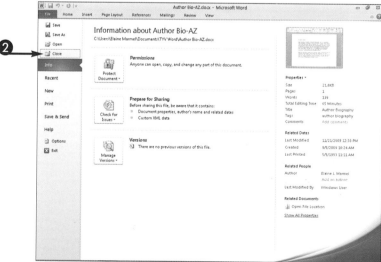

Inspect a Document Before Sharing

You can remove any personal information that Word stores in a document. You may want to remove this information before you share a document with anyone.

Inspect a Document Before Sharing

1 Click the **File** tab.

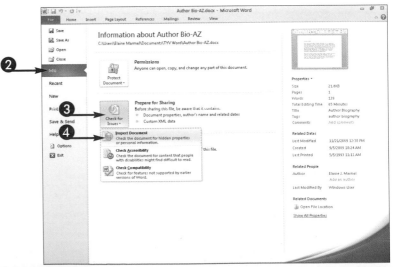

The Backstage view appears.

2 Click **Info**.

3 Click **Check for Issues**.

4 Click **Inspect Document**.

Note: If you have unsaved changes, Word prompts you to save the document, which you do by clicking **Yes**.

The Document Inspector window appears.

● You can click to deselect check marks to avoid inspecting for these elements.

5 Click **Inspect**.

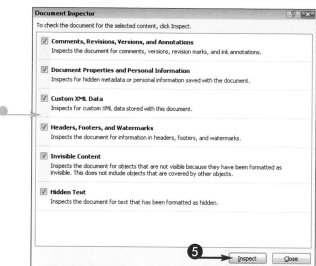

The Document Inspector looks for the information you specified and displays the results.

● You can remove any identified information by clicking **Remove All** beside that element.

● You can click **Reinspect** after removing identifying information.

6 Click **Close**.

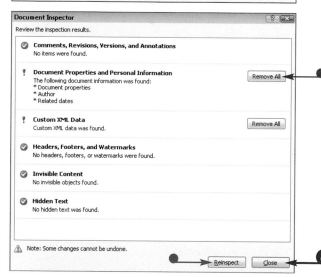

TIPS

Can I review the information that the Document Inspector displays before I remove it?

No. The only way to review the information before you remove it is to close the Document Inspector *without* removing information, use the appropriate Word features to review the information, and then rerun the Document Inspector as described in this section.

What happens if I remove information and then decide that I really want that information?

You cannot undo the effects of removing the information using the Document Inspector. However, to restore removed information, you can close the document *without* saving changes and then reopen it.

Work with Protected Documents

You can limit the changes others can make to a document by protecting it with a password. Word offers two kinds of protection: Password and User Authentication. User authentication, not shown in this section, relies on Windows authentication.

You can limit the styles available to format the document, the kinds of changes users can make, and the users who can make changes.

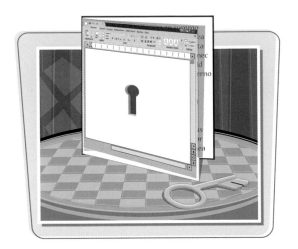

Work with Protected Documents

1 Click the **Review** tab.

2 Click **Restrict Editing**.

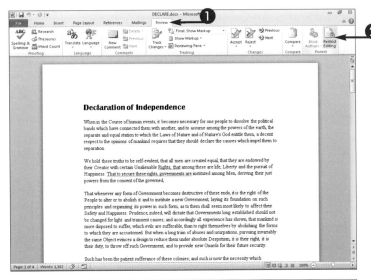

The Restrict Formatting and Editing pane appears.

3 Select this option to limit document formatting to the styles you select (☐ changes to ☑).

4 Click the **Settings** link.

The Formatting Restrictions dialog box appears.

5 Select the styles you want unavailable (☑ changes to ☐).

6 Click **OK**.

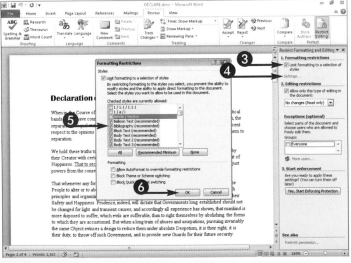

7 Select this option to specify editing restrictions (☐ changes to ☑).

8 Click here and select the type of editing to permit.

You can select parts of the document to make them available for editing.

9 Click here to identify users who are allowed to edit the selected parts of the document (☐ changes to ☑).

10 Click **Yes, Start Enforcing Protection**.

The Start Enforcing Protection dialog box appears.

11 Type a password.

12 Retype the password.

13 Click **OK**.

14 Click the **Save** button (🖫).

Word protects the document and saves the protection.

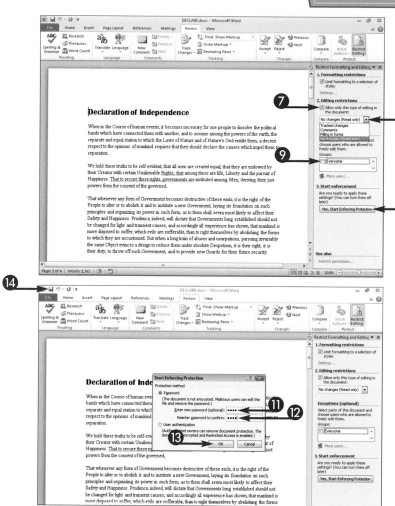

How do I open a protected document and work in it?

Open a protected document like you open any other document. Areas you can edit are highlighted. If you try to change an area that is not highlighted, a message appears in the status bar, explaining that you cannot make the modification because that area of the document is protected. Follow Steps **1** and **2** in this section to display the Protect Document pane and click **Show All Regions I Can Edit** to find areas you can change. To turn off protection, you need the protection password.

What happens when I click Restrict permission at the bottom of the Protect Document pane?

Word offers to install Windows Rights Management, a service that helps prevent documents and e-mail messages from being forwarded, edited, or copied unless authorized. You can click the **Learn more about this feature** link to get more information.

Mark a Document as Final

When you mark a document as final, Word makes the document read-only; you cannot make changes to it or inspect it.

Marking a document as final is not a security feature; instead, it is a feature that helps you focus on reading rather than editing because it makes editing unavailable.

Mark the Document

1 Click the **File** tab.

The Backstage view appears.

2 Click **Protect Document.**

3 Click **Mark As Final.**

A message explains that Word will mark the document as final and then saved.

4 Click **OK**.

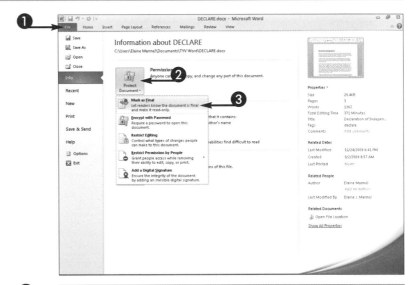

● Word saves the document and confirms that the document has been marked as final and editing commands are unavailable.

5 Click **OK**.

6 Click the **File** tab.

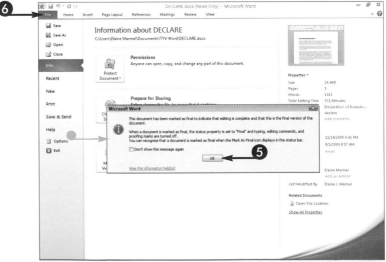

Editing a Final Document

- The document is now read-only and the Save button (🖫) on the QAT becomes unavailable.

- Word hides the Ribbon buttons because most editing commands are not available.

- This gold bar appears, indicating that the document has been marked as final.

- The Marked as Final button (🖺) appears in the status bar.

7 Click **Edit Anyway** in the red bar at the top of the document.

- Word no longer marks the document as read-only.

- Word redisplays and makes available all Ribbon buttons.

- 🖫 is available.

- 🖺 disappears from the Status Bar.

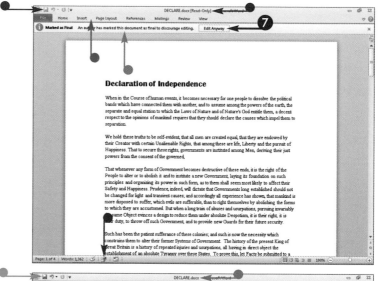

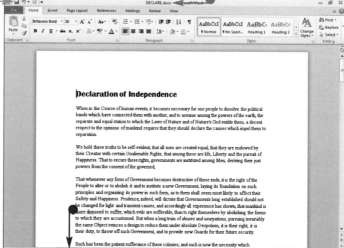

TIPS

Can any user remove the "Mark As Final" status from a document?

Yes. If you absolutely do not want others to edit or change your document, consider other security options. If you share a document without permitting changes, you can protect the document. You can also consider saving your document as a PDF or XPS document, which is discussed earlier in this chapter in the section "Save a Document in PDF or XPS format."

In the Backstage view, I noticed the Protect Document button? What does this do?

You can use this button to assign a password or add a digital signature to a document. If you assign a password, no one can open the document without the password. You use a digital signature to indicate that a document has not changed since you signed it.

Convert Word Documents from Prior Versions to Word 2010

You can convert existing Word 97-Word 2003 documents to the new format introduced by Word 2007. You also can convert Word 2007 to Word 2010 documents using the same approach.

1 Open any prior version Word document; this example uses a Word 2003 document.

Note: See the section "Open Documents" earlier in this chapter for details.

● In the title bar, Word indicates that the document is open in Compatibility Mode.

2 Click the **File** tab.

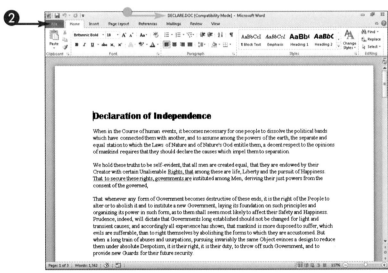

The Backstage view appears.

3 Click **Info**.

4 Click **Convert**.

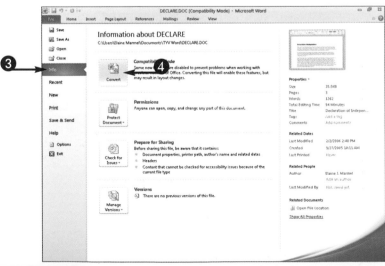

Word closes Backstage view and displays a message indicating it will convert the document to the newest file format.

● If you do not want to view this message in the future when you convert documents, select this option (□ changes to ☑).

⑤ Click **OK**.

● Word converts the document and removes the Compatibility Mode indicator from the title bar.

⑥ Click .

The Save As dialog box appears.

● Word suggests the same file name but the new file format extension .docx

⑦ Click **Save**.

Word saves the document in Word 2010 format.

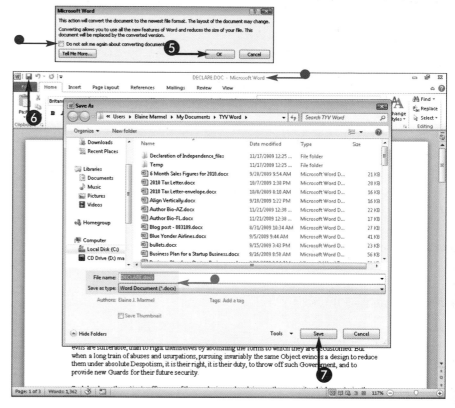

TIPS

Do I need to convert my documents from earlier versions of Word before I work on them in Word 2010?

No. You can work on a document created in an older version of Word and even incorporate Word 2010 features not available in earlier versions of Word. You only need to convert documents in which you expect to include features available only in Word 2010.

Is there any difference between using the method described in this section and opening a Word 97-Word 2003 document and then using the Save As command?

Not really; if you use the Save As method and choose Word Document (*.docx), Word prompts you to convert the older version document to the Word 2010 format using the Convert command as described in this section.

CHAPTER 3

Editing Text

Once you know how to navigate around Word, it is time to work with the text that you type on a page. In this chapter, you learn editing techniques that you can use to change text in documents you create.

You can insert text into a document by adding to existing text or replacing existing text. In Insert mode, Word adds to existing text. In Overtype mode, Word replaces existing text to the right of the insertion point, character for character.

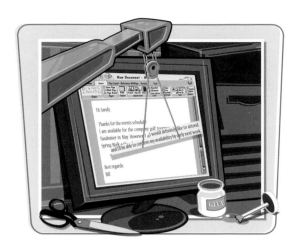

Insert and Add Text

1 Click the location where you want to insert text.

The insertion point flashes where you clicked.

You can press ➡, ⬅, ⬆, or ⬇ to move the insertion point one character or line.

You can press Ctrl + ➡ or Ctrl + ⬅ to move the insertion point one word at a time to the right or left.

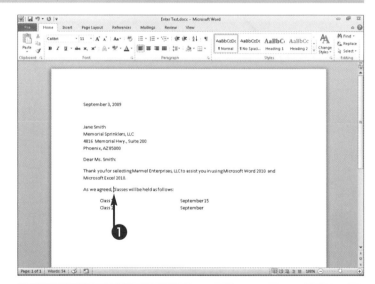

2 Type the text you want to insert.

Word inserts the text to the left of the insertion point, moving existing text to the right.

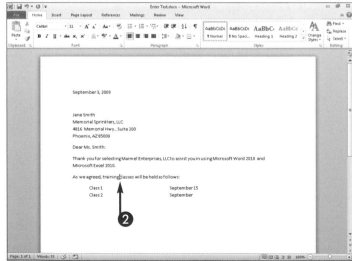

Insert and Replace Text

① Right-click the status bar.

② Click **Overtype**.

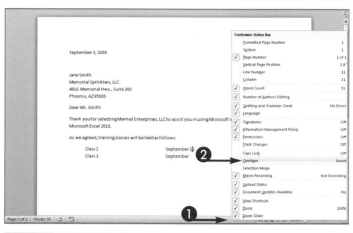

An indicator appears in the status bar.

③ Click the indicator to switch to Overtype mode.

Each time you click the indicator, you switch between Overtype and Insert mode.

④ Position the insertion point where you want to replace existing text and type the new text.

TIPS

Can I control switching between Insert mode and Overtype mode using the keyboard?

Yes. Follow these steps:

① Click the **File** tab and click **Options** to display the Word Options dialog box.

② Click **Advanced**.

③ Select the **Use the Insert key to control overtype mode** option (☐ changes to ☑).

④ Click **OK** and then press **Insert** on your keyboard.

Word switches between Insert mode and Overtype mode.

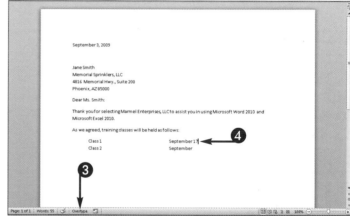

Delete
Text

You can easily remove text from a document using either the Delete or Backspace keys on your keyboard.

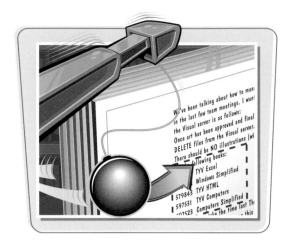

Using the Delete Key

1 Click to the left of the location where you want to delete text.

The insertion point flashes where you clicked.

You can press →, ←, ↑, or ↓ to move the insertion point one character or line.

You can press Ctrl + → or Ctrl + ← to move the insertion point one word at a time to the right or left.

2 Press Del on your keyboard.

● Word deletes the character immediately to the right of the insertion point.

You can hold Del to repeatedly delete characters to the right of the insertion point.

You can press Ctrl + Del to delete the word to the right of the insertion point.

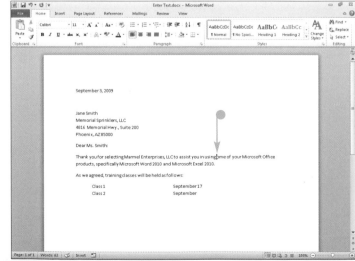

Using the Backspace Key

1 Click to the right of the location where you want to delete text.

The insertion point flashes where you clicked.

2 Press **Backspace** on your keyboard.

● Word deletes the character immediately to the left of the insertion point.

You can hold **Backspace** to repeatedly delete characters to the left of the insertion point.

You can press **Ctrl** + **Backspace** to delete the word to the left of the insertion point.

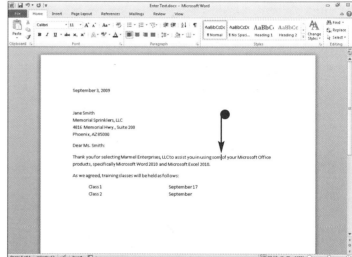

TIPS

Do I have to delete a large block of text one character or one word at a time?

No. You can select the block of text and then press either **Del** or **Backspace**; either key deletes selected text. For details on selecting text, see the section "Select Text" later in this chapter.

What should I do if I mistakenly delete text?

You should use the Undo feature in Word to restore the text you deleted. For details on how this feature works, see the section "Undo Changes" later in this chapter.

Insert Blank Lines

You can insert blank lines in your text to signify new paragraphs by inserting line breaks or paragraph marks. You use line breaks to start a new line without starting a new paragraph.

Word stores paragraph formatting in the paragraph mark shown in this section. When you start a new paragraph, you can change the new paragraph's formatting without affecting the preceding paragraph's formatting. For more information on styles and displaying paragraph marks, see Chapter 6.

Start a New Paragraph

1 Click where you want to start a new paragraph.

2 Press Enter.

● Word inserts a paragraph mark and moves any text to the right of the insertion point into the new paragraph.

3 Repeat Steps **1** and **2** for each blank line you want to insert.

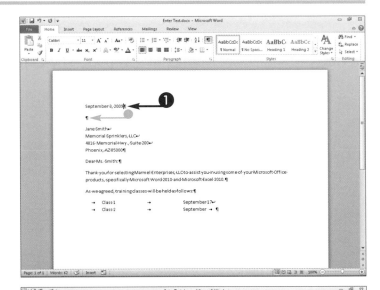

Insert a Line break

1 Click where you want to start a new paragraph.

2 Press Shift + Enter.

● Word inserts a line break and moves any text to the right of the insertion point onto the new line.

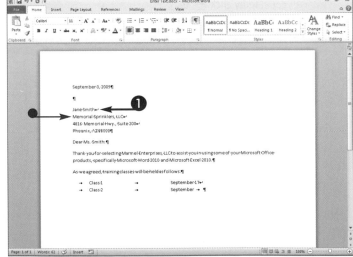

Undo Changes

You can use the Undo feature to reverse actions you take while working in a document, such as deleting or formatting text.

The Undo feature is particularly useful if you mistakenly delete text; when you use the Undo feature, you can recover the text.

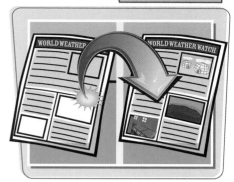

Undo Changes

1 Click the **Undo** button (↺).

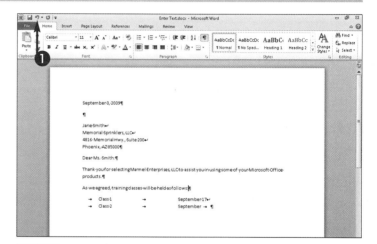

● Word reverses the effects of the last change you made.

You can repeatedly click ↺ to reverse each action you have taken, from last to first.

You can also press Ctrl + Z to reverse an action.

● If you decide not to reverse an action after clicking ↺, click the **Redo** button (↻).

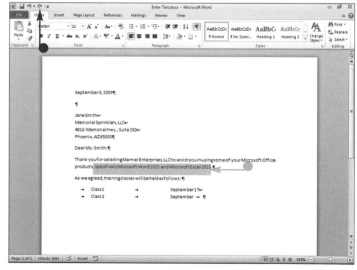

Before performing many tasks in Word, you identify the existing text on which you want to work by selecting it. For example, you select existing text to underline it, align it, change its font size, or apply color to it.

Select a Block of Text

1 Position the mouse pointer to the left of the first character you want to select.

2 Click and drag to the right and down over the text you want to select and release the mouse button.

● The selection appears highlighted and the Mini toolbar appears faded in the background.

To cancel a selection, you can press ▶, ◀, ▲, or ▼, or click anywhere on-screen.

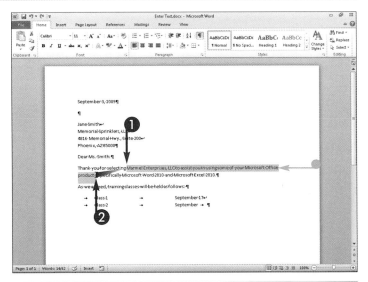

Select a Word

1 Double-click the word you want to select.

● Word selects the word and the Mini Toolbar appears faded in the background.

You can slide the mouse pointer closer to the Mini Toolbar to make its options available.

Note: See Chapter 1 for details on using the Mini Toolbar.

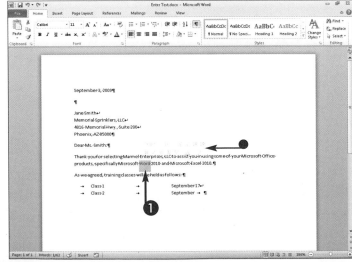

Select a Sentence

1 Press and hold **Ctrl**.

2 Click anywhere in the sentence you want to select.

● Word selects the entire sentence and the Mini Toolbar appears faded in the background.

You can slide the mouse pointer closer to the Mini Toolbar to make its options available.

Note: *See Chapter 1 for details on using the Mini Toolbar.*

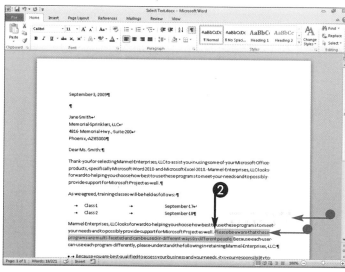

Select the Entire Document

1 Click the **Home** tab.

2 Click **Select**.

3 Click **Select All**.

● Word selects the entire document.

You also can press and hold **Ctrl** and press **A** to select the entire document.

To cancel the selection, click anywhere.

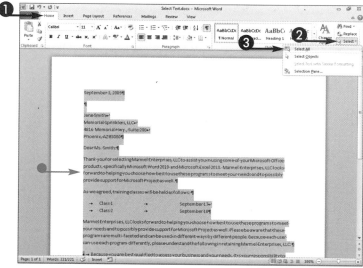

TIPS

Can I select text using the keyboard?

Yes. Press and hold **Shift** while pressing **←**, **→**, **↑**, or **↓**. You also can press **Shift** + **Ctrl** to select, for example, several words in a row. If you press and hold **Shift** + **Ctrl** while pressing **→** five times, you select five consecutive words to the right of the insertion point.

Can I select noncontiguous text?

Yes. You select the first area using any of the techniques described in this section. Then press and hold **Ctrl** as you select the additional areas. Word selects all areas, even if text appears between them.

Mark and Find Your Place

You can use the Bookmark feature to mark a location in a document so that you can easily return to it later.

You can also use bookmarks to store text; and Word uses bookmarks behind the scenes to operate some of its features.

Mark Your Place

1 Click the location you want to mark.

Note: If you select text instead of clicking at the location you want to mark, Word creates a bookmark containing text.

2 Click the **Insert** tab.

3 Click **Bookmark**.

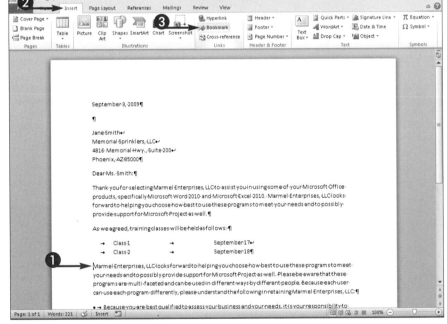

The Bookmark dialog box appears.

4 Type a name for the bookmark.

5 Click **Add**.

Word saves the bookmark and closes the Bookmark dialog box.

Find Your Place

1. Click the **Home** tab.

2. Click the down arrow beside **Find**.

3. Click **Go To**.

   The Go To tab of the Find and Replace dialog box appears.

4. Click **Bookmark**.

5. Click here and select a bookmark.

6. Click **Go To**.

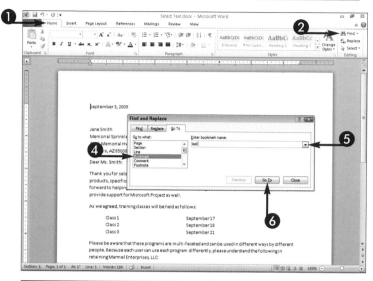

● Word moves the insertion point to the bookmark.

Note: If the bookmark contains text, Word selects the text in the bookmark.

7. Click **Close** or press Esc.

   Word closes the Find and Replace dialog box.

 TIP

Can I display bookmarks in my document?

Yes. Follow these steps.

1. Click the **File** tab.

2. Click **Options**.

3. Click **Advanced**.

4. Select the **Show bookmarks** option (☐ changes to ☑).

5. Click **OK**.

   Word displays open and close brackets representing the bookmark.

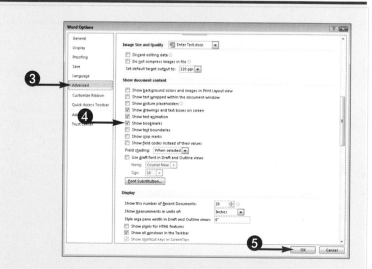

Move or Copy Text

You can reposition text in your document by cutting and then pasting it. You also can repeat text by copying and then pasting it.

When you move text by cutting and pasting it, the text disappears from the original location and appears in a new one. When you copy and paste text, it remains in the original location and also appears in a new one.

Using Ribbon Buttons

1. Select the text you want to move or copy.

   Note: To select text, see the section "Select Text."

2. Click the **Home** tab.

3. To move text, click the **Cut** button ( ); to copy text, click the **Copy** button ( ).

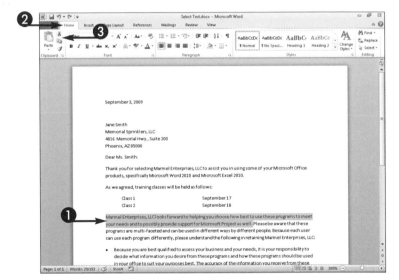

4. Click to place the insertion point at the location where you want the text to appear.

5. Click the **Paste** button ( ).

   The text appears at the new location.

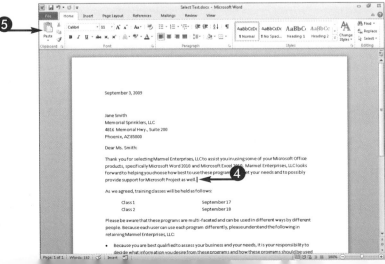

Dragging and Dropping

① Select the text you want to move or copy.

② Position the mouse pointer over the selected text (⌶ changes to ⬦).

③ Either move or copy the text.

To move text, drag the mouse (⌶ changes to ⬦).

To copy text, press and hold **Ctrl** and drag the mouse (⌶ changes to ⬦).

● The text appears at the new location.

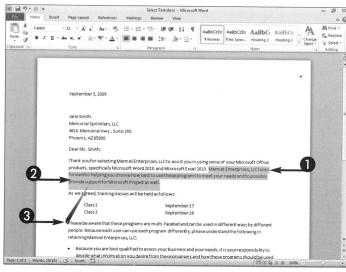

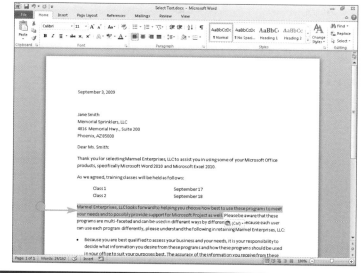

TIPS

Is there a way I can move or copy text using menus?

Yes. You can select the text that you want to move or copy and then right-click it. The context menu and the Mini toolbar appear; click **Cut** or **Copy**. Then place the insertion point at the location where you want the text to appear and right-click again. From the context menu, click **Paste**.

Can I copy or move information other than text?

Yes. You can copy or move any type of element in your Word document: text, pictures, tables, graphics, and so on. Essentially, you can copy or move any element that you can select. You also can copy or move text from one Word document to another; see the section "Share Text Between Documents" later in this chapter.

Share Text
Between Documents

When you cut, copy, and paste text, you are not limited to using the text in a single document. You can move or copy text from one document to another.

Any text that you cut disappears from its original location. Text that you copy continues to appear in its original location.

① Open the two documents you want to use to share text.

② Select the text you want to move or copy.

Note: For details on selecting text, see the section "Select Text."

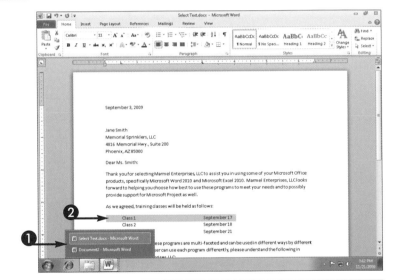

③ Click 🔲 to move text or click 🔲 to copy text.

④ Switch to the other document by clicking its button in the Windows taskbar.

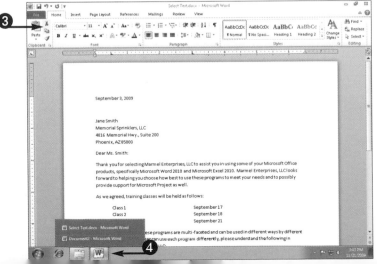

The other document appears.

5 Place the insertion point at the location where you want the text you are moving or copying to appear.

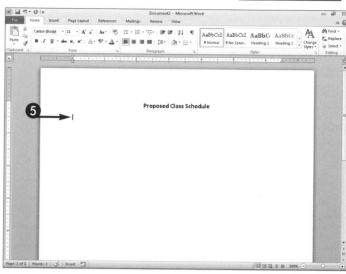

6 Click ✐.

● The text appears in the new location.

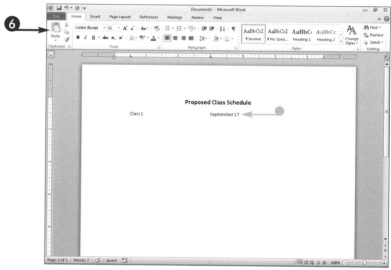

Why do I see a button when I paste?

Word displays the Paste Options button (⧉ (Ctrl)▾) to give you the opportunity to determine how to handle the formatting of the selection you are pasting. See the section "Take Advantage of Paste Options" for details on how to use Paste options.

What format will Word use by default for text I paste?

The default appearance of pasted text depends on options set in the Word Options dialog box. To view or set the default appearance, click ⧉ (Ctrl)▾ and then click **Set Default Paste** to display cut, copy, and paste options in the Word Options dialog box.

Move or Copy Several Selections

You can move or copy several selections at the same time using the Office Clipboard. The Office Clipboard is the location where information you cut or copy is stored until you paste it.

The Clipboard can hold up to the last 24 selections that you cut or copied in any Office program.

① Click the **Clipboard** 🔲.

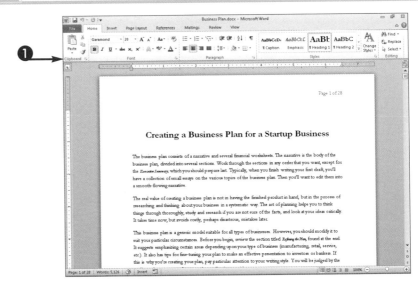

● The Office Clipboard pane appears.

Note: *If you cut or copied anything prior to this time, an entry appears in the Clipboard pane.*

② Select the text or information you want to move or copy.

③ Click ✂ or 📋.

● An entry appears in the Clipboard pane.

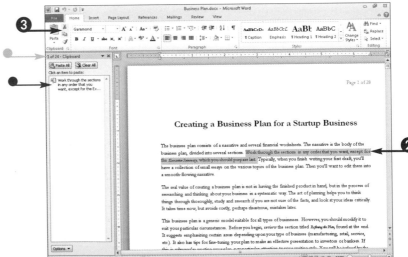

④ Repeat Steps **2** and **3** for each selection you want to move or copy.

● Word adds each entry to the Clipboard pane; the newest entry appears at the top of the pane.

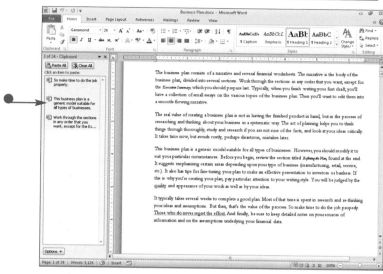

⑤ Click in the document where you want to place text you cut or copied.

⑥ Click a selection in the Clipboard pane to place it in the document.

⑦ Repeat Steps **5** and **6** to paste other items from the Clipboard.

● If you want to place all of the items in one location and the items appear in the Clipboard pane in the order you want them in your document, you can click **Paste All**.

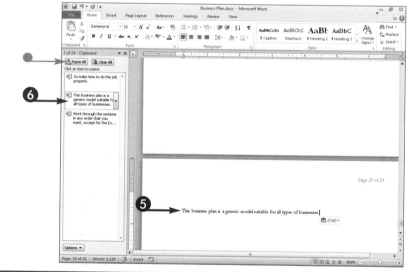
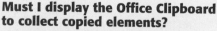

TIPS

Why does ▾ appear when I point at an item in the Clipboard pane?

If you click ▾, a menu appears. From this menu, you can click **Paste** to add the item to your document, or you can click **Delete** to remove the item from the Clipboard pane.

Must I display the Office Clipboard to collect copied elements?

No. Click the **Options** button at the bottom of the Clipboard pane and then click **Collect Without Showing Office Clipboard**. As you cut or copy, a message appears in the lower-right corner of your screen, telling you how many elements are stored on the Office Clipboard. You must display the Office Clipboard to paste any item except the one you last cut or copied.

Take Advantage of Paste Options

When you move or copy information, you can choose the formatting Word applies to the selection at its new location.

① Make a selection; this example uses an Excel spreadsheet selection, but you can select text in a Word document.

② Click 📋 or ✂.

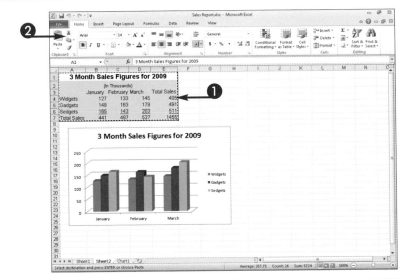

③ Position the insertion point in your Word document where you want to paste the information.

④ Click the **Paste** 🔽.

● Buttons representing paste options appear.

⑤ To preview the appearance of the selection, point at the **Keep Source Formatting** button (🖼).

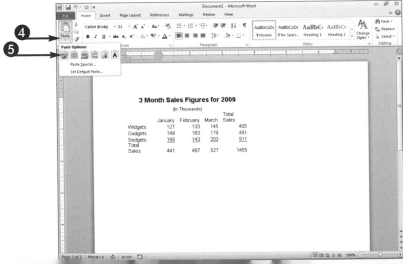

70

6 To preview the appearance of the selection, point at the **Use Destination Styles** (▯) button.

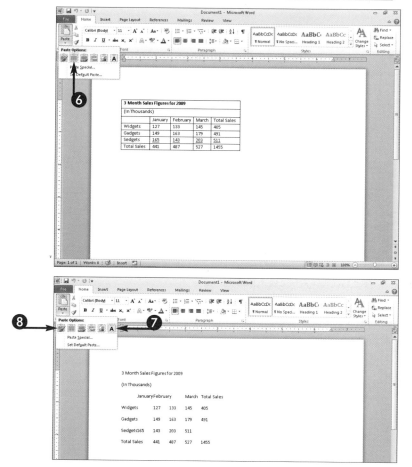

7 To preview the appearance of the selection, point at the **Keep Text Only** button (▤).

8 Click a **Paste Options** button to paste the selection and specify its format in your Word document.

What do the various Paste Options buttons mean?

Paste Options Button	Function
🖼	Use the formatting of the selection you copied or cut.
▯	Formats the selection using the style of the location where you paste the selection.
🖼	Uses the formatting of the selection you cut or copied and links the selection at the new location to the selection at the original location.
🖼	Formats the selection using the style of the location where you paste the selection and links the selection at the new location to the selection at the original location.
🖼	Formats the selection as a graphic that you cannot edit in Word.
🖼	Applies no formatting to the selection; only text appears.

Switch Document Views

You can view a document five ways. The view you use depends entirely on what you are doing at the time; select the view that best meets your needs. For more on the various views, see the section "Understanding Document Views."

The button for the currently selected view appears in orange.

① Click the **View** tab.

② Click one of the Document Views buttons on the Ribbon:

Print Layout

Full Screen Reading

Web Layout

Outline

Draft

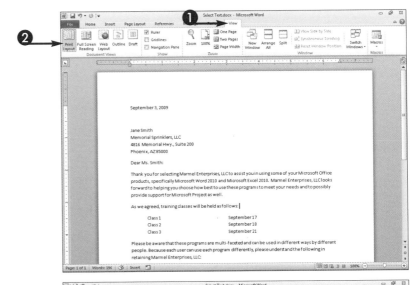

● Word switches your document to the view you selected.

● Buttons for each view also appear at the right edge of the status bar; position the mouse pointer over each button to see its function and click a button to switch views.

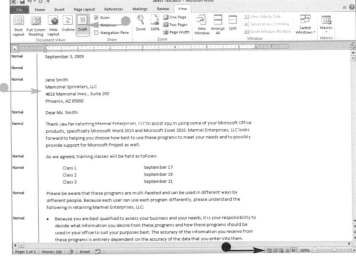

You should select the view that best meets your needs. But, which view is right for you? The purpose of each view is described in this section.

To switch between views, see the section "Switch Document Views."

Draft View

Draft view is designed for editing and formatting; it does not display your document the way it will print. Instead, you can view elements such as the Style Area on the left side of the screen, but you cannot view the document's margins, headers and footers, or graphics in the location where they will appear.

Web Layout View

Web Layout view is useful when you are designing a Web page.

Print Layout View

Print Layout view presents a "what you see is what you get" view of your document. In Print Layout view, you see elements of your document that affect the printed page, such as margins.

Outline View

Outline view helps you work with the organization of a document. Word indents text styled as headings based on the heading number; you can move or copy entire sections of a document by moving or copying the heading.

Full Screen Reading View

Full Screen Reading view is designed to minimize eye strain when you read a document on-screen. This view removes most toolbars. To return to another view, click the **Close** button (☒ Close) in the upper-right corner of the screen.

Work with the Navigation Pane

You can use the Navigation Pane to navigate through a document that contains text styled in one of the Heading styles.

The Navigation Pane is blank for documents that do not contain Heading styles. For more information on styles, see Chapter 6.

Work with the Navigation Pane

Navigate Using Headings

1 In a document containing text styled with Heading styles, click the **View** tab.

2 Click **Navigation Pane** (☐ changes to ☑).

The Navigation Pane appears.

● Heading1 styles appear at the left edge of the Navigation Pane.

● Word indents Heading2 styles slightly and each subsequent heading style a bit more.

● This icon represents a heading displaying subheadings; you can click it to hide subheadings.

● This icon represents a heading hiding subheadings; you can click it to display subheadings.

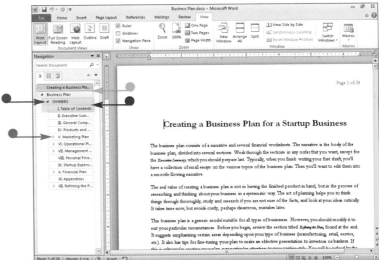

③ Click any heading in the Navigation Pane to select it.

● Word moves the insertion point to it in your document.

● You can click ▲ or ▼ to navigate one heading at a time through your document.

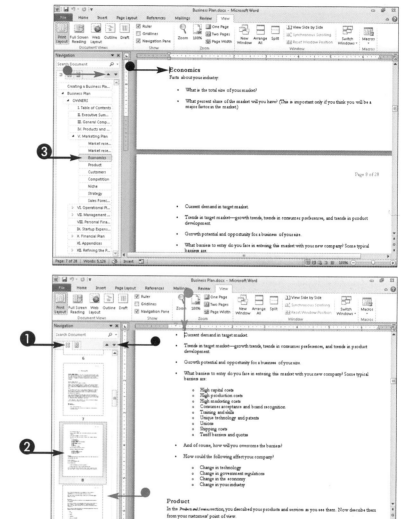

Navigate by Page

① Click here.

● Word displays each page in your document as a thumbnail.

② Click a thumbnail.

● Word selects that page in the Navigation Pane and moves the insertion point to the top of that page.

● You can click ▲ or ▼ to navigate one page at a time through your document.

What do I do with the Search Document box?

You can use the Search Document box to find text in your document; see Chapter 4 for details on using this box and on other ways you can search for information in your document.

I realize I can close the Navigation Pane by clicking ☒ in the upper-right corner of the pane. What does ▾ beside ☒ do?

When you click ▾, a menu appears. You can use the menu to move or size the Navigation Pane. The menu also contains a Close command that you can use instead of ☒ to close the Navigation Pane.

Zoom In or Out

You can use the Zoom feature to enlarge or reduce the size of the text on-screen. Zooming in enlarges text. Zooming out reduces text, providing more of an overview of your document.

1 Click the **View** tab.

2 Click **Zoom**.

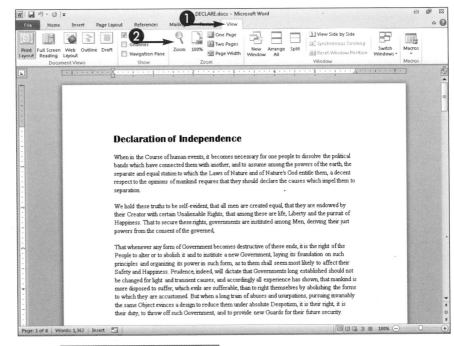

The Zoom dialog box appears.

3 Click a zoom setting.

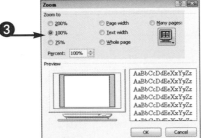

● You can click the **Many pages** button and select to display multiple pages.

Note: The number of pages you can view depends on the resolution you set for your monitor.

④ Click **OK**.

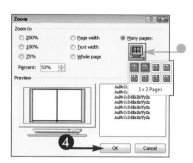

The document appears on-screen using the new zoom setting.

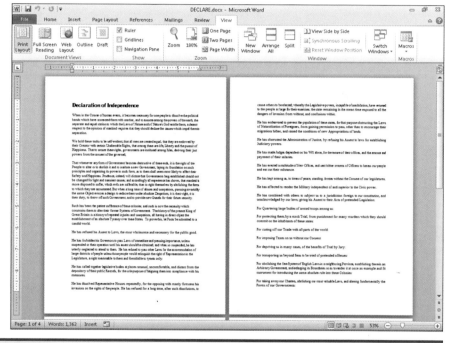

What do the Page width and Text width options do?

You can select the **Page width** option (changes to) to fit the page, including margins, across the width of the screen, or **Text width** to fit text, excluding margins, across the width of the screen. The Page Width button on the Ribbon serves the same purpose as the Page width option in the Zoom dialog box, and the One Page button and the Two Pages button on the Ribbon are the most common choices when using the Many pages option in the Zoom dialog box.

Can I use the mouse to zoom?

Yes. Drag the Zoom slider in the status bar or click the plus or minus signs at either end of the Zoom slider. Each click of the plus sign zooms in 10 percent; each click of the minus sign zooms out 10 percent.

Insert a Symbol

Using the Symbol feature, you can insert characters into your documents that do not appear on your keyboard.

Insert a Symbol

① Click the location in the document where you want the symbol to appear.

② Click the **Insert** tab.

③ Click **Symbol**.

A list of commonly used symbols appears. If the symbol you need appears in the list, you can click it and skip the rest of these steps.

④ Click **More Symbols**.

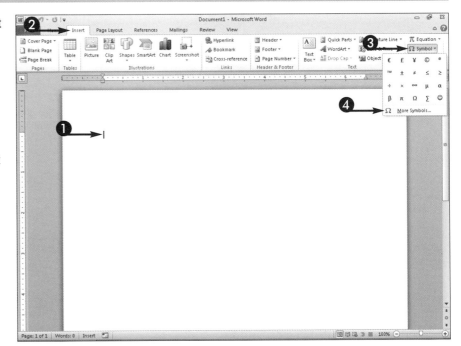

The Symbol dialog box appears.

⑤ Click here and select the symbol's font.

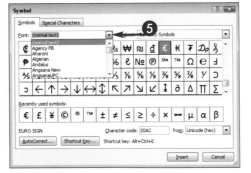

The available symbols change to match the font you selected.

6 Click a symbol.

7 Click **Insert**.

8 Click **Close** to close the Symbol dialog box.

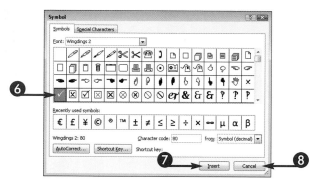

● The symbol appears in the document.

Note: *You can control the size of the symbol the same way you control the size of text; see Chapter 5 for details.*

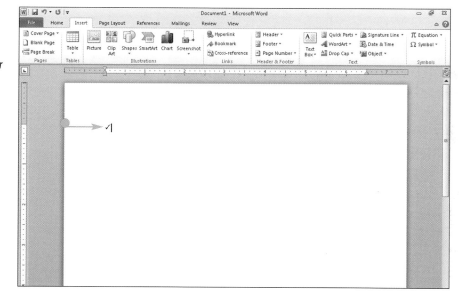

TIP

If I have a particular symbol I use frequently, how can I easily insert it?
You can assign a keyboard shortcut, which you can then use to place the symbol.

1 Complete Steps **1** to **6** in this section and then click **Shortcut Key**.

2 In the Customize Keyboard dialog box, press **Alt** or **Ctrl** and any other key; the combination should be unassigned in the selected template.

3 Click **Assign**.

4 Click **Close** in both dialog boxes.

You can now position the insertion point and press the assigned keyboard shortcut to place the symbol.

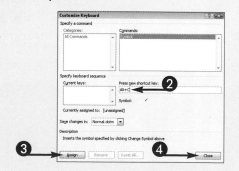

Work with Equations

You can easily create complex equations in Word 2010 using the Equation Tools Design tab on the Ribbon. You no longer need to use add-in products as you did in versions of Word prior to Word 2007.

If you add a structure to an equation, Word supplies dotted box placeholders for you to click and substitute constants or variables. Note that the Equation feature does not function when you work in Compatibility Mode.

Work with Equations

Insert an Equation

① Position the insertion point where you want to insert an equation.

② Click the **Insert** tab.

③ Click ▼ on the **Equation** button.

● The Equation Gallery, a list of commonly used equations, appears.

You can click an equation to insert it and then skip Steps **4** and **5**.

④ Click **Insert New Equation**.

Word inserts a blank equation box.

● The Equations Tools Design tab appears on the Ribbon.

⑤ Type your equation.

You can click the tools on the Ribbon to help you type the equation.

⑥ Press ➡ or click outside the equation box.

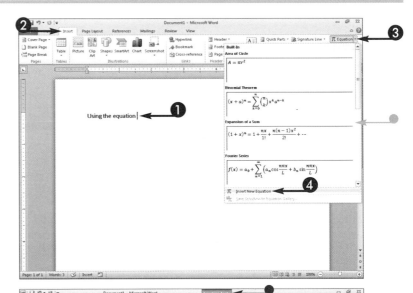

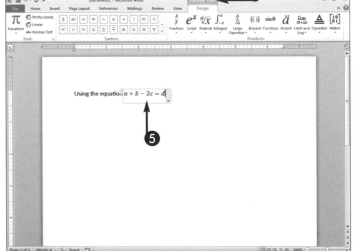

Word hides the equation box and
you can continue typing.

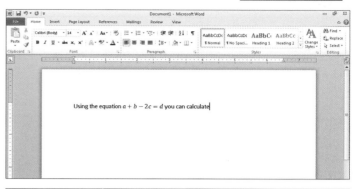

Delete an Equation

1 Click anywhere in the equation to
display it in the equation box.

2 Click the three dots on the left
side of the box.

Word highlights the contents of
the equation box.

3 Press Del.

Word deletes the equation from
your document.

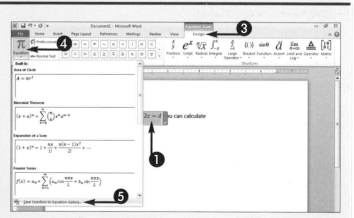

 TIP

**Can I save an equation I use regularly
so that I do not have to create it each
time I need it?**

Yes. Follow these steps:

1 Click anywhere in the equation.

2 Click the three dots on the left side of the box.

3 Click the **Equation Tools Design** tab.

4 Click **Equation**.

5 Click **Save Selection to Equation Gallery**.

6 In the Create New Building Block dialog box
that appears, click **OK**.

The next time you display the Equation Gallery,
your equation appears on the list.

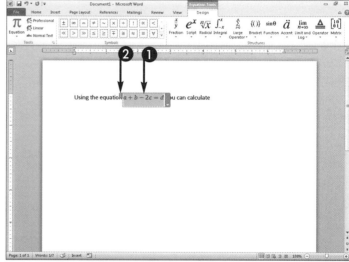

Set Options for Additional Actions

You can control the kinds of information Word recognizes and identifies for additional actions that can save you time.

You also can turn off additional action recognition entirely.

Set Options for Additional Actions

1 Click the **File** tab.

The Back Stage view appears.

2 Click **Options**.

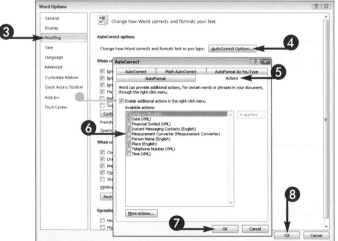

The Word Options dialog box appears.

3 Click **Proofing**.

4 Click **AutoCorrect Options**.

The AutoCorrect dialog box appears.

5 Click the **Actions** tab.

● You can click here (☑ changes to ☐) to turn off smart tag recognition.

6 Click the check box beside an item to turn additional action recognition on (☑) or off (☐).

7 Click **OK** to close the AutoCorrect dialog box.

8 Click **OK** to close the Word Options window.

Word saves your preferences.

Using Additional Actions

You can use the Additional Actions feature, formerly called "Smart Tags," to save time. Using this feature, Word can convert measurements, add a telephone number to Outlook Contacts, or schedule a meeting.

This feature may not be on by default; see the section, "Set Options for Additional Actions."

Using Additional Actions

① Right-click text for which you have enabled additional actions. In this example uses an address.

● A context menu appears.

② Click **Additional Actions.**

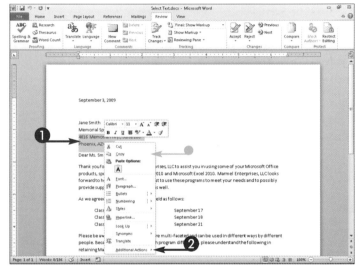

● Word displays a list of actions you can take using the text.

③ Click an action.

Word performs the action; or, the program that performs the action you selected appears on-screen.

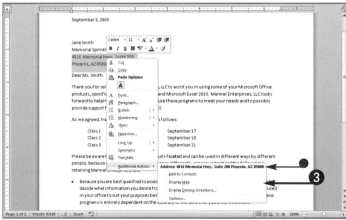

Translate Text

Using the Translation feature, you can translate a word from one language to another using language dictionaries installed on your computer.

If you are connected to the Internet, the Translation feature searches the dictionaries on your computer as well as online dictionaries.

Translate Text

Translate a phrase

1 Select a phrase to translate.

2 Click the **Review** tab.

3 Click **Translate**.

4 Click **Translate Selected Text**.

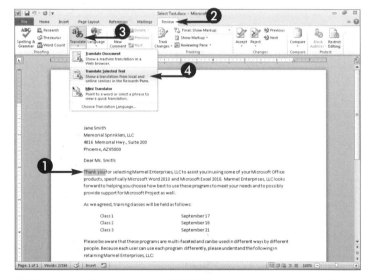

● The Research task pane appears.

● The phrase you selected appears here.

● The current language translation languages appear here.

● You can click ▼ to display available translation languages.

● The translation appears here.

Use the Mini Translator

1 Click the **Review** tab.

2 Click **Translate**.

3 Click **Mini Translator**.

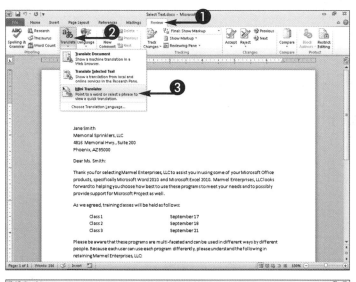

4 Move the mouse pointer over any word.

● A translation of the word appears.

5 Repeat Step 4 for each word you want to translate.

To stop translating, repeat Steps **1** to **3**.

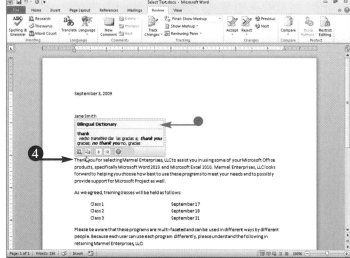

TIPS

How do I set a translation language for the Mini Translator?

Click the **Review** tab and then click **Translate**; from the drop-down menu, click **Choose Your Translation Language**. On the left side of the Translation Language Options dialog box, click **Mini Translator** and then use ⬛ to select the originating and target languages to use for translation.

Can the Translation feature translate my entire document?

Yes and no. While the feature is capable of fairly complex translations, it may not grasp the tone or meaning of your text. You can choose **Translate Document** from the Translate drop-down menu to send the document over the Internet for translation, but be aware that Word sends documents as unencrypted HTML files. If security is an issue, do not choose this route; instead, consider hiring a professional translator.

4

Proofreading in Word

This chapter shows you how to handle proofreading tasks in Word. You can search through text to find something in particular, as well as search for particular text to replace it. Word contains some features to help you with spelling and grammar issues as well as researching aids. This chapter also shows you how to track revisions and work with revisions provided by multiple reviewers.

Search for Text

Occasionally, you need to search for a word or phrase in a document. You can search for all occurrences simultaneously or for each single occurrence.

This section focuses on finding text; see the next section, "Substitute Text" for information on finding and replacing text.

Search for Text

Search for All Occurrences

1 Click the **Home** tab.

2 Click **Find**.

● The Navigation Pane appears.

3 Type the word or phrase for which you want to search.

● Word highlights all occurrences of the word or phrase in yellow.

4 Click **Close (X)** to clear the search and results.

5 Click **Close (X)** to close the Navigation Pane.

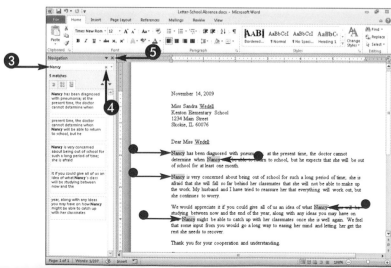

Search for One Occurrence at a Time

1 Complete Steps **1** and **2** in the subsection "Search for All Occurrences."

2 Click the **magnifying glass** button ( ).

3 From the menu that appears, click **Find** to display the Find and Replace dialog box.

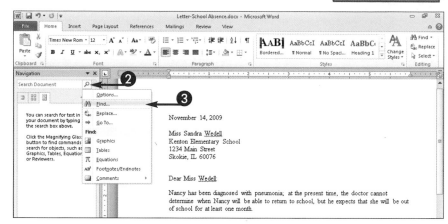

4 Click here and type the word or phrase for which you want to search.

● You can click **Reading Highlight** and then click **Highlight All** to highlight each occurrence of the word in yellow.

● You can click **Find in** to limit the search to the main document or the headers and footers.

5 Click **Find Next** to view each occurrence.

When Word finds no more occurrences, a dialog box appears telling you that the search is finished; click **OK**.

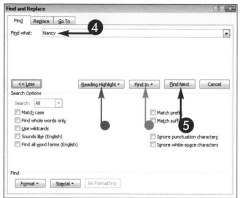

How can I set options to limit my search in the Navigation Pane?

1 Complete Steps **1** and **2** in the subsection "Search for All Occurrences."

2 Click .

3 From the menu that appears, click **Options** to display the Find Options dialog box.

4 Select the options you want to use (changes to).

5 Click **OK** and complete the rest of the steps in the section.

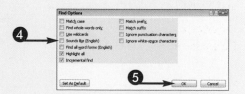

Substitute Text

Often, you want to find a word or phrase because you need to substitute some other word or phrase for it.

You can substitute a word or phrase for all occurrences of the original word or phrase, or you can selectively substitute.

① Click the **Home** tab.

② Click **Replace**.

The Find and Replace dialog box appears.

③ Type the word or phrase you want to replace here.

④ Type the word or phrase you want Word to substitute here.

● You can click **More** to display additional search and replace options; the More button changes to Less.

⑤ Click **Find Next**.

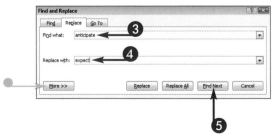

● Word highlights the first occurrence of the word or phrase that it finds.

● If you do not want to change the highlighted occurrence, you can click **Find Next** to ignore it.

6 Click **Replace**.

● To change all occurrences in the document, you can click **Replace All**.

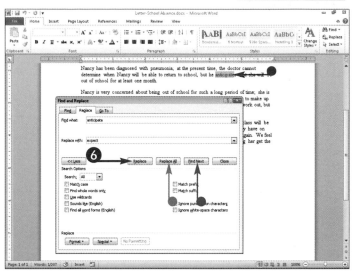

● Word replaces the original word or phrase with the word or phrase you specify as the substitute.

7 Repeat Steps **5** and **6** as needed.

8 When Word finds no more occurrences, a dialog box appears telling you that the search is finished; click **OK**.

● The Cancel button changes to Close.

9 Click **Close** to close the Find and Replace dialog box.

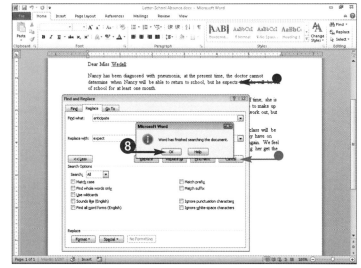

Can I find italic text and change it to boldface text?

Yes. Follow Steps **1** and **2** and click **More** to expand the window. Follow Steps **3** and **4**, but, instead of typing text, click **Format** and then click **Font**. In the Font style list of the Font dialog box that appears, click **Italic** for Step **3** and **Bold** for Step **4**. Then complete Steps **5** to **9**.

Can I search for and replace special characters such as tabs or paragraph marks?

Yes. Follow Steps **1** and **2** and click **More** to expand the window. Then follow Steps **3** and **4**, but instead of typing text, click **Special** to display a menu of special characters. For Step **3**, select the special character you want to find. For Step **4**, select the special character you want to substitute. Then complete Steps **5** to **9**.

Count Words in a Document

You can count the number of words in a document or in any portion of a document. This is particularly handy when you must limit the number of words in a section of a document. Make use of this feature when a work or school project requires a specific number of words.

Display the Word Count

1 Right-click the status bar.

● The Status Bar Configuration menu appears.

● The number across from Word Count is the number of words in the document.

2 If no check mark appears beside Word Count, click **Word Count**; otherwise, skip this step.

3 Click anywhere outside the menu.

● Word closes the menu and the number of words in the document appears on the status bar.

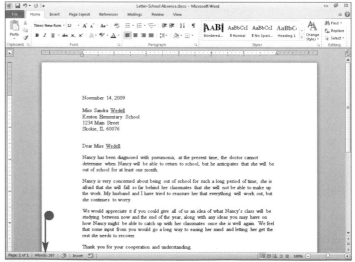

Display Count Statistics

1 Click the word count on the status bar.

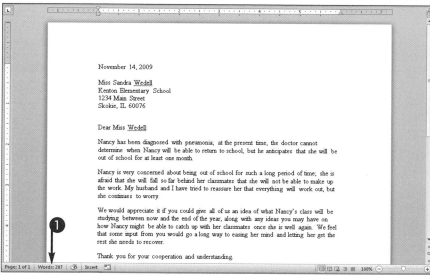

The Word Count dialog box appears.

The Word Count dialog box reports the number of pages, words, characters with and without spaces, paragraphs, and lines in your document.

2 When you finish reviewing count statistics, click **Close**.

Can I count the number of words in just one paragraph?

Yes. Do the following:

1 Select the text containing the words you want to count.

● Both the number of words and the total words in the document appear in the Word Count box on the status bar.

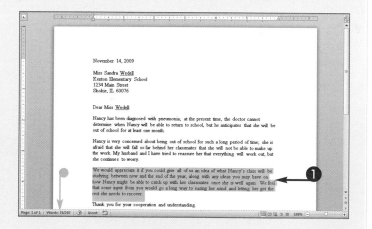

Automatically Correct Mistakes

Using the AutoCorrect feature, Word automatically corrects hundreds of common typing and spelling mistakes as you work. You can also add your own set of mistakes and the corrections to the list Word references.

Automatically Correct Mistakes

① Click the **File** tab.

The Backstage view appears.

② Click **Options**.

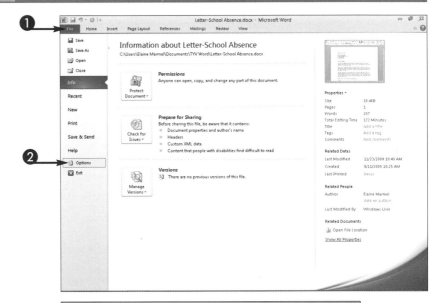

The Word Options dialog box appears.

③ Click **Proofing** to display proofing options.

④ Click **AutoCorrect Options**.

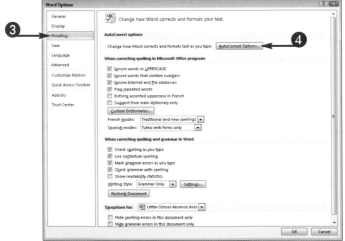

The AutoCorrect dialog box appears.

● The corrections Word already makes automatically appear in this area.

⑤ Click here and type the word you typically mistype or misspell.

⑥ Click here and type the correct version of the word.

⑦ Click **Add**.

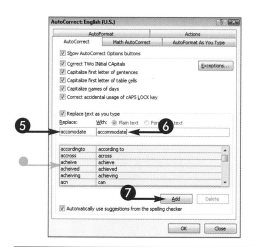

● Word adds the entry to the list to automatically correct.

You can repeat Steps **5** to **7** for each automatic correction you want to add.

⑧ Click **OK** to close the AutoCorrect dialog box.

⑨ Click **OK** to close the Word Options dialog box.

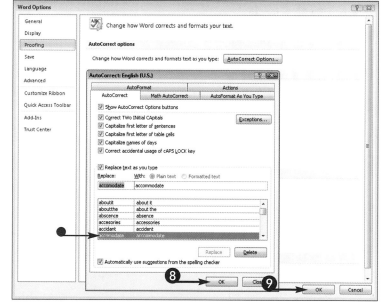

TIPS

How does the automatic correction work?

You do not need to do anything unusual — just type. If you mistype or misspell a word stored as an AutoCorrect entry, Word corrects the entry when you press Spacebar, Tab, or Enter.

What should I do if Word automatically replaces an entry that I do not want replaced?

Position the insertion point at the beginning of the AutoCorrected word and click the **AutoCorrect Options** button (⊞ ▾) that appears. From the list of choices displayed, click **Change back to**. To make Word permanently stop correcting an entry, follow Steps **1** to **4**, click the stored AutoCorrect entry in the list, and then click **Delete**.

Automatically Insert Frequently Used Text

Using the Quick Parts feature, you can store and then insert phrases you use frequently. The Quick Parts feature is particularly useful for phrases that take up more than one line, such as a name, title, and company name that appears at the bottom of a letter.

Quick Parts were known as AutoText entries in versions of Word prior to Word 2007. Any AutoText entries you created appear in Word 2010, but unless you remember their names, you can insert them only using the AutoText Gallery. For Word 2010, Quick Parts are faster and easier to use.

Automatically Insert Frequently Used Text

Create a Quick Part Entry

1 Type the text that you want to store, including all formatting that should appear each time you insert the entry.

2 Select the text you typed.

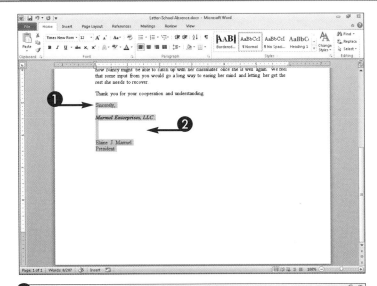

3 Click the **Insert** tab.

4 Click **Quick Parts**.

5 Click **Save Selection to Quick Part Gallery**.

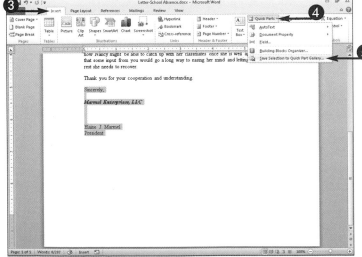

The Create New Building Block dialog box appears.

⑥ Type a name that you want to use as a shortcut for the entry.

⑦ Click **OK**.

Word stores the entry on the Quick Part Gallery.

Insert a Quick Part Entry

① Position the insertion point where you want the Quick Part entry to appear.

② Click **Quick Parts**.

All building blocks you define as Quick Parts appear on the Quick Part Gallery.

③ Click the entry.

Word inserts the Quick Part entry.

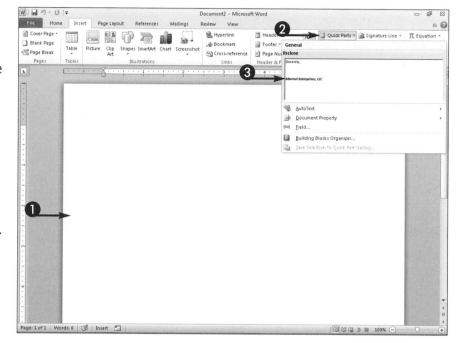

 TIPS

Is there a way to use the Quick Part without using the mouse?

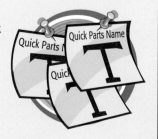

Yes. Type the name you assigned to the entry and press F3. Word inserts the Quick Part.

How can I find and use an AutoText entry?

AutoText entries do not appear when you open the Quick Part Gallery. To find an AutoText entry, click **Quick Parts** and then click **Building Blocks Organizer**. In the Building Blocks Organizer window that appears, click the entry and click **Insert**.

Check Spelling and Grammar

Using the Spelling and Grammar Checker, you can search for and correct all spelling and grammar mistakes in your document. On-screen, Word places a red squiggly underline beneath spelling errors, a green squiggly underline beneath grammar errors, and a blue squiggly line under correctly spelled but misused words.

Check Spelling and Grammar

① Click the **Review** tab.

② Click **Spelling and Grammar**.

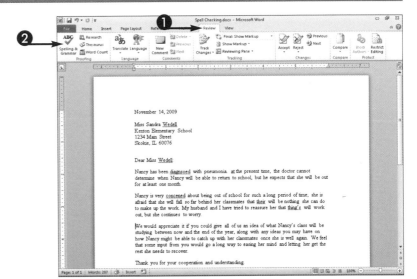

● Word selects the first spelling or grammar mistake and displays the Spelling and Grammar window.

Note: *If your document contains no errors, this window does not appear.*

● This area displays the spelling or grammar mistake.

● This area displays suggestions to correct the error.

③ Click the suggestion you want to use.

④ Click **Change**.

● You can click **Ignore Once** or **Ignore All** to leave the selected word or phrase unchanged.

Word selects the next spelling or grammar mistake.

⑤ Repeat Steps **3** and **4** for each spelling or grammar mistake.

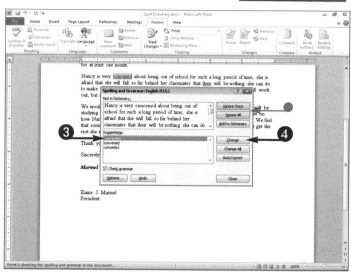

Word displays a dialog box when it finishes checking for spelling and grammar mistakes.

⑥ Click **OK**.

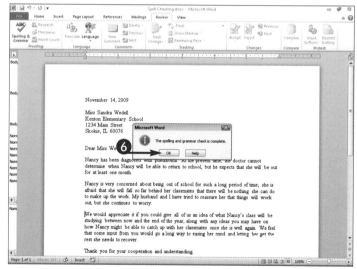

TIPS

Can I correct spelling and grammar mistakes as I work instead of checking them all at once?

Yes. Each time you see a red, green, or blue squiggly underline, right-click the word or phrase. Word displays a menu of suggestions; you can click one to correct the error.

When should I use the Add to Dictionary button?

Word identifies misspellings by comparing words in your document to its own dictionary. When a word you type does not appear in Word's dictionary, Word flags the word as misspelled. If the word is a term you use regularly, click **Add to Dictionary** so that Word stops flagging the word as a misspelling.

Disable Grammar and Spell Checking

By default, Word automatically checks spelling and grammar by displaying red and green squiggly lines whenever it identifies a spelling or grammar mistake. If the red and green squiggly underlines annoy you, you can turn off automatic spelling and grammar checking.

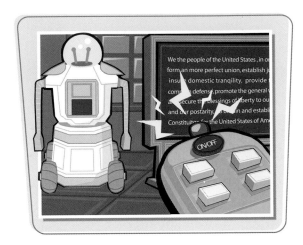

Disable Grammar and Spell Checking

1 Click the **File** tab.

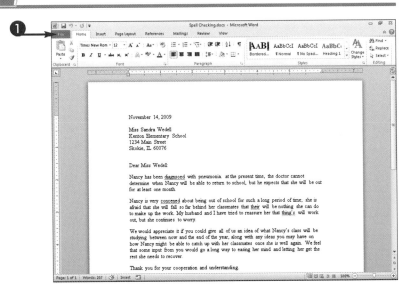

The Backstage view appears.

2 Click **Options**.

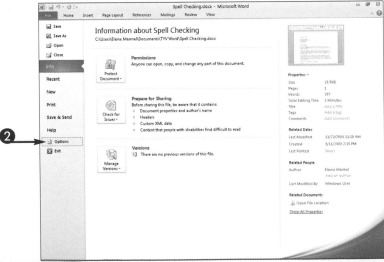

The Word Options dialog box appears.

3 Click **Proofing**.

4 Deselect the **Check spelling as you type** option (☑ changes to ☐) to disable automatic spell checking.

5 Deselect the **Mark grammar errors as you type** option (☑ changes to ☐) to disable automatic grammar checking.

6 Click **OK**.

● Word no longer identifies the spelling and grammar errors in your document.

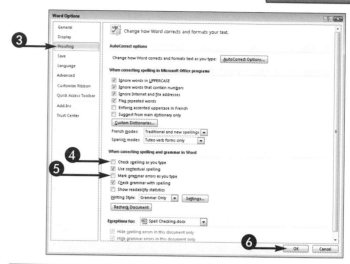

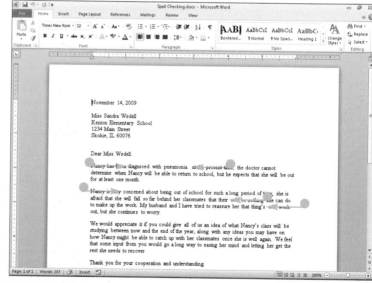

If I disable automatic spelling and grammar checking, is there a way to check spelling and grammar?

Yes. Use the procedure described in the section "Check Spelling and Grammar." When you follow the procedure in that section, you disable only the portion of the feature where Word automatically identifies misspellings or grammar mistakes with squiggly red or green underlines.

What should I do if I change my mind and decide that I want to see the red and green squiggly lines?

Repeat the steps in this section, selecting the options you deselected previously (☐ changes to ☑).

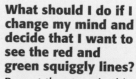

Find a Synonym or Antonym with the Thesaurus

Using the thesaurus, you can search for a more suitable word than the word you originally chose. The thesaurus can help you find a synonym — a word with a similar meaning — for the word you originally chose, as well as an antonym, which is a word with an opposite meaning.

Find a Synonym or Antonym with the Thesaurus

1 Click the word for which you want to find an opposite or substitute.

2 Click the **Review** tab.

3 Click **Thesaurus**.

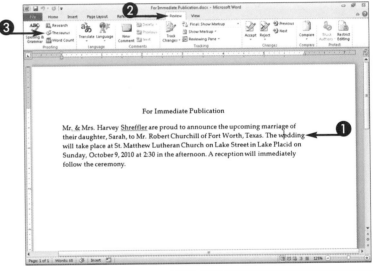

The Research task pane appears.

● The word you selected appears here.

● Click here to display a list of resources you can use to search for information.

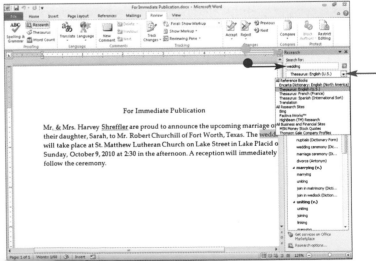

A list of words with similar meanings appears.

● Each bold word represents a part of speech — a noun, a verb, an adjective — with a similar meaning to the word you selected.

● Each word listed below a bold word is a synonym for the bold word.

● Antonyms are marked.

④ Point the mouse at the word you want to use in your document.

☑ appears beside the word.

⑤ Click here to display a list of choices.

⑥ Click **Insert**.

Word replaces the word in your document with the one appearing in the Research task pane.

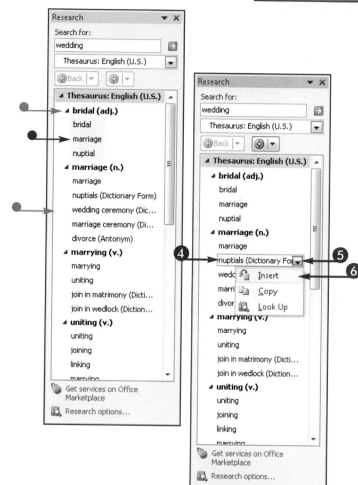

TIP

Is there a faster way I can display synonyms and antonyms?

Yes. Follow these steps:

❶ Click the word for which you want a synonym or antonym.

❷ Press Shift + F7 or right-click the word and click **Synonyms**.

❸ Click a choice to replace the word in your document.

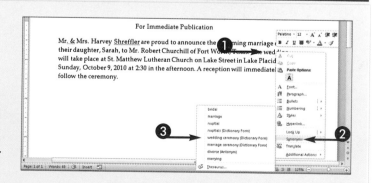

Research Information

Using the Research task pane, you can look up a word in the dictionary or search online resources for information on a variety of subjects using encyclopedias or online business resources.

Using online resources, you can search for essential business news and information to help you make better decisions faster, and you can get a stock quote.

Research Information

① Click a word in your document that you want to research.

② Click the **Review** tab.

③ Click **Research**.

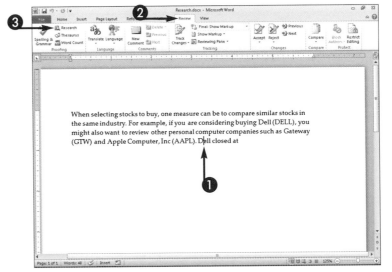

● The Research task pane appears.

● The word you clicked in Step **1** appears here.

④ Click here to display a list of resources available for research.

⑤ Click the resource you want to use.

Note: This example uses MSN Money Stock Quotes.

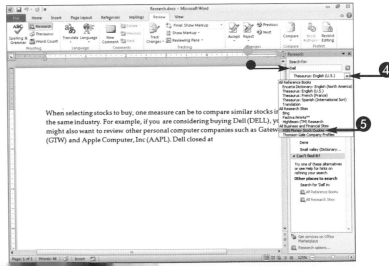

● Information from the research tool you selected appears in the Research task pane.

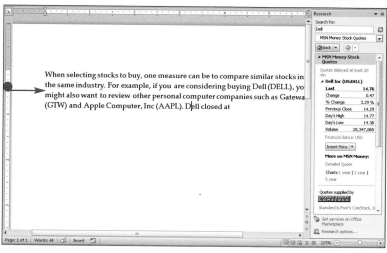

● Some of the research tools offer you a way to include the research in your document; for example, using MSN Money Stock Quotes, you can click  and then click **Insert Price**.

 TIPS

Can I find all the research information for free?

No. If you must pay for the information, a link appears in the Research pane.

How can Factiva iWorks help me?

Factiva iWorks provides free Web search capabilities and is designed to provide access to content that helps employees make quicker, more informed business decisions. It is a streamlined version of Factiva.com, the fee-based search engine built into Microsoft Office 2003 and later.

Add Comments to a Document

You can add comments to clarify your documents. For example, you can use a comment to explain a statement, add a note of clarification, or remind you to take an action.

Add a Comment

① On the status bar, click the **Full Screen Reading** button (▯), the **Web Layout** button (▯), or the **Print Layout** button (▯) to view your document.

You alternatively can click ▯, ▯, or ▯ on the View tab.

② Select the text about which you want to comment.

③ Click the **Review** tab.

④ Click **New Comment**.

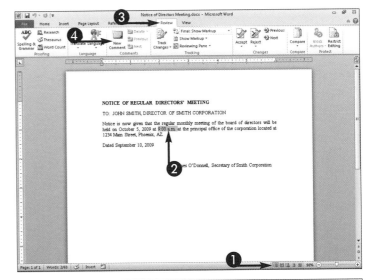

● A comment balloon appears in the markup area on the right side of the document.

● The comment balloon is attached to the text you selected, which is highlighted in the color of the balloon.

Note: *In the comment, Word inserts the initials stored in the Personalize section of the Word Options dialog box along with a comment number.*

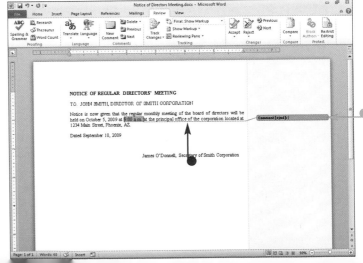

⑤ Type the text you want to store in the comment.

⑥ Click outside the comment balloon to save your comment.

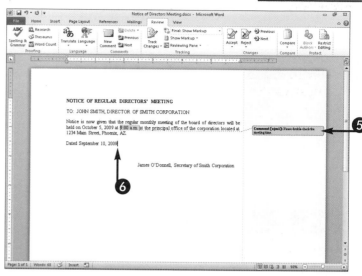

Delete a Comment

① Click anywhere in the comment balloon you want to delete.

② On the Review tab, click **Delete**.

Word deletes the comment balloon and removes the highlighting from the associated text.

TIP

Can I insert a comment in Draft view or Outline view?

Yes. Do the following:

① Follow Steps **1** to **4** in this section, selecting **Draft** view (▨) or **Outline** view (▨) in Step **1**.

② Type your comment.

③ To continue working, click in the document.

● To hide the pane, click the **Close** button (▨).

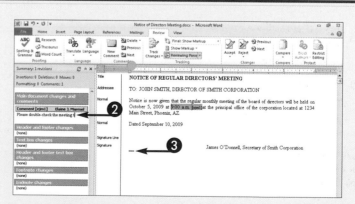

Track Document Changes During Review

Word can track the editing and formatting changes made to your document. This feature is particularly useful when more than one person works on the same document.

When Word tracks document revisions, it tracks the changes made and who made them so that you can easily identify who did what to a document.

Track Document Changes During Review

① Click ▣.

The document appears in Print Layout view.

② Click the **Review** tab.

③ Click **Track Changes**.

● The Track Changes button appears pressed.

④ Make changes to the document as needed.

● A vertical bar appears in the left margin beside lines containing changes.

● Deleted text changes appear with strikethrough formatting.

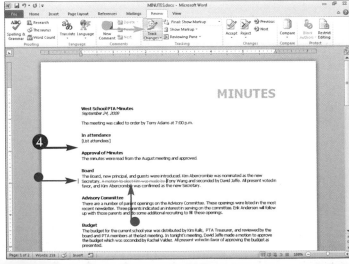

● Added text appears underlined and in a color other than black.

Each reviewer's changes appear in a different color.

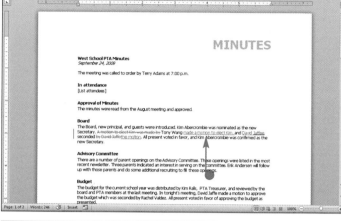

● You can view details about a change and who made it by positioning the mouse pointer over a change.

You can stop tracking changes by repeating Steps **2** and **3**.

Note: To review changes and accept or reject them, see the section "Review Tracked Changes."

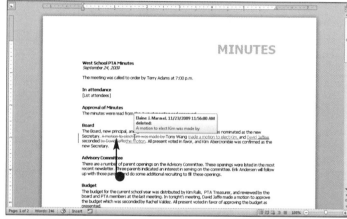

Can I print revisions?

Yes, you can print revisions in the document as they appear on-screen, or print a separate list of revisions.

1 Click the **File** tab.

The Backstage view appears.

2 Click **Print**.

3 Click the button below **Settings**.

4 Click **List of Markup**.

5 Click **Print**.

Review Tracked Changes

When you review a document containing tracked changes, you decide whether to accept or reject the changes. As you accept or reject changes, Word removes the revision marks.

Review Tracked Changes

1. Open a document in which changes were tracked.

2. Click the **Review** tab.

3. Click **Reviewing Pane**.

● For each change, Word displays the reviewer's name, the date and time of the change, and the details of the change.

● You can click ☒ to close the pane.

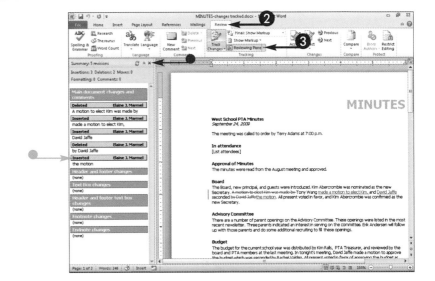

4. Press Ctrl + Home to place the insertion point at the beginning of the document.

5. Click **Next** to review the first change.

● Word highlights the change.

You can click **Next** again to skip over the change without accepting or rejecting it.

6 Click **Accept** to incorporate the change into the document or **Reject** to revert the text to its original state.

Word accepts or rejects the change, removes the revision marks, and highlights the next change.

7 Repeat Step **6** to review all revisions.

● If you need to move backward to a change you previously skipped, you can click **Previous**.

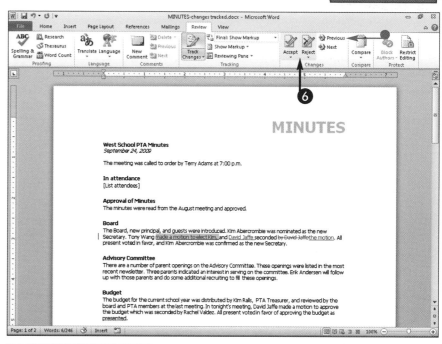

When you have reviewed all changes, this dialog box appears.

8 Click **OK**.

TIP

Is there a way I can work in the document without addressing the changes or viewing the tracking marks?

Yes. You can work viewing the original document before changes or viewing the edited document after changes.

1 Click the **Display for Review** drop-down menu.

2 Click **Final** to view the edited document without revision marks or click **Original** to view the document without revision marks, before any changes were made.

Combine Reviewers' Comments

You can combine two versions of the same document; this feature is particularly useful when two reviewers have each reviewed the same original and you want to work from the combined changes of both reviewers.

Combine Reviewers' Comments

① Click the **Review** tab.

② Click **Compare**.

③ Click **Combine**.

The Combine Documents dialog box appears.

④ Click the **Open** button (📂) for the Original document.

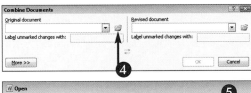

The Open dialog box appears.

⑤ Navigate to the folder containing the original file you want to combine.

⑥ Click the file.

⑦ Click **Open**.

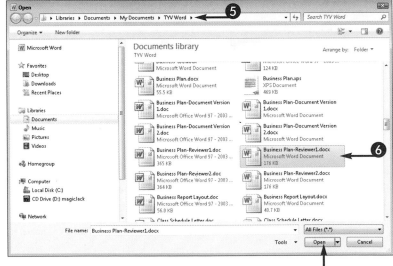

The Combine Documents dialog box reappears.

⑧ Repeat Steps **4** to **7**, clicking 🖼 for the Revised document.

● You can type a label for changes to each document in these boxes.

⑨ Click **OK**.

Word displays three panes.

● The left pane contains the results of combining both documents.

● The top-right pane displays the document you selected in Step **6**.

● The bottom-right pane displays the document you selected in Step **8**.

● You can display information about each revision by clicking **Reviewing Pane**.

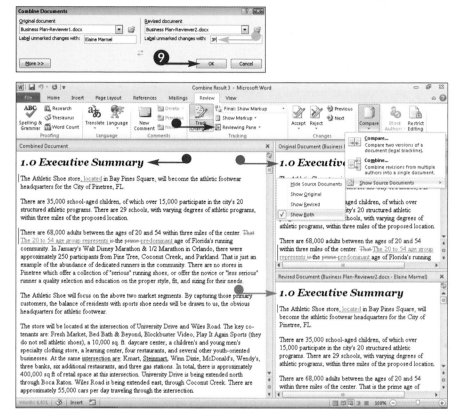

What happens when I click the More button?

Word displays a series of settings you can control. You can specify the comparisons you want to make and you can identify how to show changes. For example, you can control whether Word displays changes in the original document, the revised document, or a new document.

Two reviewers reviewed same document but they forgot to track changes; can I somehow see their changes?

You can compare the documents with the original or with each other. Follow the steps in this section, but, in Step **3**, click **Compare**. Word again displays three panes; the results of comparing the two documents appears in the left pane, while the document you select in Step **6** appears in the top-right pane, and the document you select in Step **8** appears in the bottom-right pane.

Formatting Text

You can format text for emphasis and for greater readability. And although the individual types of formatting are discussed separately, you can perform each of the tasks in this chapter on a single selection of text.

Change the Font

You can change the typeface that appears in your document by changing the font. Changing the font can help readers better understand your document.

Use serif fonts — fonts with short lines stemming from the bottoms of the letters — to provide a line that helps guide the reader's eyes. Use sans serif fonts — fonts without short lines stemming from the bottoms of the letters — for headlines.

Change the Font

1 Select the text that you want to change to a different font.

If you drag to select, the Mini toolbar appears faded in the background, and you can use it by moving ☐ toward the Mini toolbar.

● To use the Ribbon, you can click the **Home** tab.

2 Click here to display a list of the available fonts on your computer.

Word displays a sample of the selected text in any font at which you point the mouse.

Note: See Chapter 1 for details on Live Preview and the Mini toolbar.

3 Click the font you want to use.

● Word assigns the font you selected to the text you selected.

You can click anywhere outside the selection to continue working.

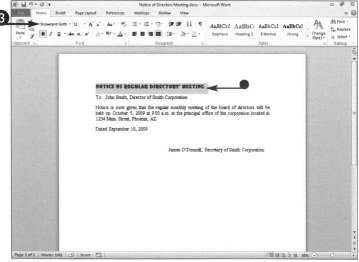

Change Text Size

You can increase or decrease the size of the text in your document. Increase the size to make reading the text easier; decrease the size to fit more text on a page.

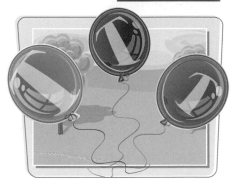

Change Text Size

① Select the text to which you want to assign a new size.

If you drag to select, the Mini toolbar appears faded in the background, and you can use it by moving ⍈ toward the Mini toolbar.

● To use the Ribbon, click the **Home** tab.

② Click here to display a list of the possible sizes for the current font.

Word displays a sample of the selected text in any font size at which you point the mouse.

Note: See Chapter 1 for details on Live Preview and the Mini toolbar.

③ Click the size you want to use.

● Word changes the size of the selected text.

You can click anywhere outside the selection to continue working.

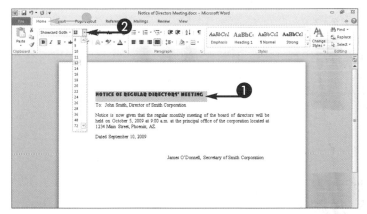

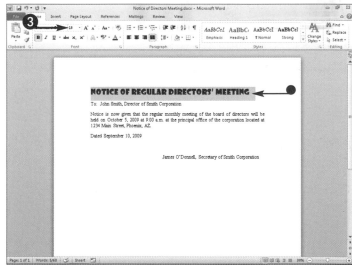

Emphasize Information with Bold, Italic, or Underline

You can apply italics, boldface, or underlining to text in your document for emphasis.

① Select the text that you want to emphasize.

● If you drag to select, the Mini toolbar appears faded in the background, and you can use it by moving toward the Mini toolbar.

Note: See Chapter 1 for details on the Mini toolbar.

● If you want to use the Ribbon, click the **Home** tab.

② Click the **Bold** button (**B**), the **Italic** button (*I*), or the **Underline** button (U) on the Ribbon or the Mini toolbar.

● Word applies the emphasis you selected.

This example shows the text after italics is selected.

You can click anywhere outside the selection to continue working.

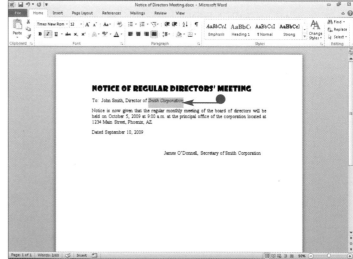

Superscript or Subscript Text

You can assign superscript or subscript notation to any text to make it appear above or below the regular line of text. Superscripting and subscripting are often used when inserting trademark symbols.

The example in this section uses superscript.

Superscript or Subscript Text

① Type the text that you want to superscript or subscript.

② Select the text that you want to superscript or subscript.

If you drag to select, the Mini toolbar appears faded in the background.

Note: See Chapter 1 for details on the Mini toolbar.

③ Click the **Home** tab.

④ Click the **Superscript** button (x²) or the **Subscript** button (x₂).

● Word superscripts or subscripts the selected text.

You can click anywhere outside the selection to continue working.

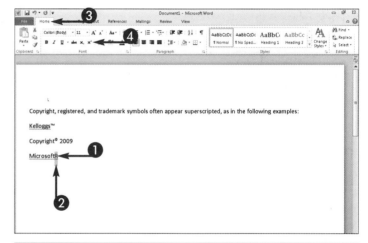

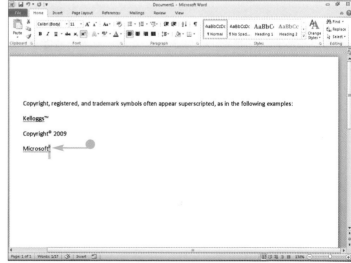

Change Text Case

You can change the case of selected text instead of retyping it with a new case applied.

Change Text Case

1. Select the text to which you want to assign a new case.

   If you drag to select, the Mini toolbar appears faded in the background.

   Note: *See Chapter 1 for details on the Mini toolbar.*

2. Click the **Home** tab.

3. Click the **Change Case** button (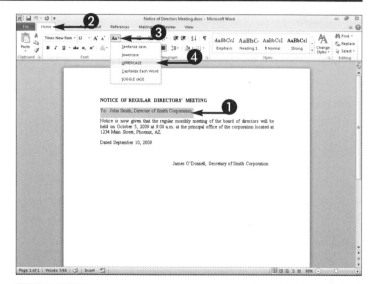).

4. Click the case you want to use.

- The selected text appears in the new case.

  You can click anywhere outside the selection to continue working.

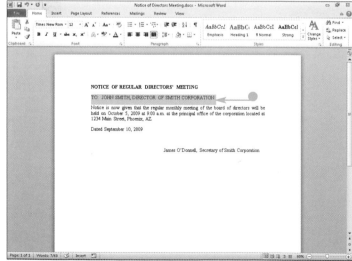

Change Text Color

You can change the color of selected text for emphasis. Color is effective when you view your document on-screen, save it as a PDF or an XPS file, or print it using a color printer.

Change Text Color

① Select the text that you want to change to a different color.

● If you drag to select, the Mini toolbar appears faded in the background, and you can use it by moving ⟍ toward the Mini toolbar.

● To use the Ribbon, click the **Home** tab.

② Click the **Font Color** button (◼) on the Ribbon or on the Mini toolbar and point at a color.

Word displays a sample of the selected text.

Note: See Chapter 1 for details on Live Preview and the Mini toolbar.

③ Click a color.

● Word assigns the color to the selected text.

You can click anywhere outside the selection to continue working.

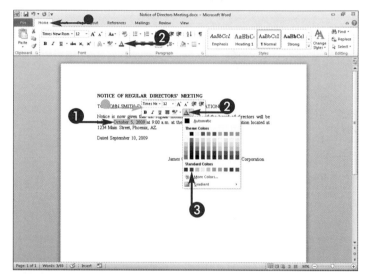

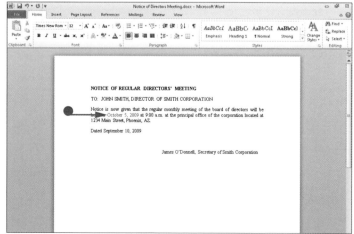

Apply Text Effects

You can apply effects to text such as outlining, shadows, reflections, glows, and beveling to draw a reader's eye to the text.

This example applies outlining to text.

Apply Text Effects

Assign a Text Effect

① Type and select the text to which you want to apply an effect.

If you drag to select, the Mini toolbar appears faded in the background.

② Click the **Home** tab.

③ Click the **Text Effects** button (▨▾).

● The Text Effects gallery appears.

Word displays a sample of the selected text in any text effect at which you point the mouse.

Note: See Chapter 1 for details on Live Preview and the Mini toolbar.

④ Click an option from the gallery to apply it.

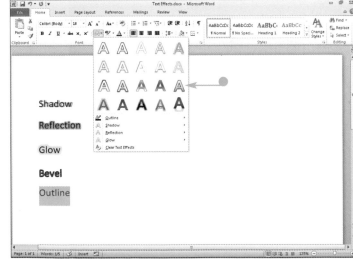

● Word applies your choice to the selected text.

You can click anywhere outside the selection to continue working.

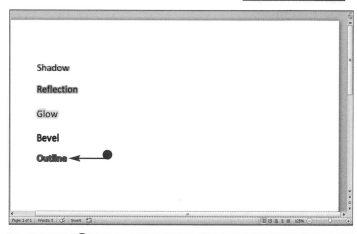

Control a Text Effect's Appearance

1 Select text to which you have applied an effect.

2 Click the **Home** tab.

3 Click 🄰 to display the Text Effects gallery.

4 Click the type of effect you applied.

● Use the menu that appears to make changes to the appearance of the text effect.

The changes you can make depend on the type of effect you applied.

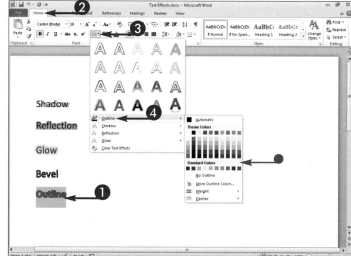

I applied a shadow to text but I cannot see it; what should I do?

Use the Format Text Effects window to adjust the distance of your shadow. While viewing the Text Effects gallery, click **Shadow** and then click **Shadow Options**.

1 Click Shadow.

2 Drag this slider bar to increase the shadow distance.

● You can type a distance here.

3 Click **Close**.

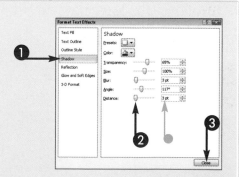

Apply a Font Style Set

You can use font style sets to enhance the appearance of OpenType fonts.

You see the biggest difference in style set changes when you select a larger number from the Stylistic Sets list box.

Get your new font styles here!

Apply a Font Style Set

① Select an OpenType font.

This example uses Gabriola.

② Type some text.

③ Select the text you typed.

If you drag to select, the Mini toolbar appears faded in the background.

④ Click the **Font** ▣.

The Font dialog box appears.

5 Click the **Advanced** tab.

6 Click the **Stylistic sets** [▾] and choose **7**.

● A preview of your choice appears here.

7 Click **OK**.

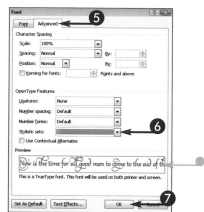

● Word applies the font style set to the text you selected.

You can click anywhere outside the selection to continue working.

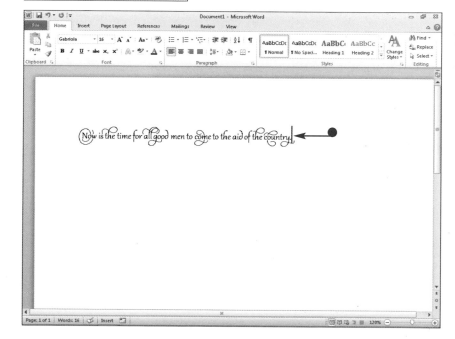

TIP

What effect does the Number forms option in the Font dialog box have?

When you click [▾], you can select either Oldstyle or Lining. This feature for OpenType fonts affects the alignment of numbers above and below an imaginary horizontal line. Oldstyle aligns numbers above and below the imaginary line, while Lining aligns numbers on the imaginary line.

| 123456789 | Old Style |
| 123456789 | Lining |

Apply Highlighting to Text

You can use color to create highlights in a document to draw attention to the text. Highlighting is effective when you view the document on-screen or when you print it using a color printer.

① Select the text that you want to highlight.

If you drag to select, the Mini toolbar appears faded in the background, and you can use it by moving 🔖 toward the Mini toolbar.

② To use the Ribbon, click the **Home** tab.

③ Click 🔽 beside the Text Highlight Color button (🖍️) on the Ribbon or the Mini toolbar and point at a color.

Word displays a sample of the selected text highlighted in any color at which you point the mouse.

Note: *See Chapter 1 for details on Live Preview and the Mini toolbar.*

④ Click a color.

● Word highlights the selected text using the color you select.

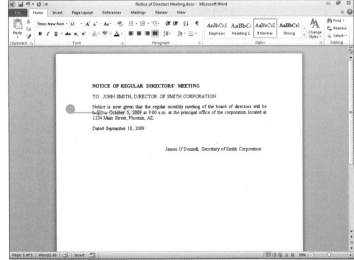

Apply Strikethrough to Text

Strikethrough formatting is often used in the legal community to identify text the reviewer proposes to delete.

If you need to track both additions and deletions and want to update the document in an automated way, use Word's review tracking features as described in Chapter 4.

Apply Strikethrough to Text

① Select the text to which you want to apply strikethrough formatting.

If you drag to select, the Mini toolbar appears faded in the background.

Note: See Chapter 1 for details on the Mini toolbar.

② Click the **Home** tab.

③ Click the **Strikethrough** button (abc).

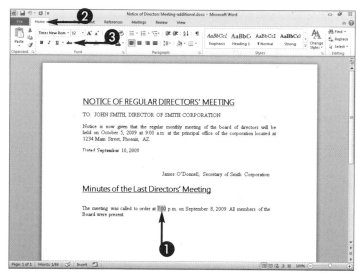

● Word applies strikethrough formatting to the selected text.

You can click anywhere outside the selection to continue working.

You can repeat these steps to remove strikethrough formatting.

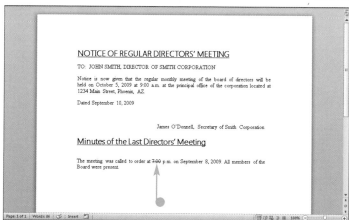

Copy Text Formatting

To save time, you can copy formatting that you apply to text in one portion of your document to another portion of your document.

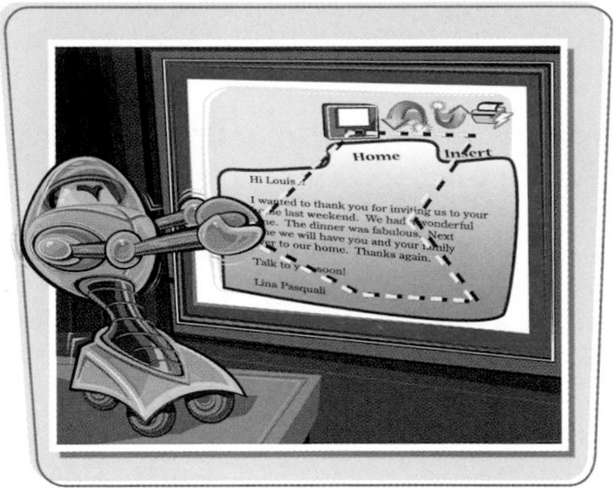

Copy Text Formatting

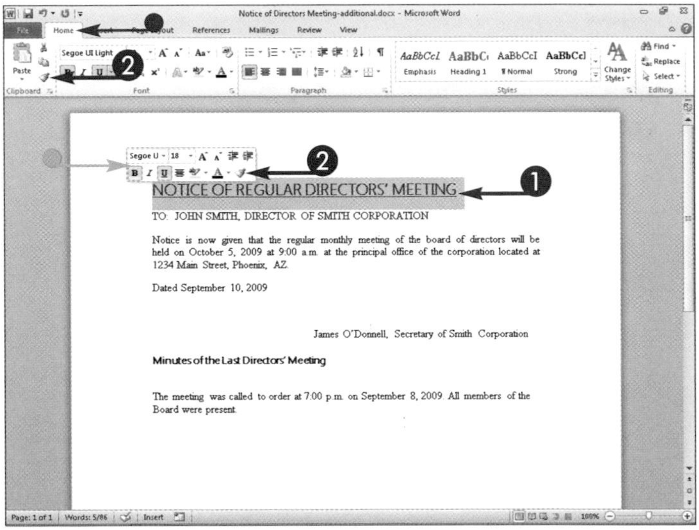

1. Select the text containing the formatting that you want to copy.

- If you drag to select, the Mini toolbar appears faded in the background, and you can use it by moving toward the Mini toolbar.
- To use the Ribbon, click the **Home** tab.

2. Click the **Format Painter** button ( ).

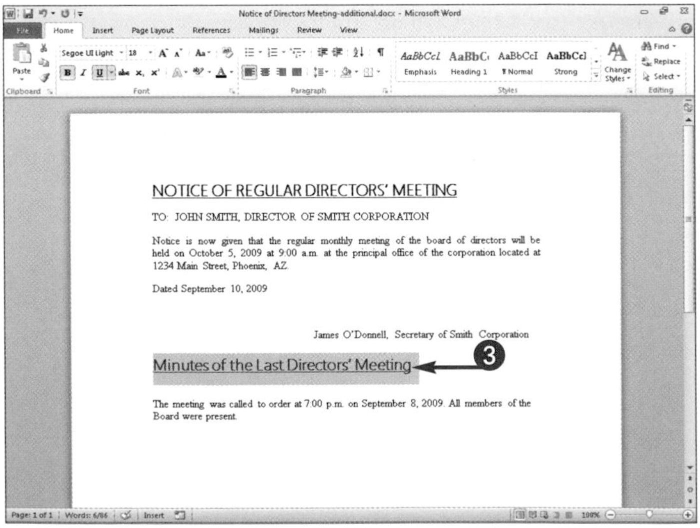

The mouse pointer changes to when you move the mouse over your document.

3. Select the text to which you want to assign formatting.

The newly selected text changes to the format used for the original selection.

You can click anywhere outside the selection to continue working.

Remove Text Formatting

You can quickly and easily remove formatting that you have applied to text in your document.

Remove Text Formatting

① Select the text from which you want to remove formatting.

Note: *If you do not select text, Word removes text formatting from the entire document.*

The Mini toolbar appears faded in the background.

② Click the **Home** tab.

③ Click the **Clear Formatting** button (⟺).

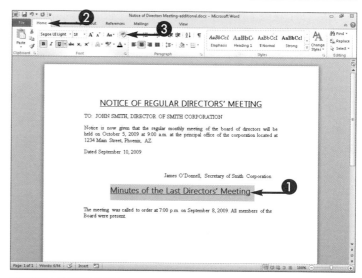

● Word removes all formatting from the selected text.

Click anywhere outside the selection to continue working.

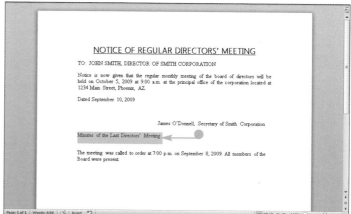

Set the Default Font for All New Documents

You can change the default font that Word uses for all new documents you create. The default font that ships with Word is Calibri, 11 point.

Changing the default font does not affect documents you have already created.

Set the Default Font for All New Documents

❶ Click the **Home** tab.

❷ Right-click the Normal style.

❸ Click **Modify**.

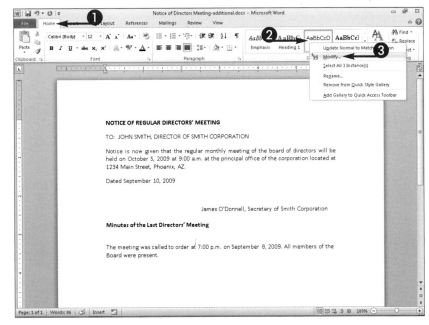

The Modify Style dialog box appears.

❹ Click ▼ to select the font that you want to use for all new documents.

❺ Click ▼ to select the font size that you want to use for all new documents.

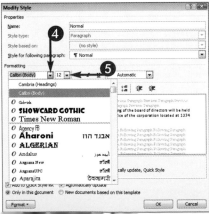

● A preview of the new selections appears here.

6 Select the **New documents based on this template** option (○ changes to ◉).

7 Click **OK**.

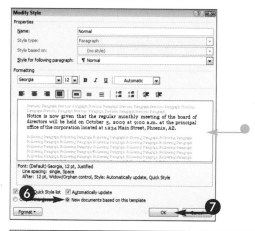

● When you open a new document, the default font is the font you selected.

Note: To open a new document, see Chapter 2.

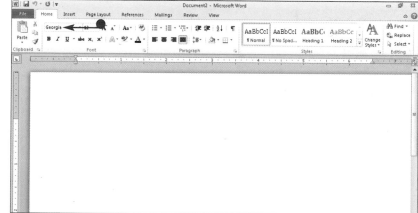

I like the default font, but I want to indent the first line of each paragraph by default. Can I do that?

Yes. Follow these steps:

1 Complete Steps **1** to **3**.

2 Click **Format**, and from the list that appears, click **Paragraph**.

3 Click here and click **First line**.

4 Click **OK** twice.

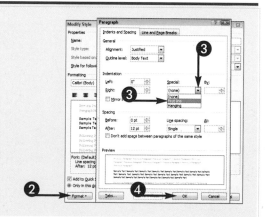

Formatting Paragraphs

Instead of formatting individual words in your document, you can apply changes to entire paragraphs to help certain sections of your text stand out. You can apply formatting such as line spacing, bullets, or borders to the paragraphs in your document to enhance the appearance of the document.

You can change the alignment of various paragraphs in your document to enhance the document's appearance.

You can align text with the left or right margins, center it horizontally between both margins, or justify it so that the text aligns with both the left and right margins. To align text vertically, see Chapter 7. The example in this section centers a headline between the left and right margins.

Change Text Alignment

① Click anywhere in the paragraph that you want to align.

② Click the **Home** tab.

③ Click an alignment button.

The **Align Left** button (▤) aligns text with the left margin, the **Center** button (▤), centers text between the left and right margins, the **Align Right** button (▤) aligns text with the right margin, and the **Justify** button (▤) aligns text between the left and right margins.

Word aligns the text.

● This text is aligned with the left margin.

● This text is centered between both margins.

● This text is aligned with the right margin.

● This text is justified between both margins.

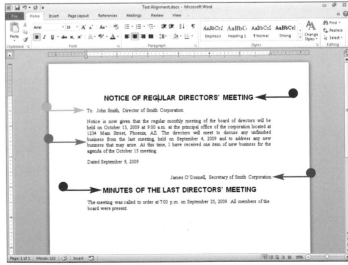

Set Line Spacing Within a Paragraph

You can change the amount of space Word places between the lines of text within a paragraph. Word 2010 uses a different default line spacing than Word 2003 and earlier.

Word can measure line spacing in inches, but it is typically easiest to measure in points, specified as pts. 12 pts equal approximately one line of space.

1. Click in the paragraph for which you want to change line spacing.

2. Click **Home**.

3. Click the **Line Spacing** button (≡).

4. Click a number.

   1 represents single spacing, the default in Word 97–2003; **1.15** is the default spacing in Word 2010; **1.5** places ½ blank line between lines of text; **2** represents double spacing; **2.5** places 1½ blank lines between lines of text; and **3** represents triple spacing.

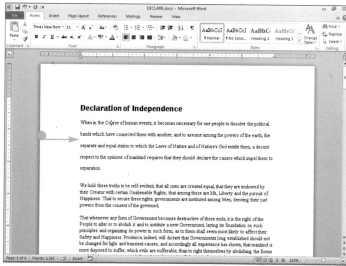

● Word applies the line spacing you specified to the selected text.

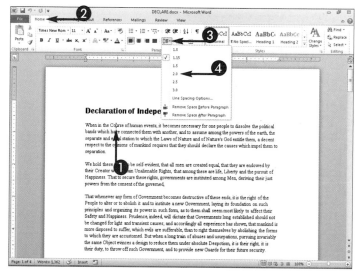

Set Line Spacing Between Paragraphs

You can change the amount of space Word places between paragraphs of text. For example, you can use this technique to set double spacing between paragraphs while maintaining single spacing within each paragraph.

By default, Word 2010 uses different settings than Word 2003 and earlier for space between paragraphs.

Set Line Spacing Between Paragraphs

① Select the paragraph or paragraphs for which you want to define spacing.

② Click the **Home** tab.

③ Click the **Paragraph** ◻.

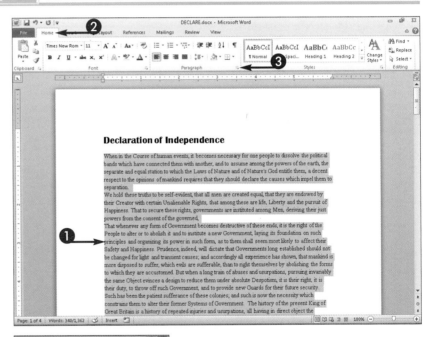

The Paragraph dialog box appears.

④ Click here to increase or decrease the space before the selected paragraph.

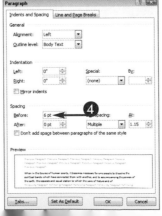

5 Click here to increase or decrease the space after the selected paragraph.

6 Click **OK**.

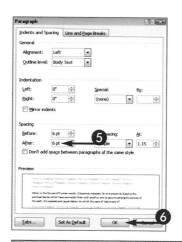

● Word applies the spacing before and after the selected paragraph.

7 Click anywhere outside the selection to continue working.

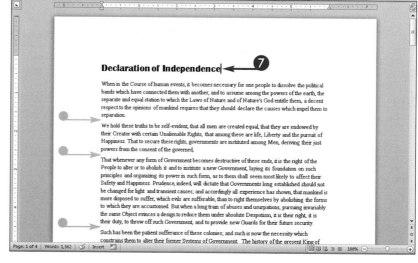

TIPS

What does the Do not add space between paragraphs of the same style check box do?

As described later in this chapter, you can use styles to assign predefined sets of formatting information, such as font and paragraph information. By default, Word assigns the Normal style to each paragraph of text. You can use the Do not add space between paragraphs of the same style check box to use the same spacing both within a paragraph and between paragraphs to which you have assigned the same style.

How many points should I use before and after paragraphs to leave one blank line between paragraphs?

Assign 6 points before and after each paragraph. The 6 points of space at the bottom of Paragraph 1 plus the 6 points of space at the top of Paragraph 2 equal 12 points, or one line space. A point is 1/72 of an inch. A 72-point line of text is approximately 1 inch high. Measure 1 inch of text vertically; in most cases, six lines of text fill 1 vertical inch of space. One line equals about 1/6 inch, and 1/6 inch equals 12 points of vertical line space.

Create a Bulleted or Numbered List

You can use bullets or numbers to call attention to lists that you present in your documents.

Use numbers when the items in your list follow a particular order. Use bullets when the items in your list do not follow any particular order.

Create a List from Existing Text

1 Select the text to which you want to assign bullets or numbers.

2 Click the **Home** tab.

3 Click the **Numbering** button (⊞) or the **Bullets** button (⊞).

● Word applies numbers or bullets to the selection.

This example uses bullets.

4 Click anywhere outside the selection to continue working.

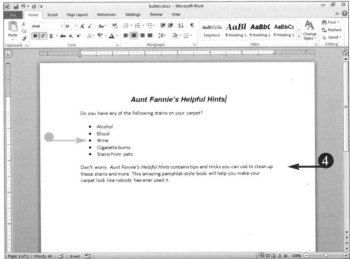

Create a List as You Type

1 Type **1.** to create a numbered list or ***** to create a bulleted list.

2 Press **Spacebar** or **Tab**.

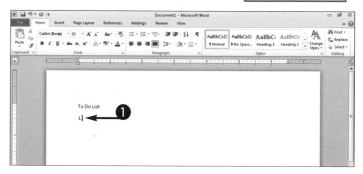

Word automatically formats the entry as a list item and displays the AutoCorrect Options button so that you can undo or stop automatic numbering.

3 Type a list item.

4 Press **Enter** to prepare to type another list item.

● Word automatically adds a bullet or number for the next list item.

5 Repeat Steps **3** and **4** for each list item.

To stop entering items in the list, press **Enter** twice.

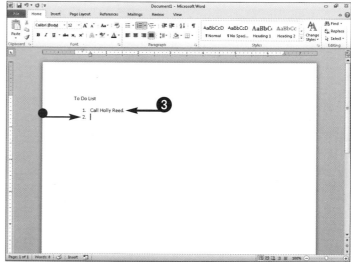

Can I create a bulleted or numbered list with more than one level, like the type of list you use when creating an outline?

Yes. You can use the Multilevel List button (▦).

1 Click ▦.

2 Click a format.

3 Type your list.

● You can press **Enter** to enter a new list item at the same list level.

● Each time you press **Tab**, Word indents a level in the list.

● Each time you press **Shift** + **Tab**, Word outdents a level in the list.

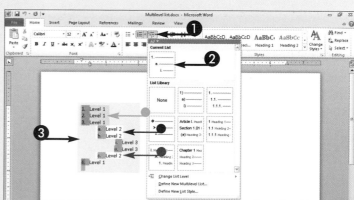

Display Formatting Marks

You can display formatting marks that do not print but help you identify formatting in your document.

Word can display formatting marks that represent spaces, tabs, paragraphs, hidden text, and optional hyphens.

1 Open any document.

2 Click the **Home** tab.

3 Click the **Show/Hide** button (¶).

Word displays all formatting marks in your document.

● Single dots (·) appear each time you press **Spacebar**.

● Paragraph marks (¶) appear each time you press **Enter**.

● Arrows (→) appear each time you press **Tab**.

● Hidden text appears underlined with dots.

● Optional hyphens, inserted by pressing **Ctrl** + **·**, appear as ⊡.

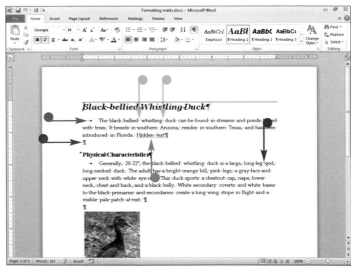

Hide or Display the Ruler

You can hide or display horizontal and vertical rulers to help you identify the position of the insertion point or to align text.

You can use the ruler to indent paragraphs or set tabs in your document; see the sections "Indent Paragraphs" and "Set Tabs."

Hide or Display the Ruler

1 Click the **View** tab.

2 Click **Ruler**.

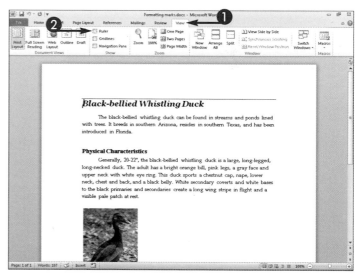

● A ruler appears above your document.

● A ruler appears on the left side of your document.

● You can click the **Ruler** button (🔲) to hide or display the rulers.

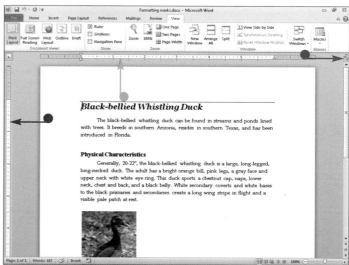

Indent Paragraphs

You can indent paragraphs in your document from the left and right margins. You also can indent only the first line of a paragraph or all lines *except* the first line of the paragraph.

① Select the text that you want to indent.

② Click the **Home** tab.

③ Click the **Paragraph** ▣.

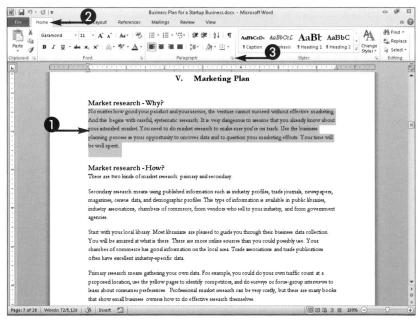

The Paragraph dialog box appears.

④ Click here to specify the number of inches to indent the left and right edge of the paragraph.

● The effects of your settings appear here.

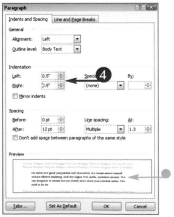

5 Click here and select an indenting option.

First line indents only the first line of the paragraph, and **Hanging** indents all lines *except* the first line of the paragraph.

6 Click here to set the amount of the first line or hanging indent.

● The effects of your settings appear here.

7 Click **OK**.

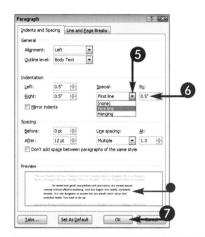

● Word applies your settings to the selected paragraph.

You can click anywhere outside the selection to continue working.

Can I set paragraph indentations without using a dialog box?

Yes. You can use buttons in the ruler. On the ruler, drag the **Left Indent** button (□) to indent all lines from the left margin, drag the **Hanging Indent** button (▣) to create a hanging indent, or drag the **First Line Indent** button (▢) to indent the first line only. On the right side of the ruler, drag the **Right Indent** button (△) to indent all lines from the right margin.

What do the Decrease Indent button and the Increase Indent button do?

The **Increase Indent** button (▤) indents all lines from the left margin. The **Decrease Indent** button (▤) decreases the indent of all lines from the left margin.

Set Tabs

You can use left, center, right, decimal, or bar tabs to line up columnar information. Using tabs ensures that information lines up properly within a column.

By default, Word places tabs every .5 inch across the page between the left and right margins.

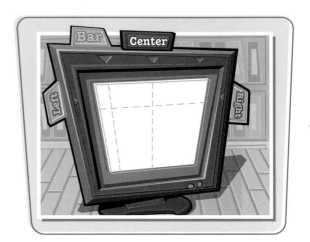

Add a Tab

① Click here until the type of tab you want to add appears.

- ⊔   Left tab
- ⊥   Center tab
- ⊣   Right tab
- ⊥   Decimal tab
- ⊥   Bar tab

② Select the lines to which you want to add a tab.

③ Click the ruler where you want the tab to appear.

Word displays a tab at the location you clicked on each selected line.

Using a Tab

1 Click to the left of the information you want to appear at the tab.

2 Press **Tab**.

3 Type your text.

The text appears at the tab.

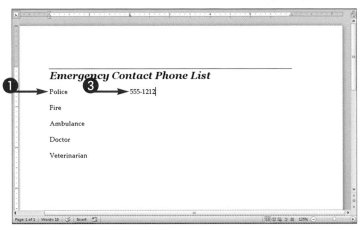

Move a Tab

1 Click the line using the tab or select the lines of text affected by the tab.

2 Drag the tab to the left or right.

● A vertical line marks its position as you drag.

When you click and drag a tab, the text moves with the tab.

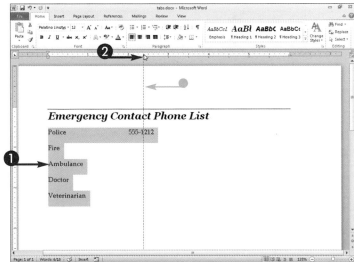

How can I delete a tab?

Yes. Follow these steps:

1 Click in or select the paragraphs containing the tab.

2 Drag the tab off the ruler.

● When you delete a tab, text aligned at the tab moves to the first preset tab on the line.

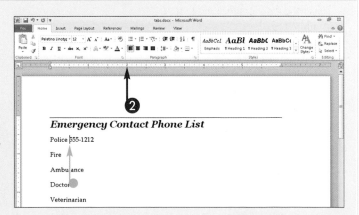

You can use dot leader tabs to help your reader follow information across a page.

Add Leader Characters to Tabs

① Follow Steps **1** to **3** in the subsection "Add a Tab" to create a tab stop.

② Select the text containing the tab to which you want to add dot leaders.

③ Click the **Home** tab.

④ Click the **Paragraph** 🖼.

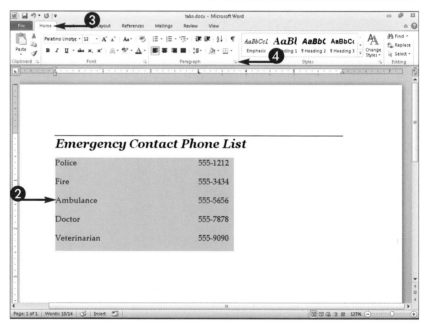

The Paragraph dialog box appears.

⑤ Click **Tabs**.

The Tabs dialog box appears.

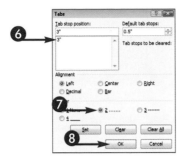

6 Click the tab setting to which you want to add leaders.

7 Select a leader option (☐ changes to ☉).

8 Click **OK**.

● Word adds leading characters from the last character before the tab to the first character at the tab.

Click anywhere outside the selection to continue working.

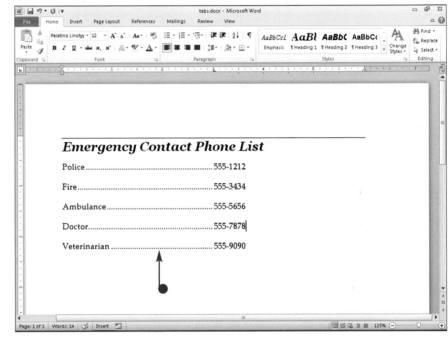

Emergency Contact Phone List

Police...555-1212

Fire..555-3434

Ambulance...555-5656

Doctor...555-7878

Veterinarian 555-9090

Can I set tabs using the Tabs dialog box instead of the ruler?
Yes. Follow these steps:

1 Follow Steps **2** to **5** on this page to display the Tabs dialog box.

2 Click here and type a tab stop position.

3 Click here and select a tab alignment option (☐ changes to ☉).

4 Click **Set**.

5 Repeat Steps **2** to **4** for each tab stop you want to set.

6 Click **OK** to have the tabs you set appear on the ruler.

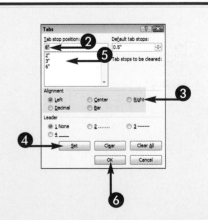

Add a Paragraph Border

You can draw attention to a paragraph containing important information by adding a border to it.

1. Select the text that you want to surround with a border.

2. Click the **Home** tab.

3. Click ⯆ beside the **Borders** button (⊞).

4. Click **Borders and Shading**.

The Borders and Shading dialog box appears.

5. Click the **Borders** tab.

6. Click here to select a type of border.

This example uses 3-D.

⑦ Click here to select the style for the border line.

⑧ Click here and select a color for the border line.

⑨ Click here and select a thickness for the border line.

This area shows the results of the settings you select.

⑩ Click **OK**.

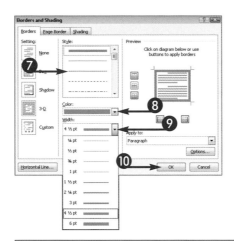

● The border appears around the text you selected in Step **1**.

⑪ Click anywhere outside the selection to continue working.

How do I remove a border?

Yes. Follow these steps, and if you are willing to use the same color, style, and thickness for the border, you also can use these steps to quickly apply a border to any paragraph, clicking the type of border you want to apply in Step **4**.

① Click anywhere in the text surrounded by a border.

② Click the **Home** tab.

③ Click ▾ on ▦.

④ Click **No Border**.

Word removes the border.

Check for Formatting Inconsistencies

You can have Word display wavy blue underlines to mark text you have formatted inconsistently in your document. This feature is useful when you want to make sure that you have applied direct formatting, such as italics, consistently or that you have used styles whenever possible.

For each formatting inconsistency, Word suggests a way that you can make the formatting consistent and give your document a more professional-looking appearance.

Display Format Inconsistencies

1 Click the **File** tab.

The Backstage view appears.

2 Click **Options**.

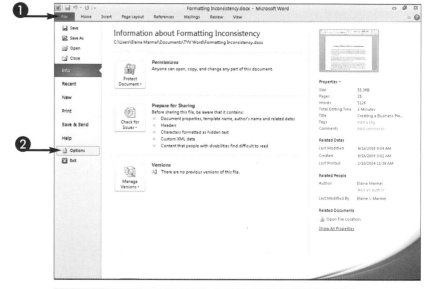

The Word Options dialog box appears.

3 Click **Advanced**.

4 In the Editing options section, select **Keep track of formatting** (☐ changes to ☑).

5 Select **Mark formatting inconsistencies** (☐ changes to ☑).

6 Click **OK**.

Word saves your settings.

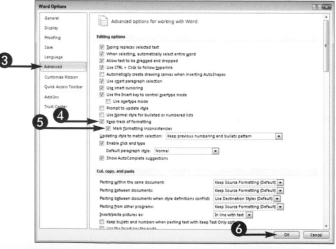

Correct Formatting Inconsistencies

1 Right-click a formatting inconsistency to display a context menu.

● Formatting inconsistencies appear with wavy blue underlines.

2 To correct the inconsistency, click the first option on the menu.

● You can ignore this inconsistency by clicking **Ignore Once**, or you can ignore all occurrences of this inconsistency by clicking **Ignore Rule**.

● Word selects the inconsistency, corrects or ignores it, and removes the wavy blue underline.

You can click anywhere outside the selection to continue working.

3 Repeat Steps **1** and **2** for each inconsistency.

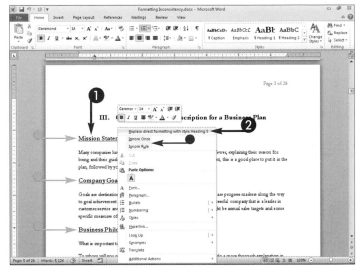

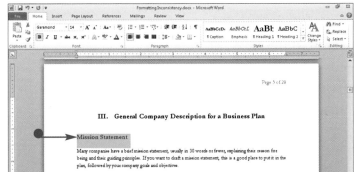

TIPS

What kinds of formatting inconsistencies does Word check for?

Word looks for occurrences of similar, but not identical, formatting that you applied directly to text or lists. Word also looks for occurrences of formatting you applied directly to text that matches styles you applied elsewhere in your document.

I do not want Word to check for formatting inconsistencies any longer. How do I turn off this feature?

Repeat Steps **1** to **5** in the subsection "Display Format Inconsistencies." Deselect the **Mark formatting inconsistencies** option in Step **4** (☑ changes to ☐). When you click **OK** in Step **5**, Word disables the feature.

Review and Change Formatting

You can review the formatting associated with text in your document to see the details of exactly what formatting is applied to the text.

1. Select the text containing the formatting you want to review.

2. Click the **Home** tab.

3. Click the **Styles** 🔲.

   The Styles pane appears.

4. Click the **Style Inspector** button (🗐).

   The Style Inspector pane appears.

5. Click the **Reveal Formatting** button (🔍).

   The Reveal Formatting pane appears.

6. Click the **Close** buttons (🗷) to close the Styles pane and the Style Inspector pane.

● A portion of the selected text appears here.

● Formatting details for the selected text appear here.

● You can click a plus sign (⊞) beside a bold heading in the Reveal Formatting pane to display links.

7. Click the link for the type of change you want to make.

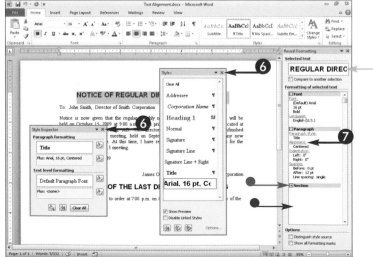

In this example, the Indents and Spacing tab of the Paragraph dialog box appears.

8 Select the options you want to change.

9 Click **OK**.

● Word applies the formatting changes.

● The information in the Reveal Formatting task pane updates.

10 Click anywhere to continue working.

● You can click ⊠ to close the Reveal Formatting task pane.

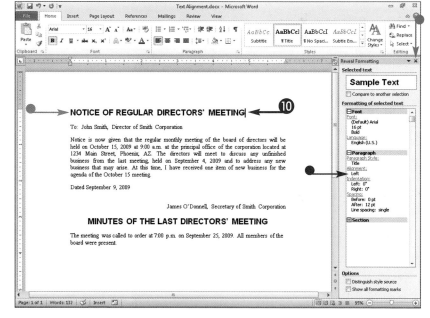

TIP

What happens if I select the Distinguish style source option below the Reveal Formatting task pane?

When you select this option (☐ changes to ☑), Word changes the appearance of the Reveal Formatting task pane to include the names of any styles used in your document. For more information on using styles, see the section "Apply Formatting Using Styles."

Options

☑ Distinguish style source

☐ Show all formatting marks

Compare Formatting

You can compare the formatting of one selection to another and have Word update the second selection so that it matches the first selection. This feature is useful for ensuring that you apply consistent manual formatting to multiple selections.

① Select the text containing the formatting that you want to compare.

② Click the **Home** tab.

③ Click the **Styles** 🔲.

The Styles task pane appears.

④ Click 🔁.

The Style Inspector pane appears.

⑤ Click 🔁.

● The Reveal Formatting pane appears.

⑥ Click 🗙 to close the Styles pane and the Style Inspector pane.

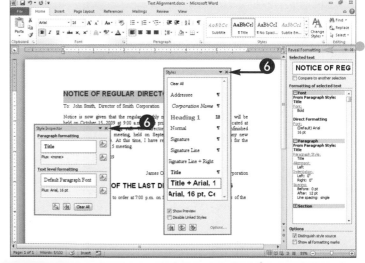

7 Select the **Compare to another selection** option (☐ changes to ☑).

● A second box for selected text appears.

8 Select the text that you want to compare to the text you selected in Step **1**.

● Formatting differences between the selections appear here.

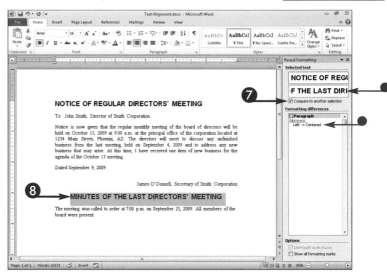

9 To match the formatting of the selections, slide the mouse pointer over the second selection.

10 Click ▼.

11 Click **Apply Formatting of Original Selection**.

Word applies the formatting of the first selection to the second selection.

You can click anywhere to continue working.

● You can click ☒ to close the Reveal Formatting task pane.

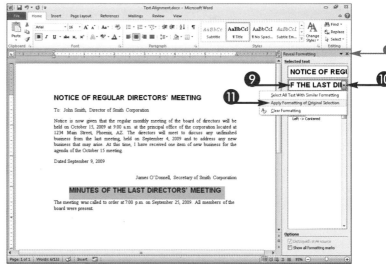

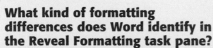

TIPS

What kind of formatting differences does Word identify in the Reveal Formatting task pane?

For any two selections, Word identifies differences in font, paragraph style, alignment, outline level, spacing before and after the paragraphs, line and page breaks, and bullets and numbering. You can make changes to any of these formatting differences by following the steps in the section "Review and Change Formatting."

What happens if I select the Show all formatting marks option below the Reveal Formatting task pane?

When you select this option, Word displays formatting marks in your document that represent tabs, spaces, paragraphs, line breaks, and so on.

Apply Formatting Using Styles

You can quickly apply formatting and maintain formatting consistency by using styles to format text. Styles are predefined sets of formatting that can include font, paragraph, list, and border and shading information.

You can store styles you use frequently in the Quick Style gallery, but you also can easily use styles not stored in the Quick Style gallery.

Apply Formatting Using Styles

Using the Quick Style Gallery

① Select the text to which you want to apply formatting.

② Click the **Home** tab.

③ Click ▲ and ▼ to scroll through available Quick Styles.

④ Click ▼.

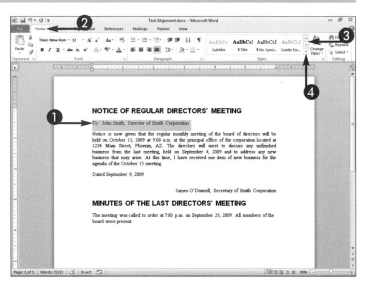

Word displays the Quick Style gallery.

● The style of the selected text appears highlighted.

● As you position the mouse pointer over various styles, Live Preview shows you the way the selected text would look in each style.

You can click a style to apply it to the selected text.

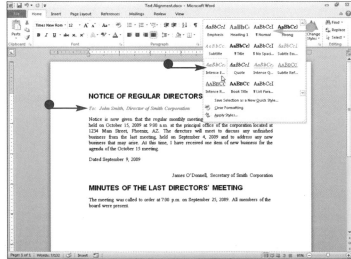

Using other Styles

1 Complete Steps **1** to **3** in the subsection "Using a Style from the Quick Style Gallery."

2 Click **Apply Styles**.

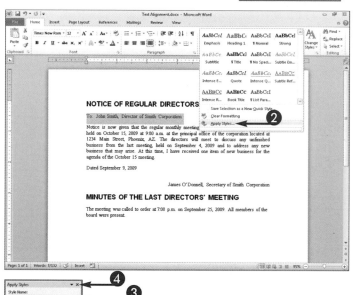

The Apply Styles pane appears.

3 Click ▾ to open the Style Name list and then select a style.

Word applies the style to the selected text.

4 Click ☒ to close the Apply Styles pane.

You can click anywhere to continue working.

Can I view the styles in the Apply Styles pane using Live Preview?

Yes. Follow these steps:

1 Click the **Styles** ☐.

2 In the Styles task pane, select the **Show Preview** option (☐ changes to ☑).

The next time that you open the Apply Styles pane, Word shows a preview of the style in the pane.

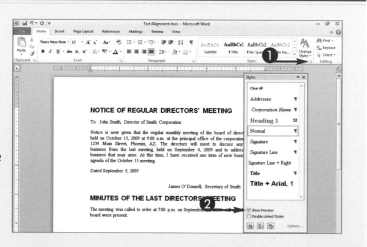

Switch Styles

You can easily change all text that is formatted in one style to another style. Using this technique can help you maintain formatting consistency in your documents.

Switch Styles

1 Place the insertion point in or select one example of text containing the formatting that you want to change.

2 Click the **Home** tab.

3 Click the **Styles** ▣.

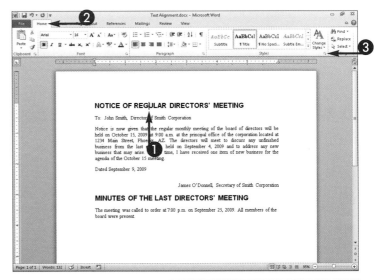

Word displays the Styles pane.

● The style for the selected text appears highlighted.

● You can position ▷ over any style to display its formatting information.

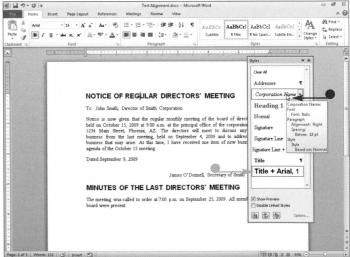

④ Position the mouse pointer over a style until ⊡ appears.

⑤ Click ⊡ to display a list of options.

⑥ Click **Select All Instance(s)**.

● Word selects all text in your document formatted using the style of the text you selected in Step **1**.

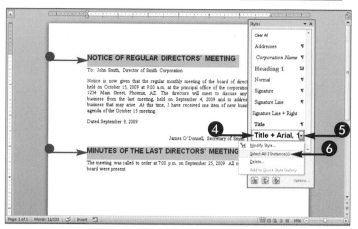

⑦ Click the style you want to apply to all selected text.

● Word changes all selected text to the style you selected in Step **7**.

You can click anywhere to continue working.

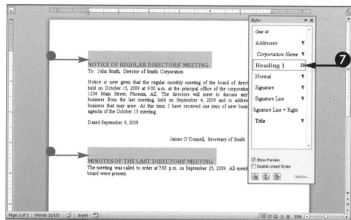

Is there an easy way to see the style assigned to each paragraph of my document?

Yes. You can use the Style area pane on the left side of the Draft view.

① Click 🔲 on the Status Bar to switch to Draft view.

② Click the **File** tab.

③ In the Backstage view, click **Options** to open the Word Options dialog box.

④ Click **Advanced**.

⑤ Click here and select a value of at least .5 inches.

⑥ Click **OK**.

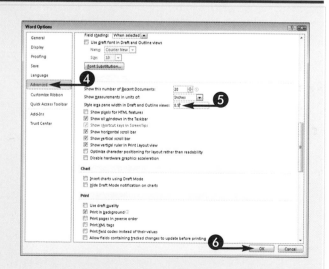

Save Formatting in a Style

You can easily create your own styles to store formatting information if you cannot find a built-in style that exactly suits your needs.

When you create a new style, you can make it appear in the Quick Style gallery.

① Format text in your document using the formatting you want to save.

② Select the text containing the formatting you want to save.

③ Click ▼.

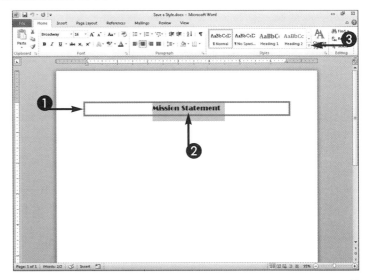

The Quick Style gallery appears.

④ Click **Save Selection as New Quick Style.**

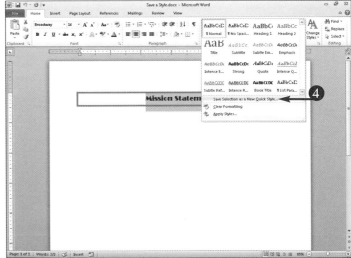

160

The Create New Style from Formatting dialog box appears.

⑤ Type a name for the style.

⑥ Click **Modify**.

Word displays additional options in the dialog box.

⑦ Click here and select the style of the paragraph that follows the style you are creating.

⑧ Select the font formatting options for the style.

⑨ Select paragraph alignment, spacing, and indentation options.

⑩ Select this option to make your style available in new documents (○ changes to ◉).

⑪ Click **OK**.

Word saves your newly created style.

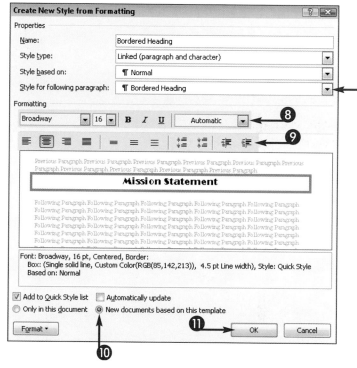

 TIPS

What happens if I click Format?

A menu appears that you can use to specify additional formatting. Select the type of formatting, and Word displays a dialog box where you can add more formatting characteristics to the style.

What does the Style based on option do?

Every style you create is based on a built-in Word style. Changing a built-in style can result in many styles changing. For example, many styles are based on the Normal style. If you change the font of the Normal style, you change the font of all styles based on the Normal style.

Modify a Style

At some point you may decide that the formatting of a style is close to but not exactly what you want. You do not need to create a new style; you can modify the existing one.

You can modify a style so that Word automatically updates the style's definition if you apply manual formatting to a paragraph using this style.

Modify a Style

1. Open a document containing the style you want to change.

2. Click the **Home** tab.

3. Click the **Styles** to display the Styles pane.

4. Position the mouse pointer over the style you want to change to display .

5. Click .

6. Click **Modify**.

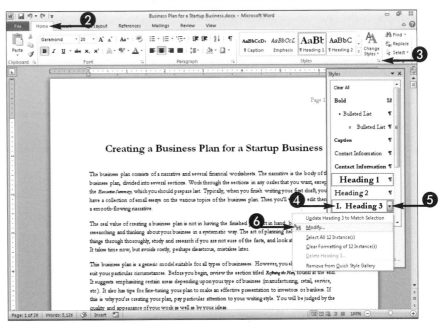

The Modify Style dialog box appears.

7. Select any font or paragraph formatting changes you want to make.

8. Select this option (changes to) to make the modified style available in new documents.

9. Select this option (changes to) to add the style to the Quick Style gallery.

10. Click **OK**.

Word updates all text in the document formatted with the style you changed.

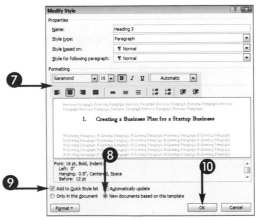

Add Paragraph Shading

Shading is another technique you can use to draw your reader's attention. Shading appears when you print your document; if you do not use a color printer, make sure you select a shade of gray for your shading.

Add Paragraph Shading

❶ Place the insertion point in the paragraph that you want to shade.

❷ Click the **Home** tab.

❸ Click ▾ on the **Shading** button (▨).

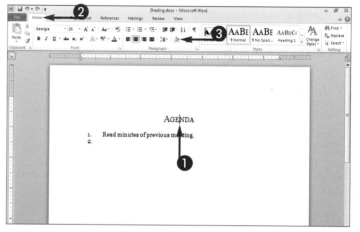

The Shading gallery appears.

❹ Point at a color.

Live Preview highlights the paragraph containing the insertion point with the color at which the mouse points.

❺ Click a color to select it as the shading color for the paragraph.

Note: *If Word applies shading to more text than you intended, click ↩ and Word reduces the amount of text to which it applies shading.*

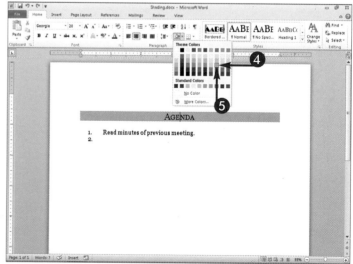

Formatting Pages

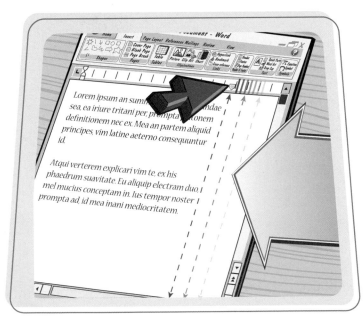

In addition to applying formatting to characters and paragraphs, you can apply formatting to pages of your Word document. Find out how to get your page to look its best in this chapter.

Adjust Margins

You can adjust the right, left, top, and bottom margins of your document. When you adjust margins, Word sets the margins from the position of the insertion point to the end of the document.

By default, Word sets all margins — left, right, top, and bottom — to 1 inch.

Adjust Margins

① Click anywhere in the document or section where you want to change margins.

② Click the **Page Layout** tab.

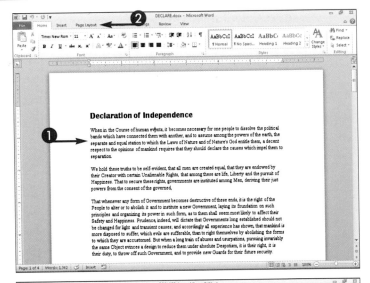

③ Click **Margins**.

The Margins Gallery appears.

If the margins you want to use appear in the Margins Gallery, click them and skip the rest of these steps; otherwise, proceed with Steps **4** to **9**.

④ Click **Custom Margins**.

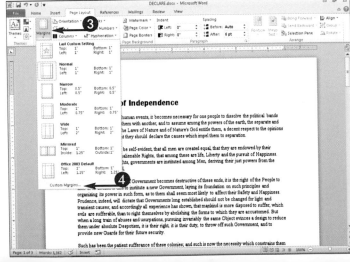

The Page Setup dialog box appears, displaying the Margins tab.

5 Drag the mouse pointer over any margin setting.

6 Type a new margin setting.

7 Repeat Steps **5** and **6** for each margin setting.

8 Click **OK**.

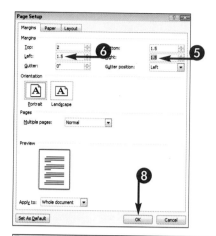

Word saves your changes and applies them to your document.

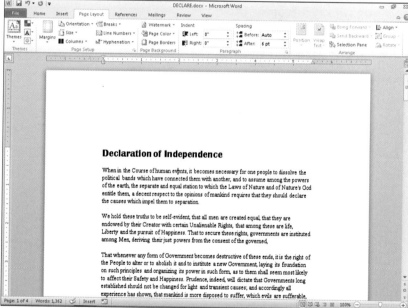

TIPS

Can I change the margins for just one part of my document?

Yes, you can if you divide your document into sections using section breaks. You can set distinct margins for each section of a document. See the section "Insert a Section Break" for more information.

Can I use the mouse to change margins?

In Print Layout view, Word displays margins in blue on the ruler. Select the text you want to change. To reposition the left margin, point the mouse at ☐ on the ruler and drag to the right or left. To adjust the right margin, drag △ to the right or left. To adjust top and bottom margins, move the mouse into the ruler area on the left side of the window, between the white and blue portions of the ruler. ☖ changes to ⁑. Drag ⁑ up or down to reposition the margin.

Insert a Page Break

You can insert a page break to force Word to start text on a new page. Word automatically starts a new page when the current page becomes filled with text.

You can insert a page break using either the mouse or the keyboard.

Insert a Page Break

Using the Mouse

1 Position the insertion point immediately before the text that you want to appear on a new page.

2 Click the **Insert** tab.

3 Click **Page Break**.

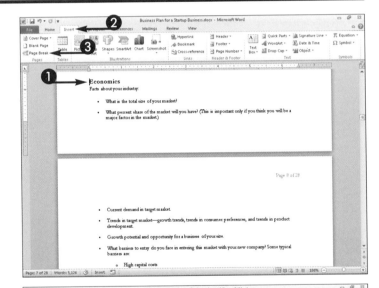

● Word inserts a page break and moves all text after the page break onto a new page.

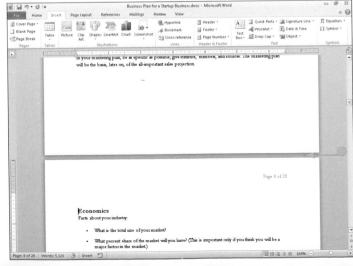

Using the Keyboard

1 Position the insertion point immediately before the text that you want to appear on a new page.

2 Press **Ctrl** + **Enter**.

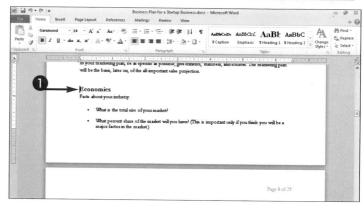

● Word inserts a page break and moves all text after the page break onto a new page.

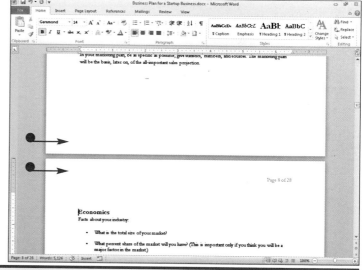

Can I delete a page break?
Yes. You can delete page breaks that you insert into your document.

1 Click the **Draft view** button (⊞).

2 Click **Home**.

3 Click the **Paragraph** button (¶).

● Lines representing page breaks appear.

● Dotted lines without "Page Break" in them are page breaks inserted automatically by Word.

4 Click at the left edge of the page break line.

5 Press **Del**.

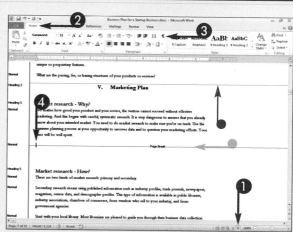

Control Text Flow and Pagination

You can control the placement of the automatic page breaks that Word inserts when you fill a page with text.

You can eliminate widows and orphans, keep an entire paragraph on one page, keep one paragraph with the next paragraph on a page, or insert a page break before a paragraph.

Control Text Flow and Pagination

1 Select the text whose flow you want to affect.

Note: To control widows and orphans, you do not need to select any text.

2 Click the **Page Layout** tab.

3 Click the **Paragraph** (🔲).

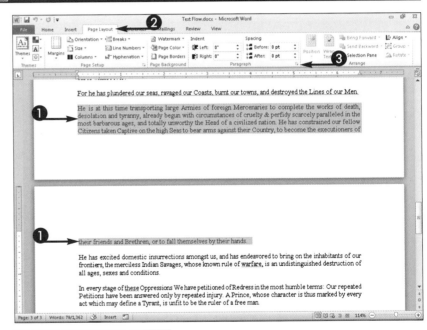

The Paragraph dialog box appears.

4 Click the **Line and Page Breaks** tab.

● This area contains the options you can use to control text flow and automatic pagination.

⑤ Select an option (☐ changes to ☑).

⑥ Repeat Step **5** as needed.

⑦ Click **OK**.

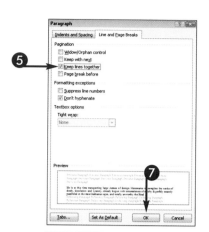

● Word groups the selected text in the manner you specified.

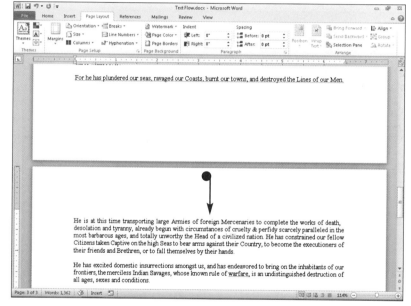

What is a widow?

Widow is the term used to describe text grouped so that the first line of a paragraph appears at the bottom of a page and subsequent lines appear on the following page. Widows are distracting to reading comprehension.

What is an orphan?

Orphan is the term used to describe text grouped so that the last line of a paragraph appears at the top of a new page and all preceding lines appear at the bottom of the previous page. Like widows, orphans are distracting to reading comprehension.

Align Text Vertically on the Page

You can align text between the top and bottom margins of a page if the text does not fill the page. For example, centering text vertically often improves the appearance of short business letters or report cover pages.

By default, Word applies vertical alignment to your entire document, but you can limit the alignment if you divide the document into sections. See the section "Insert a Section Break" for more information.

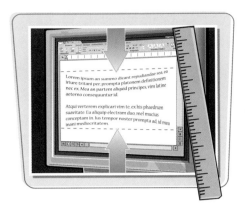

Align Text Vertically on the Page

1 In the document you want to align, click the **Page Layout** tab.

2 Click the **Page Setup** 🔲.

The Page Setup dialog box appears.

3 Click the **Layout** tab.

4 Click the **Vertical alignment** 🔽 and select a vertical alignment choice.

● To align all pages from the insertion point to the end of the document, click the **Apply to** 🔽 and select **This point forward**.

5 Click **OK**.

● Word applies vertical alignment.

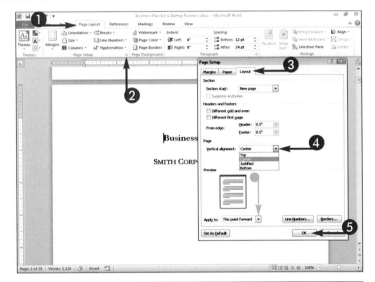

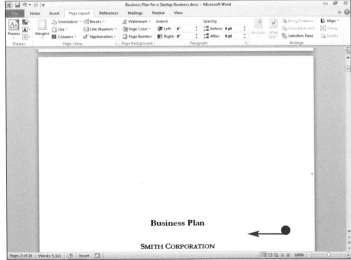

Change Page Orientation

You can change the direction that text prints from the standard portrait orientation of 8½ inches × 11 inches to landscape orientation of 11 inches × 8½ inches.

To remember the difference between the orientations, think of paintings. Leonardo da Vinci painted his famous Mona Lisa portrait with the canvas oriented vertically. Georges Seurat painted his famous Sunday Afternoon on the Island of La Grande Jatte landscape with the canvas oriented horizontally.

Change Page Orientation

1 Click anywhere in the document.

Note: *The document in this example appears zoomed out to show orientation changes more clearly.*

2 Click the **Page Layout** tab.

3 Click **Orientation**.

● The current orientation appears highlighted.

4 Click an option.

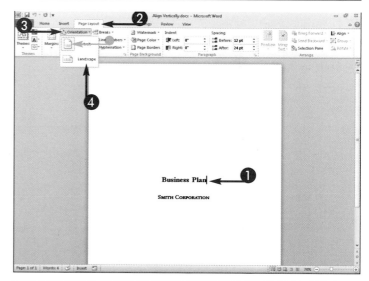

● Word changes the orientation.

Note: *By default, Word changes the orientation for the entire document. To limit orientation changes, divide the document into sections. See the section "Insert a Section Break."*

Insert a
Section Break

You can insert a section break in a document to establish different margins, headers, footers, vertical page alignment, and other page formatting settings in different portions of your document.

① Click in the location where you want to start a new section in your document.

② Click the **Page Layout** tab.

③ Click **Breaks**.

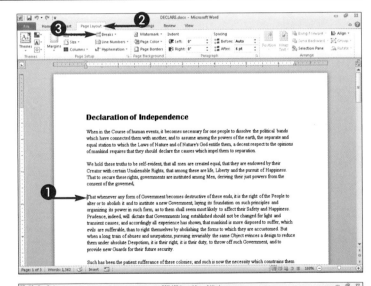

The Breaks Gallery appears.

④ Click an option to select the type of section break you want to insert.

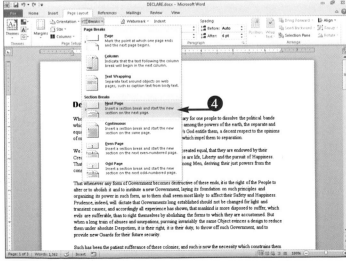

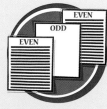

- Word inserts the type of break you selected.

5 Click  to display the document in Draft view.

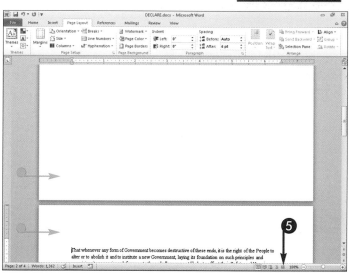

- A section break line appears.

  You can remove the section break by clicking the section break line and pressing the Del key on your keyboard.

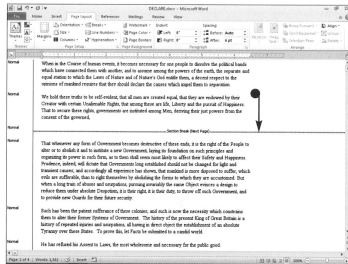

TIPS

How does Word handle printing when I insert a section break?

Section breaks are formatting marks that do not print; instead, the effects of the section break are apparent when you print. For example, if you insert a Next Page section break as shown in the example in this section, Word starts the text that immediately follows the section break on a new page.

What happens if I select Even page or Odd page?

Word starts the next section of your document on the next even or odd page. If you insert an Even page section break on an odd page, Word leaves the odd page blank. Similarly, if you insert an Odd page section break on an even page, Word leaves the even page blank.

175

Add Page Numbers to a Document

You can have Word automatically print page numbers on the pages of your document. As you edit your document to add or remove text, Word adjusts the document and the page numbers accordingly.

Page numbers appear on-screen only in Print Layout view.

Add Page Numbers to a Document

1 Click the **Insert** tab.

2 Click **Page Number**.

Page number placement options appear.

3 Click a placement option.

A gallery of page number alignment and formatting options appears.

4 Click an option.

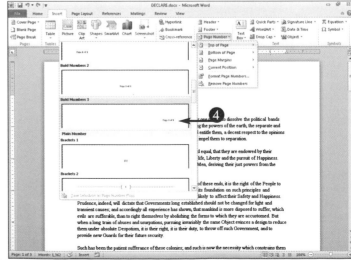

● The page number appears in the header or footer.

⑤ Click the **Print Layout** button (🖫) to display the document in Print Layout view and continue working on the document.

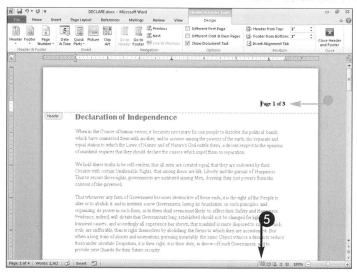

● The page number appears in the location and formatting you selected.

Note: *The page number appears gray and is unavailable for editing in Print Layout view. To work with the page number, you must open the header. See the section "Add a Header or Footer" later in this chapter.*

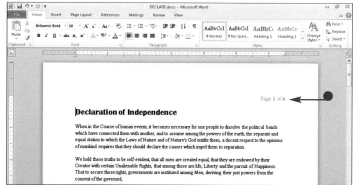

TIP

How can I start each section of my document with Page 1?

You can break the document into sections and use these steps to start each section on Page 1.

① Complete Steps **1** to **4** in this section.

② Place the insertion point in the second section of your document and repeat Steps **1** to **3**, selecting **Format Page Numbers** in Step **3**.

③ In the Page Numbering section, select the **Start at** option (🔘 changes to ⊙) and type **1** in the box.

④ Click **OK**.

⑤ Repeat these steps for each subsequent section of your document.

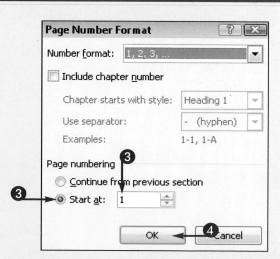

Add Line Numbers to a Document

You can add numbers to the left edge of every line of your document. Line numbers are particularly useful for proofreading; proofreaders can refer to locations in the document by their line numbers.

Line numbers appear on-screen only in Print Layout view.

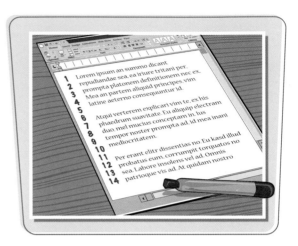

Add Line Numbers to a Document

Add Line Numbers

① Click ▦ to display the document in Print Layout view.

② Click the **Page Layout** tab.

③ Click Line Numbers.

④ Click a line numbering option.

This example shows Continuous.

● Word assigns line numbers to each line of your document.

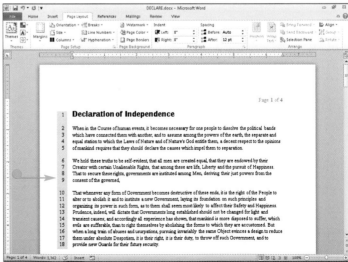

Number in Unusual Increments

1 Add line numbers using Steps **1** to **3** above.

2 Repeat Steps **1** to **3**, selecting **Line Numbering Options** in Step **3**.

The Layout tab of the Page Setup dialog box appears.

3 Click **Line Numbers** to display the Line Numbers dialog box.

4 Click the **Count by** ⬍ to specify an increment for line numbers.

5 Click **OK** twice.

● Line numbers in the increment you selected appear on-screen.

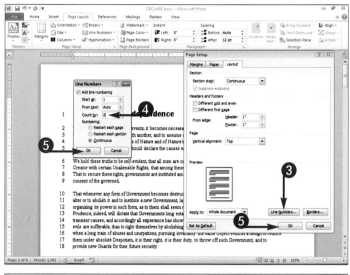

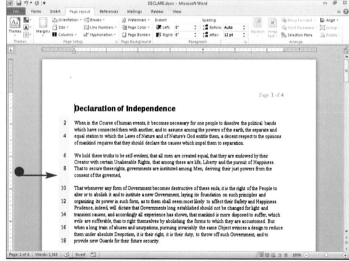

What does the From text option control in the Line Numbers dialog box?

Using this option, you can specify the position in inches in the left margin where line numbers will appear. Exercise caution, however; if you specify too large a distance, the line numbers will not appear or print.

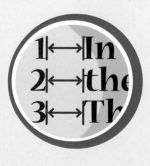

How do I remove line numbers?

Follow Steps **1** to **4** in the subsection "Add Line Numbers," clicking **None** in Step **4**. Word removes line numbers from the document.

Using the Building Blocks Organizer

Building blocks are preformatted text and graphics that quickly and easily add a splash of elegance and pizzazz to your documents. Some building blocks appear by default as gallery options in Word.

Word organizes building blocks into different galleries, such as cover pages, headers, footers, tables, and text boxes, so that you can easily find something to suit your needs. This section adds a header building block to a document.

Using the Building Blocks Organizer

1 Open a document to which you want to add a building block.

Note: Depending on the type of building block you intend to use, you may need to position the insertion point where you want the building block to appear.

2 Click the **Insert** tab.

3 Click **Quick Parts.**

4 Click **Building Block Organizer**.

The Building Blocks Organizer window appears.

● Building blocks appear here.

● You can preview a building block here.

5 Click a column heading to sort building blocks by that heading.

Sorting by Gallery is most useful to find a building block for a specific purpose.

6 Click a building block.

7 Click **Insert**.

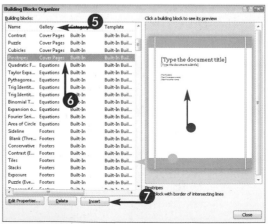

● The building block appears in your document.

8 Fill in any information required by the building block.

This example incorporates a place for a date in the header.

● For headers and footers, you can make the building block appear on all pages of your document if you do not select **Different First Page**.

● You can zoom out to see multiple pages of your document and confirm the appearance of a header or footer on all pages.

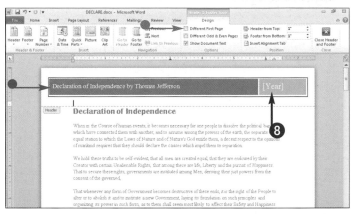

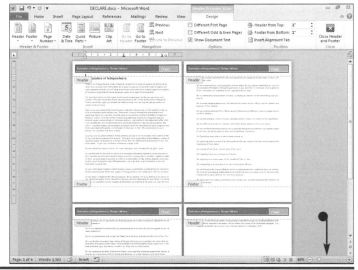

How do I know where in my document Word will insert a building block?

Word places a building block in your document based on the building block's properties. Follow these steps:

1 Follow Steps **1** to **4** in this section to display the Building Blocks Organizer window.

2 Click **Edit Properties**.

The Modify Building Block dialog box appears.

3 Click the **Options** ⏷ to determine where a particular building block will appear in your document.

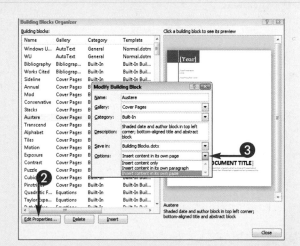

Add a Header or Footer

You can use headers at the top of the page and footers at the bottom of the page to add information that you want to appear on each page of your document.

This section shows how to add a footer, but you can use the steps in this section to add a header by substituting "header" everywhere that "footer" appears.

Add a Header or Footer

1 Click the **Insert** tab.

2 Click **Footer**.

The Footer Gallery appears.

3 Click a footer style.

Note: *The headers and footers that appear in the Header Gallery and the Footer Gallery are building blocks that also appear in the Building Blocks Organizer. See the section "Using the Building Blocks Organizer" for details.*

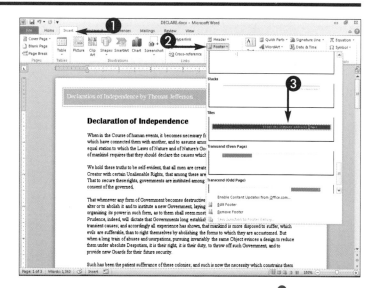

● The text in your document appears dimmed.

● The insertion point appears in the Footer area.

● Header & Footer Tools appear on the Ribbon.

● Some footers contain information prompts.

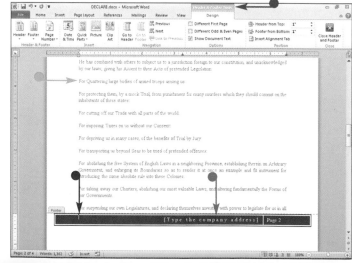

4 Click or select an information prompt.

5 Type footer information.

6 Click **Close Header and Footer**.

Word saves your footer.

● You can zoom out to view the footer on multiple pages of your document.

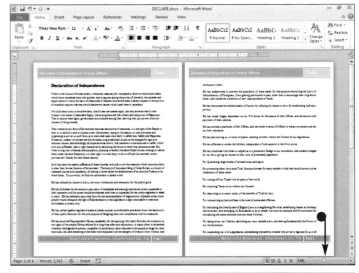

Can I change the style of header or footer?

Yes. If you closed the header or footer pane, perform Steps **1** to **3**, clicking **Edit Header** or **Edit Footer** in Step **3**. Then click **Header** or **Footer** at the left side of the Ribbon to redisplay the Header Gallery or Footer Gallery and make a different selection.

Can I format text in a header or footer?

Yes. You can apply boldface, italics, underlining, and other character formatting the same way that you apply them in the body of a document. And, the Header area and the Footer area each contain two predefined tabs so that you can center or right-align text you type.

Using Different Headers or Footers Within a Document

You can use different headers or footers in different portions of your document. If you plan to use more than one header or footer, insert section breaks before you begin. See the section "Insert a Section Break" for details.

This section shows how to create different headers in your document, but you can use the steps to create different footers by substituting "footer" everywhere that "header" appears.

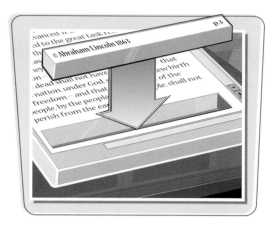

Using Different Headers or Footers Within a Document

1 Click in the first section for which you want to create a header.

2 Click the **Insert** tab.

3 Click **Header**.

The Header Gallery appears.

4 Click a header.

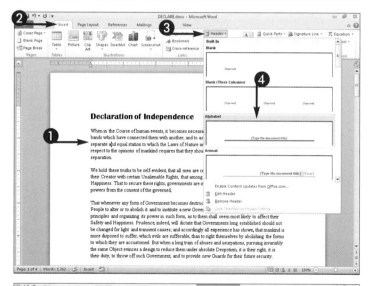

Word inserts the header.

● The text in your document appears dimmed.

● The insertion point appears in the Header-Section 1 box.

5 Type any necessary text in the header.

6 Click **Next**.

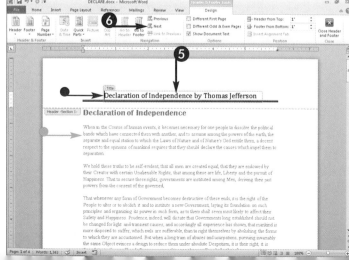

Word moves the insertion point into the header for Section 2.

● The Header-Section 2 box appears.

● Word identifies the header or footer as "Same as Previous."

7 Click **Link to Previous,** to deselect it and unlink the headers of the two sections.

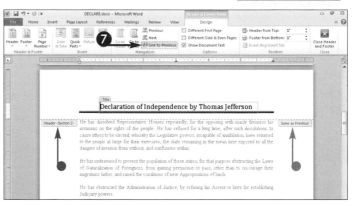

Word removes the "Same as Previous" marking from the right side of the header box.

8 Repeat Steps **2** to **5** to insert a new header in the second section.

9 Repeat Steps **6** to **8** for each section for which you want a different header.

● You can zoom out to preview the different headers.

● Word displays two different headers in the document.

10 Click **Close Header and Footer**.

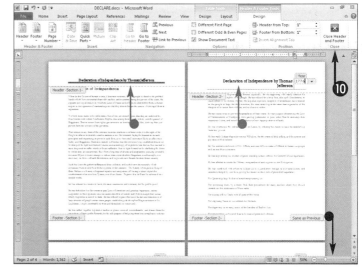

TIP

Can I create different headers or footers for odd or even pages?

Yes, and you do not need to insert section breaks.

1 Complete Steps **2** to **5** in this section.

2 On the Design tab of the Header and Footer Tools, click **Different Odd & Even Pages.**

● Each header or footer box is renamed to Odd Page or Even Page.

3 Click **Next Section** to switch to the Even Page Header box or the Even Page Footer box and type text.

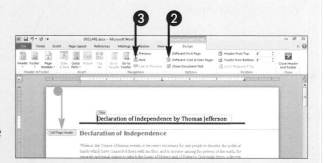

Add a Footnote

You can add footnotes to a document to provide additional explanatory information or to cite references to other works.

Footnotes are numbered 1, 2, 3, and appear within your document in Print Layout view and Full Screen Reading view. Footnote references appear in the body of your document in all views.

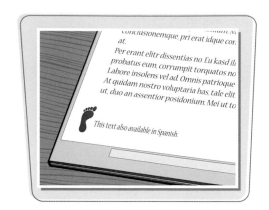

This text also available in Spanish.

Add a Footnote

① Click in the document where you want the footnote number to appear.

② Click the **References** tab.

③ Click **Insert Footnote**.

● Word displays the footnote number in the body of the document and in the note.

④ Type the text for the footnote.

⑤ Press **Shift** + **F5**.

Word returns the insertion point to the place in your document where you inserted the footnote.

You can add endnotes to a document to provide additional
explanatory information or to cite references to other works.

**Endnotes are numbered i, ii, iii, and appear at the end of your document in Print
Layout view and Full Screen Reading view. Endnote references appear in the body
of your document in all views.**

Add an Endnote

① Click in the document where you
want the endnote number to
appear.

● In this example, the endnote
number appears on Page 1.

② Click the **References** tab.

③ Click **Insert Endnote**.

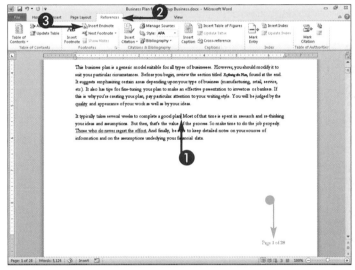

Word inserts the endnote number
in the body of your document.

● Word inserts the endnote number
at the end of your document and
displays the insertion point in the
endnote area.

④ Type the text for the endnote.

⑤ Press Shift + F5.

Word returns the insertion point
to the place in your document
where you inserted the endnote.

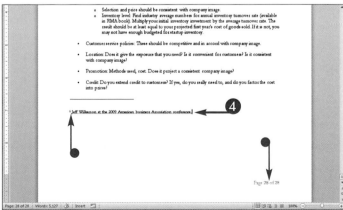

Find, Edit, or Delete Footnotes or Endnotes

Working in any view, you can find a footnote or endnote, modify its text, or delete the footnote or endnote.

Find Footnotes or Endnotes

1 Press **Ctrl** + **Home** to move the mouse pointer to the top of the document.

2 Click **References**.

3 Click ▼ beside **Next Footnote**.

4 Click an option to find the next or previous footnote or endnote.

Word moves the insertion point to the next or previous footnote or endnote.

Edit Footnotes or Endnotes

1 Select the footnote or endnote reference number in your document.

2 Double-click the selection.

Note: To easily edit endnotes, press **Ctrl** + **End** to move the insertion point to the end of the document.

● In Print Layout view, Word moves the insertion point into the footnote or endnote.

● In Draft view, Word displays footnotes in the Footnotes pane.

③ Edit the text of the note as needed.

④ In Draft view, click the **Close** button (⊠) when you finish editing.

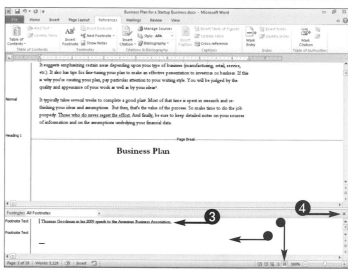

Delete a Footnote or Endnote

① Select the reference number of the footnote or endnote you want to delete.

② Press Del on your keyboard.

Word removes the footnote or endnote number and related information from the document and automatically renumbers subsequent footnotes or endnotes.

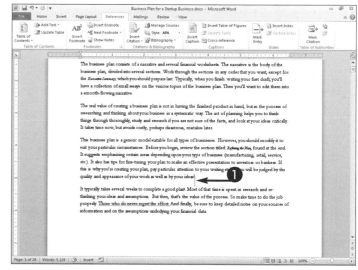

TIP

Can I print endnotes on a separate page?
Yes. Follow these steps:

① Click in your document before the first endnote.

② Click the **Insert** tab.

③ Click **Page Break**.

Word inserts a page break immediately before the endnotes, placing them on a separate page at the end of your document.

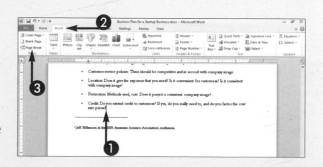

Convert Footnotes to Endnotes

If you change your mind and want to use endnotes instead of footnotes or footnotes instead of endnotes, you can convert one to the other.

1 Click the **References** tab.

2 Click the **Footnotes** ⬜.

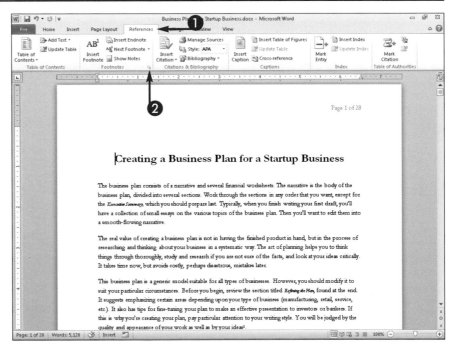

The Footnote and Endnote dialog box appears.

3 Click **Convert**.

The Convert Notes dialog box appears.

④ Select the option that describes what you want to do (◯ changes to ◉).

⑤ Click **OK** to redisplay the Footnote and Endnote dialog box.

In the Footnote and Endnote dialog box, **Cancel** changes to **Close**.

⑥ Click **Close**.

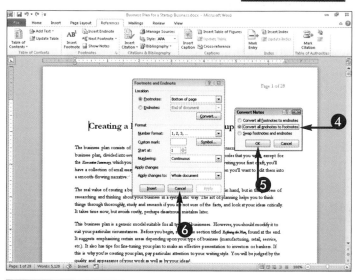

● Word makes the conversion and renumbers footnotes and endnotes appropriately.

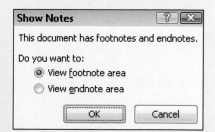

TIP

What does the Show Notes button do?

If your document contains only footnotes or only endnotes, Word jumps to the footnote section on the current page or the endnote section at the end of the document. If your document contains both footnotes and endnotes, Word displays this dialog box so that you can select an option to view.

Show Notes

This document has footnotes and endnotes.

Do you want to:
- ◉ View **f**ootnote area
- ◯ View **e**ndnote area

OK   Cancel

Generate a Table of Contents

You can create a table of contents that automatically updates as you update your document. Table of contents entries can come from text styled as Heading 1, Heading 2, and Heading 3 or from text you mark to appear in the table of contents.

You can create a table of contents at any time, continue working, and update the table of contents automatically with new information whenever you want. This section shows a table of contents created using heading styles.

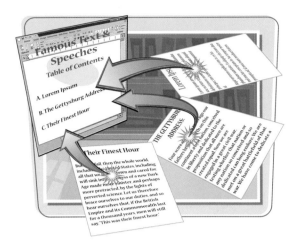

Generate a Table of Contents

Insert a Table of Contents

1 Place the insertion point in your document where you want the table of contents to appear.

● This example places the table of contents on a blank page after the cover page of a report.

2 Click the **References** tab.

3 Click **Table of Contents**.

The Table of Contents gallery appears.

4 Click a table of contents layout.

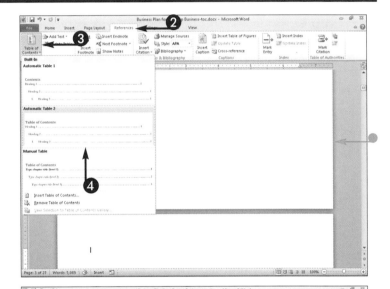

● Word inserts a table of contents at the location of the insertion point.

The information in the table of contents comes from text to which Heading styles 1, 2, and 3 are applied.

You can continue working in your document, adding new text styled with heading styles.

Note: *Do not type directly in the table of contents; make corrections in the document.*

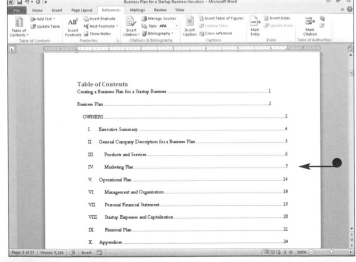

Update the Table of Contents

1. Add or change text styled with heading styles or remove heading styles from text in your document.

2. Click anywhere in the table of contents.

3. Click the **References** tab.

4. Click **Update Table**.

● You can click the **Update Table** button at the top of the table of contents.

The Update Table of Contents dialog box appears.

5. Select **Update entire table** (○ changes to ●).

6. Click **OK**.

Word updates the table of contents to reflect your changes.

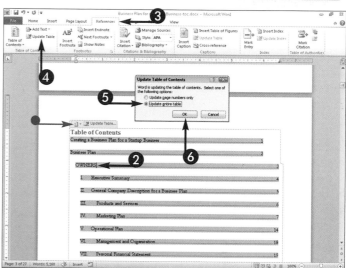

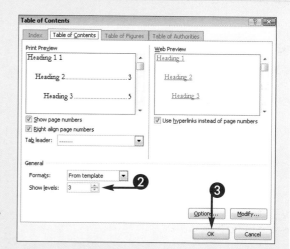

Can I include additional heading styles, such as Heading 4, in the table of contents?

Yes. Simply follow these steps:

1. Complete Steps **2** to **4** in the subsection "Insert a Table of Contents," selecting **Insert Table of Contents** in Step **4** to display the Table of Contents dialog box.

2. Click the **Show levels** 🔼 to change the number of heading styles included in the table of contents.

3. Click **OK**.

Word prompts you to replace the current table of contents.

4. Click **Yes** to update the table of contents.

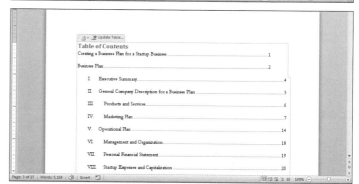

Add a Watermark

You can add a watermark, which is faint text that appears behind information in a document, to your document to add interest or convey a message.

Watermarks are visible in Print Layout view and when you print your document.

Add a Watermark

① Click 📄 to display your document in Print Layout view.

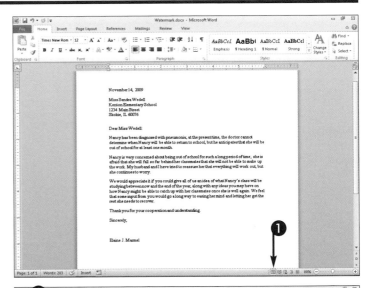

② Click the **Page Layout** tab.

③ Click **Watermark**.

● If you see the watermark you want to use in the Watermark gallery, you can click it and skip the rest of the steps in this section.

④ Click **Custom Watermark**.

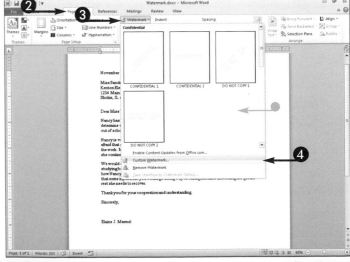

The Printed Watermark dialog box appears.

⑤ Select the **Text watermark** option (◯ changes to ◉).

⑥ Click here and select the text to use as a watermark or type your own text.

● You can use these options to control the font, size, color, intensity, and layout of the watermark.

⑦ Click **OK**.

● Word displays the watermark on each page of your document.

TIP

What happens if I select the Picture watermark option in the Printed Watermark dialog box?

Word enables you to select a picture stored on your hard drive as the watermark in your document.

① Follow Steps **1** to **5**, selecting **Picture watermark** in Step **5**.

② In the Printed Watermark dialog box, click **Select Picture**.

③ In the Insert Picture dialog box, navigate to the picture you want to use as a watermark.

④ Click **Insert**.

⑤ Click **OK** in the Printed Watermark dialog box to add the picture watermark to your document.

Add a Page Border

You can add a border around each page of your document to add interest to the document.

1 Click 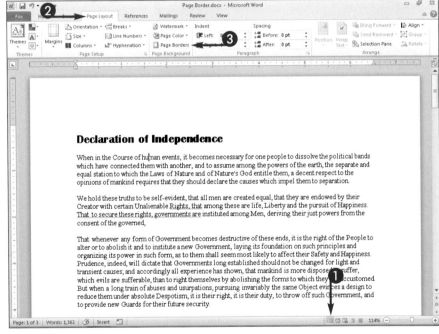 to display your document in Print Layout view.

2 Click the **Page Layout** tab.

3 Click **Page Borders**.

The Borders and Shading dialog box appears, displaying the Page Border tab.

4 Click the type of border you want to add to your document.

5 Click a style for the border line.

● This area shows a preview of the border.

● You can click here to select a color for the border.

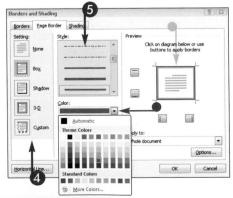

● You can click here to select a width for the border.

⑥ Click here to specify the pages on which the border should appear.

⑦ Click **OK**.

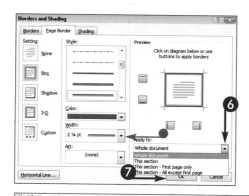

Word applies the border you specified.

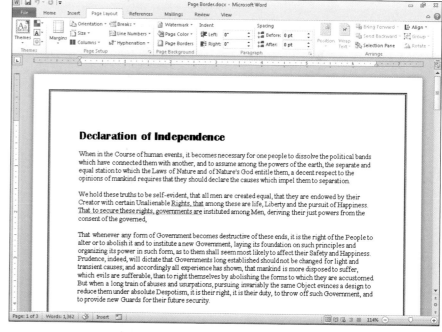

TIP

Can I add a border that does not surround the page?
Yes. Follow these steps:

① Follow Steps **1** to **6** to select the border you want to apply.

② In the Preview area, click the border lines that you do not want to appear in your document.

③ Click **OK**.

Word applies the modified page border.

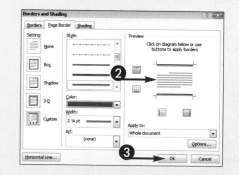

Create Newspaper Columns

You can format text in your document so that it appears in columns like the text in newspapers. Newspaper column formatting is useful when you are creating newsletters or brochures.

Text appears in newspaper columns only in Print Layout view.

Create Newspaper Columns

① Click 🔳 to display your document in Print Layout view.

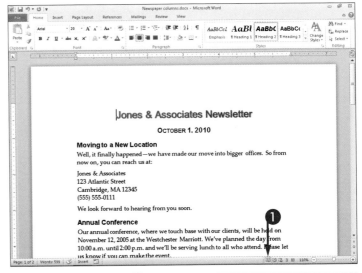

② Click the **Page Layout** tab.

③ Click **Columns**.

The Columns gallery appears.

Note: *Although you can click a column layout and skip the rest of these steps, you can control your column layout better using the rest of these steps.*

④ Click **More Columns**.

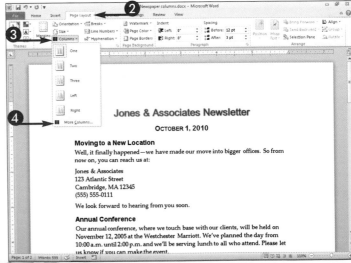

The Columns dialog box appears.

5 Click the kind of columns you want to create.

● You can use these settings to change the width of each column and the spacing between columns.

● You can select the **Line between** option (changes to) to add a line between columns.

● A preview appears here.

6 Click **OK**.

Word applies the column settings.

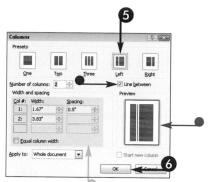

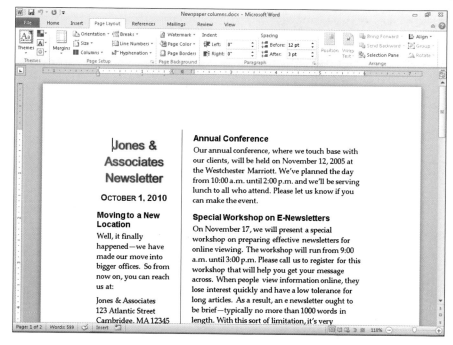

TIP

Can I force text from the left column to the top of the next column?

You can insert a column break.

1 Click at the left edge of the text you want to appear at the top of the second column.

2 Click the **Page Layout** tab.

3 Click **Breaks**.

4 Click **Column**.

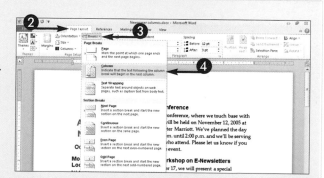

CHAPTER 8

Printing Documents

Once your document looks the way you want it to look, you are ready to distribute it. In this chapter, you learn how to preview and print documents, print envelopes, and print labels.

Preview and Print a Document

If your computer is connected to a printer that is turned on, you can preview your document to look for layout errors and other possible formatting inconsistencies and print it to produce a paper copy of it.

Preview and Print a Document

1. Open the document you want to print.

2. Click the **File** tab.

   To print only selected text, select that text.

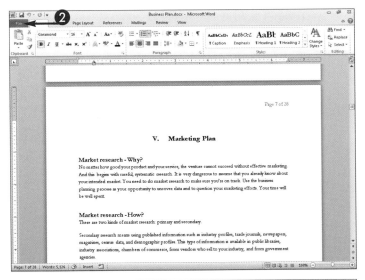

The Backstage view appears.

3. Click **Print**.

   ● A preview of your document appears here.

4. Click these arrows to page through your document.

5. To magnify an area of a page, drag the Zoom slider.

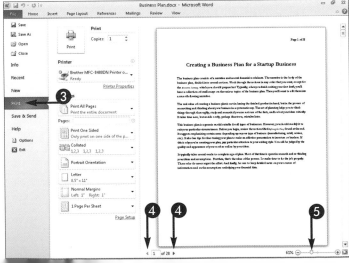

6 Click here to select a printer.

7 To print more than one copy, type the number of copies to print here.

8 Click the Settings button to print the entire document, text you selected, only the current page, or document elements such as document properties or a list of styles used in the document.

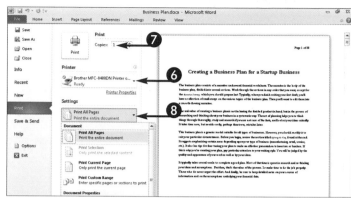

9 To print noncontiguous pages, type the pages you want to print, such as **1,5,6–9**, in the Pages box.

10 To print the document, click the **Print** button.

● If you change your mind and do not want to print, click the **File** tab to return to the document window.

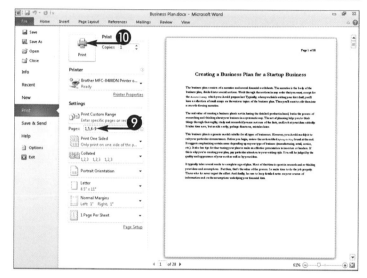

TIP

What other print options can I set?

In the Other Settings section, click buttons to select options:

Option	Purpose
Print One Sided — Only print on one side of the pa...	Determine whether to print on one or both sides of the paper.
Collated 1,2,3 1,2,3 1,2,3	When printing multiple copies, specify whether to collate the copies or print multiple copies of each page at the same time.
Portrait Orientation	Choose to print in Portrait or Landscape orientation.
Letter 8.5" x 11"	Select a paper size.
Normal Margins Left: 1" Right: 1"	Select page margins.
1 Page Per Sheet	Specify the number of pages to print on a single sheet of paper.

Print on Different Paper Sizes

You can print one part of your document on one size of paper and another part on a different size of paper. For example, you may want to print one portion of your document on legal-sized paper and another on letter-sized paper.

You must insert section breaks in your document for each portion you want to print on different paper sizes. To learn how to insert section breaks, see Chapter 7.

① After dividing your document into sections, place the insertion point in the section you want to print on a different paper size.

② Click the **Page Layout** tab.

③ Click the **Page Setup** dialog box launcher (⬚).

The Page Setup dialog box appears, displaying the Margins tab.

④ Click the **Paper** tab.

⑤ Click here and select the paper size you want to use.

- The height and width of the paper size you selected appear here.

- A preview of your selection appears here.

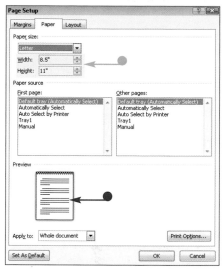

6 Click here to select a paper tray for the first page in the section.

7 Click here to select a paper tray for the rest of the section.

8 Click the **Apply to** ⊡ and click **This section**.

9 Repeat these steps for other sections of the document.

10 Click **OK** to save your changes.

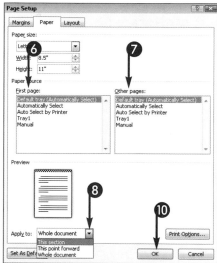

What happens when I click Print Options in the Page Setup dialog box?

The Display tab of the Word Options dialog box appears. In the Printing Options section, you can select check boxes to control the printing of various Word elements.

Printing options

☑ Print drawings created in Word ⓘ

☐ Print background colors and images

☐ Print document properties

☐ Print hidden text

☐ Update fields before printing

☐ Update linked data before printing

If your printer supports printing envelopes, Word can print a delivery and return address on an envelope for you.

Consult your printer manual to determine if your printer supports printing envelopes.

① Click the **Mailings** tab.

② Click **Envelopes**.

The Envelopes and Labels dialog box appears.

③ Click the **Envelopes** tab.

Note: If Word finds an address near the top of your document, it enters that address in the Delivery address box.

④ You can type a delivery address.

You can remove an existing address by pressing Del on your keyboard.

By default, Word displays no
return address in the Return
address box.

5 Click here to type a return
address.

6 Click **Print**.

A dialog box appears if you
supplied a return address.

Note: *If you save the return address, Word*
displays it each time you print an envelope and
does not display this dialog box.

7 Click **Yes**.

Word saves the return address as
the default return address and
prints the envelope.

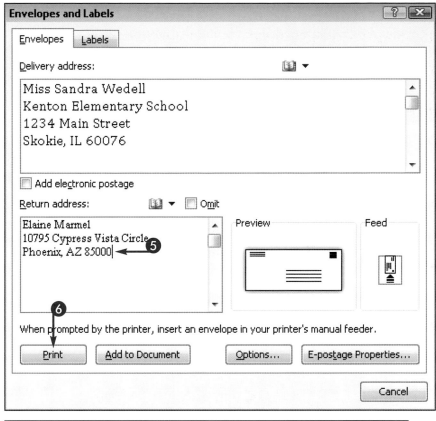

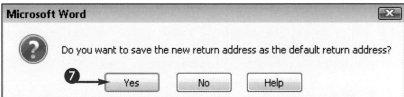

TIP

What happens if I click Options in the Envelopes and Labels dialog box?
Word displays the Envelope Options dialog box. On the Envelope Options tab, you
can set the envelope size, include a delivery bar code, and set fonts for the
delivery and return addresses. On the Printing Options tab, you can set the feed
method and tray for your printer.

Set Up Labels to Print

You can format a Word document so that you can use it to type labels. For example, you can create address, name tag, and file folder labels.

This section demonstrates how to create a blank page of address labels onto which you can type address label information.

① Click the **Mailings** tab.

② Click the **Labels** tab.

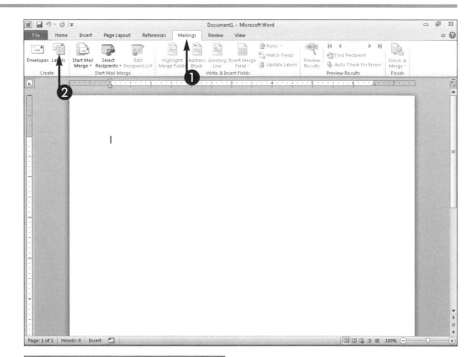

The Envelopes and Labels dialog box appears.

● This area shows the label currently selected.

③ Click **Options**.

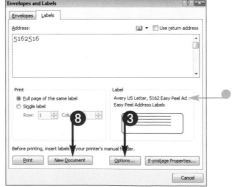

The Label Options dialog box appears.

④ In this area, select the type of printer and printer tray to print labels (○ changes to ◉).

⑤ Click here to select the maker of your labels.

⑥ Click the product number of your labels.

⑦ Click **OK**.

⑧ Click **New Document** in the Envelopes and Labels dialog box.

Word displays a blank document, set up for label information.

⑨ If you do not see gridlines to separate labels, click **Design**.

⑩ Click the **Borders** ▾ .

⑪ Click **View Gridlines**.

⑫ Type a label.

⑬ Press Tab to move to the next label and type an address.

Note: To print labels, see the section "Preview and Print a Document" earlier in this chapter.

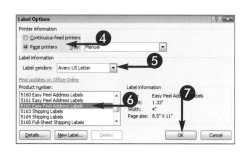

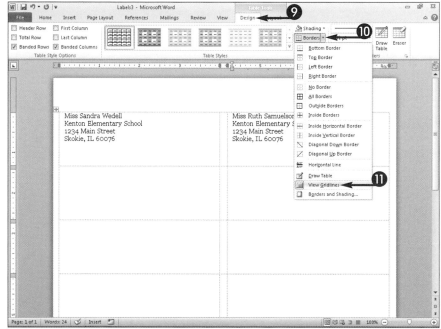

TIP

Can I print a single label?

① Complete Steps **1** and **2** in this section to open the Envelopes and Labels dialog box.

② Select the **Single label** option (○ changes to ◉).

③ Type the row and column of the label you want to use on the label sheet.

④ Type the label information here.

⑤ Click **Print**, and Word prints the single label.

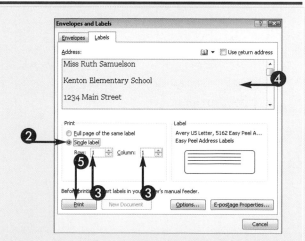

Creating Tables and Charts

Do you want to keep the information in your Word document easy to read? The answer may very well be to add a table to contain your data. In this chapter, you learn how to create and work with tables in Word.

Create a Table

You can create a table and type text into it. Tables are well suited to organize and display large amounts of data.

The initial table you create may not contain the number of rows and columns you ultimately need, but you can always add rows or columns to your table later.

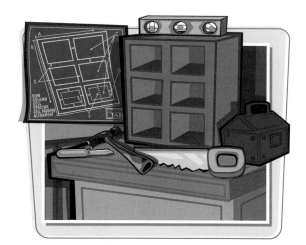

Create a Table

Set up a Table

1 Click in your document where you want the table to appear.

2 Click the **Insert** tab.

3 Click **Table**.

● Word displays a table grid.

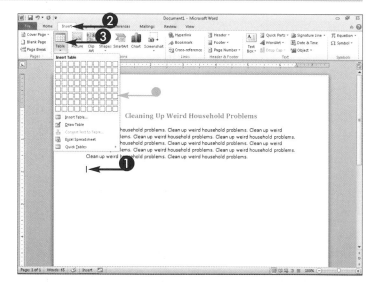

4 Slide the mouse pointer across the squares that represent the number of rows and columns you want in your table.

● Live Preview draws a sample of the table on-screen.

5 Click the square representing the lower-right corner of your table.

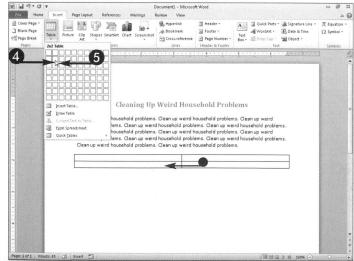

The table appears in your document.

● Table Tools appear on the Ribbon.

⑥ Click in a table cell and type information.

● If necessary, Word expands the row size to accommodate the text.

You can press **Tab** to move the insertion point to the next cell.

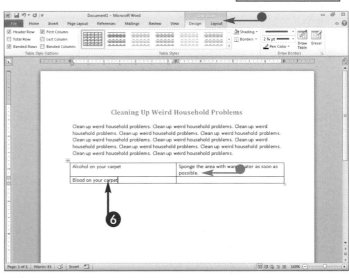

Delete a Table

① Click anywhere in the table you want to delete.

② Click the **Layout** tab.

③ Click **Delete**.

④ Click **Delete Table**.

Word removes the table and its contents from your document.

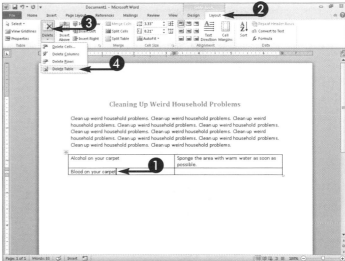

 TIPS

Can I add rows to the bottom of the table?

Yes. You can easily add rows to the bottom of a table by placing the insertion point in the last cell of the table and pressing the **Tab** key.

What, exactly, is a table cell?

A *cell* is the term used to refer to the square that appears at the intersection of a row and a column. In spreadsheet programs, columns are named with letters, rows are named with numbers, and a cell is named using the column letter and row number. For example, the cell at the intersection of Column A and Row 2 is called A2.

Change the Row Height or Column Width

You can change the height of rows or the width of columns to accommodate your table information.

Make sure that you are working from Print Layout or Web Layout view; you can use the buttons on the status bar to switch views if necessary.

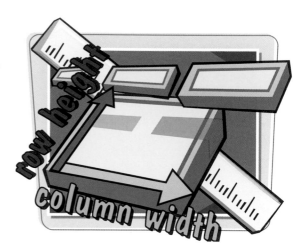

Change the Row Height

① Click the Print Layout button ( ) or the Web Layout button ( ).

② Position the mouse pointer over the bottom of the row you want to change (changes to) and drag the row edge up to shorten or down to lengthen the row height.

● A dotted line marks the proposed bottom of the row.

③ When the row height suits you, release the mouse button.

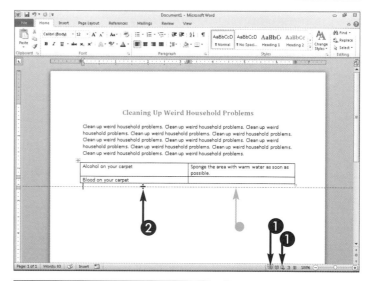

● Word adjusts the row height.

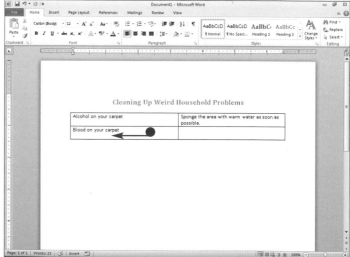

Change the Column Width

1 Position the mouse pointer over the right side of the column you want to change (⊟ changes to ⊹).

2 Drag the column edge right to widen or left to narrow the column width.

● A dotted line marks the proposed right side of the column.

3 Release the mouse.

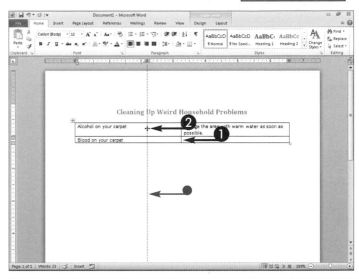

● Word adjusts the column width.

Note: For any column except the rightmost column, changing a column's width also changes the width of the column to its right, but the overall table size remains constant. When you change the width of the rightmost column, you change the width of the entire table.

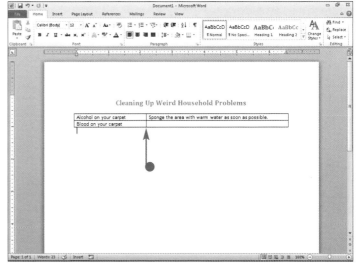

TIPS

I tried to change the row height but the mouse pointer never changed to ⊹. What did I do wrong?

You can change row height only when displaying your document in either Print Layout view or Web Layout view. Make sure you select one of those views by clicking the **Print Layout** view button (▦) or the **Web Layout** view button (▣). See Chapter 3 for more on understanding and switching between document views.

Can I easily make a column the size that accommodates the longest item in it?
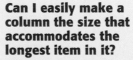
Yes. You double-click the right edge of the column. Word widens or narrows the column based on the longest entry in the column. When you use this technique, Word also adjusts the overall table size.

You can move a table to a different location in your document.

Make sure that you are working from Print Layout or Web Layout view; you can use the buttons on the status bar to switch views if necessary.

1 Click 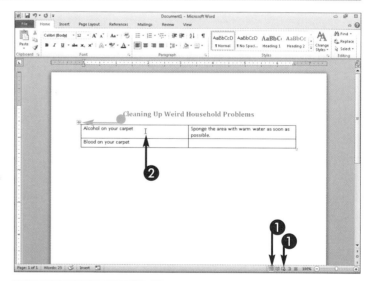 or ⬤

2 Position the mouse pointer over the table.

● A handle (⊞) appears in the upper-left corner of the table.

3 Position the mouse pointer over the handle (⌶ changes to ⬚).

4 Drag the table to a new location.

● A dashed line represents the proposed table position.

5 Release the mouse button.

The table appears in the new location.

To copy the table, perform these steps but press **Ctrl** in Step **3**.

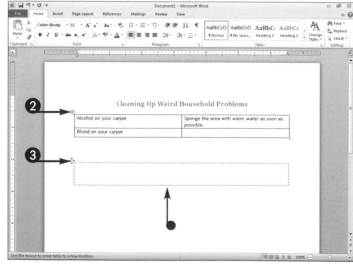

Resize a Table

If you find that your table dimensions do not suit your purpose, you can resize the table from Print Layout view or Web Layout view. For example, you may want to resize a table to make it longer and narrower.

Make sure that you are working from Print Layout or Web Layout view; you can use the buttons on the status bar to switch views if necessary.

Resize a Table

① Click ▥.

② Position the mouse pointer over the table.

● A handle (▢) appears in the lower-right corner of the table.

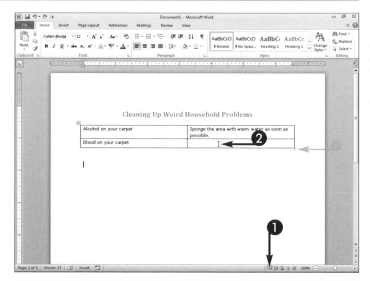

③ Position the mouse pointer over the handle (▯ changes to ⬚).

④ Drag the table up to make it shorter or down to make it larger (⬚ changes to ⊞).

Note: *You can also drag diagonally to simultaneously change both the width and height of the table.*

● A dashed line represents the proposed table size.

⑤ Release the mouse button to change the table's size.

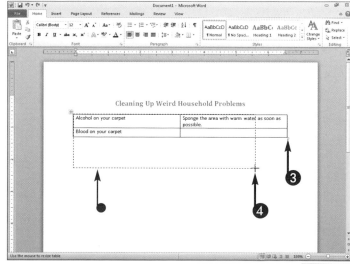

Add or Delete a Row

You can easily add rows to accommodate more information or remove rows of information you do not need.

Add a Row

1. Click in the row below where you want a new row to appear.

2. Click the **Layout** tab.

3. Click **Insert Above**.

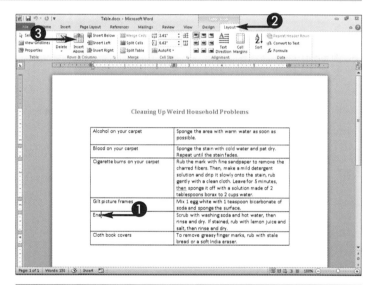

● Word inserts a row and selects it.

You can click in the row to add information to the table.

Delete a Row

1 Click anywhere in the row you want to delete.

2 Click the **Layout** tab.

3 Click **Delete**.

4 Click **Delete Rows**.

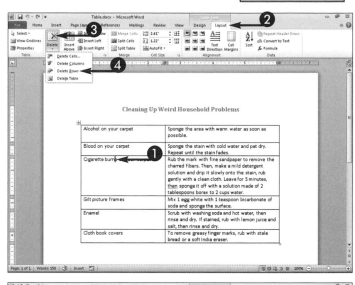

● Word removes the row and any text it contained from the table.

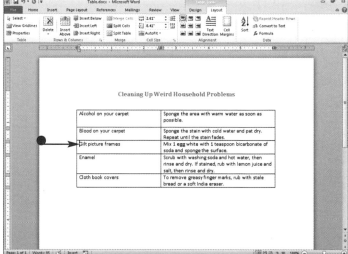

Can I delete more than one row at a time?

Yes. Select the rows you want to delete and perform Steps **2** to **4** in the subsection "Delete a Row." To select the rows, position ⫿ outside the left side of the table (⫿ changes to ⫽). Drag to select the rows you want to delete.

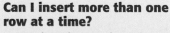

Can I insert more than one row at a time?

Yes. Select the number of rows you want to insert before you perform Steps **2** and **3** in the subsection "Add a Row." You can select rows below where you want the new rows and then perform Steps **2** and **3**, or you can select rows above where you want the new rows and, in Step **3**, click **Rows Below**.

Add or Delete a Column

You can add or delete columns to change the structure of a table to accommodate more or less information.

When you add columns, Word decreases the size of the other columns to accommodate the new column but retains the overall size of the table.

Add a Column

① Click in the column to the left of the column you want to add.

② Click the **Layout** tab.

③ Click **Insert Right**.

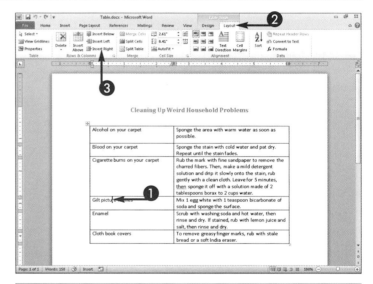

● Word inserts a new column in the table to the right of the column you clicked in Step **1** and selects the new column.

You can click in the column to add text to it.

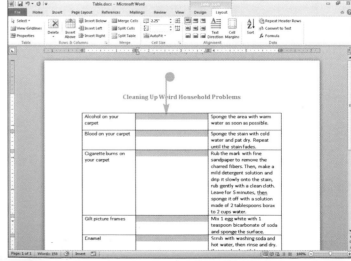

Delete a Column

1. Click anywhere in the column you want to delete.

2. Click the **Layout** tab.

3. Click **Delete**.

4. Click **Delete Columns**.

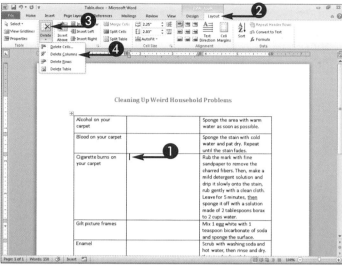

- Word removes the column and any text it contained from the table.

- The insertion point appears in the column to the right of the one you deleted.

  Word does not resize existing columns to use the space previously occupied by the deleted column.

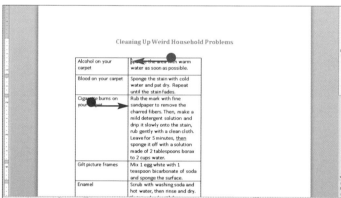

TIP

Is there a way I can easily enlarge a table to fill up the space between the left and right margins after deleting a column?

Yes. Follow these steps:

1. Click anywhere in the table.

2. Click the **Layout** tab.

3. Click **AutoFit**.

4. Click **AutoFit Window**.

   The table content and columns readjust to fill the space.

Set Cell Margins

You can set margins in table cells to make table information more legible.

① Click anywhere in the table.

② Click the **Layout** tab.

③ Click **Cell Margins**.

The Table Options dialog box appears.

④ Type margin settings here.

⑤ Click **OK**.

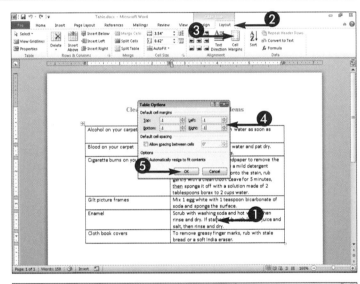

Word applies cell margin settings.

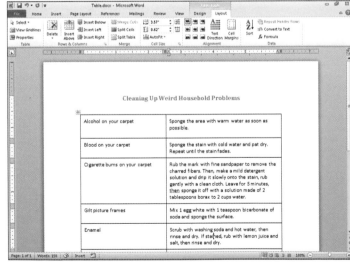

Add Space Between Cells

You can set spacing between table cells to make table information easier to read and more attractive.

Add Space Between Cells

1 Click anywhere in the table.

2 Click the **Layout** tab.

3 Click **Cell Margins**.

The Table Options dialog box appears.

4 Select the **Allow spacing between cells** option (☐ changes to ☑) and type a setting for space between cells.

5 Click **OK**.

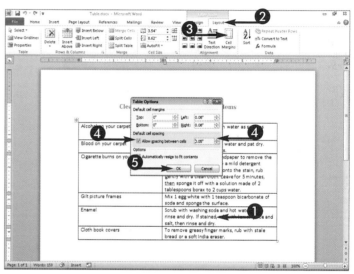

● Word adds space between cells.

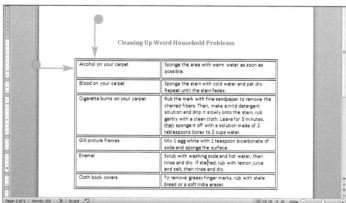

Combine Cells

You can combine two or more cells to create one large cell in which you can store, for example, a table title.

① Position the mouse pointer inside the first cell you want to merge (🏛 changes to ⟋).

② Drag ⟋ across the cells you want to merge to select them.

③ Click the **Layout** tab.

④ Click **Merge Cells**.

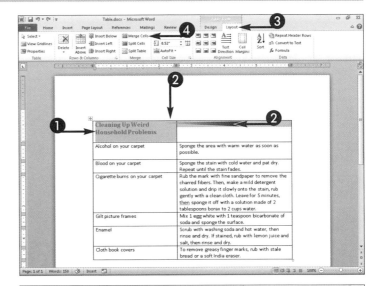

● Word combines the cells into one cell and selects that cell.

● For a table title, you can click the **Align Center** button (▤) to center text in the cell both horizontally and vertically.

⑤ Click anywhere to cancel the selection.

Split Cells

If you find that you have more information in one cell than you want, you can split the cell into two or more cells that span one or more rows, columns, or both to make room for the extra information.

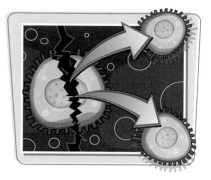

Split Cells

1 Click anywhere in the cell you want to split.

2 Click the **Layout** tab.

3 Click **Split Cells**.

The Split Cells dialog box appears.

4 Type the number of columns and rows into which you want to split the cell here.

5 Click **OK**.

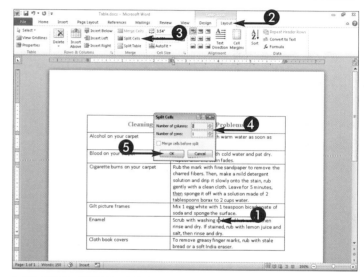

● Word splits and selects the cell.

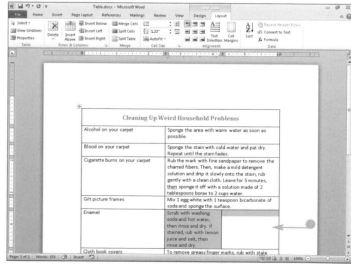

Split a Table

You can split one table into two tables. This feature is particularly useful if you discover that you should have created separate tables after you have entered a significant amount of information in one table.

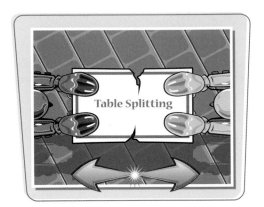

Table Splitting

Split a Table

1 Position the insertion point anywhere in the row that should appear as the first row of the new table.

2 Click the **Layout** tab.

3 Click **Split Table**.

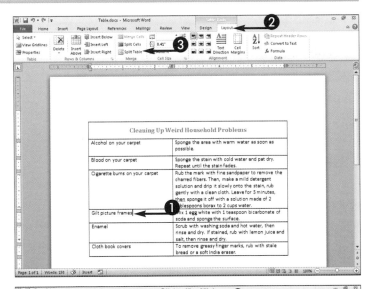

● Word separates the table into two tables and places the insertion point between the tables.

● Because the insertion point is not resting in a table cell, Table Tools no longer appears on the Ribbon.

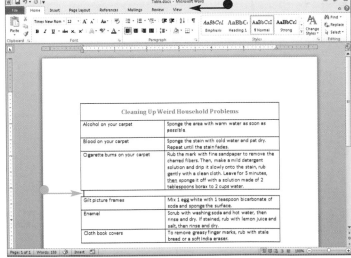

Add a Formula to a Table

You can place a formula in a cell and let Word automatically do the math for you. Word generally suggests the correct formula for the situation.

You can accept the suggested formula, as this example does, or you can select a different formula as needed.

Add a Formula to a Table

1 In a table containing numbers, click in a cell that should contain the sum of a row or a column.

2 Click the **Layout** tab.

3 Click **Formula**.

The Formula dialog box appears, suggesting a formula.

● You can click here to select a number format.

● You can click here to select a different formula.

4 Click **OK**.

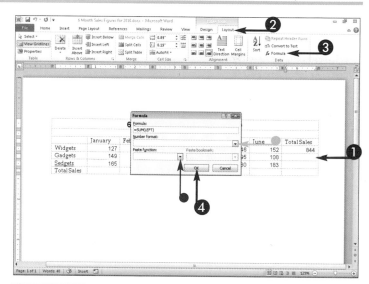

● Word places the formula in the cell containing the insertion point and displays the calculated result of the formula.

If you change any of the values in the row or column that the formula sums, you can click in the cell containing the formula and press **F9** to update the formula result.

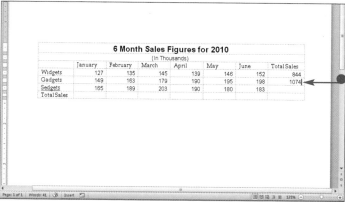

Align Text in Cells

To make your text look more uniform, you can align text or numbers with the top, bottom, left, right, or center of cells.

By default, Word aligns table entries at the top left edge of each cell.

① Click in the cell you want to align.

You can position the mouse pointer over the left edge of the cell whose alignment you want to change (⌶ changes to ▪) and drag to select multiple cells.

② Click the **Layout** tab.

③ Click an alignment button.

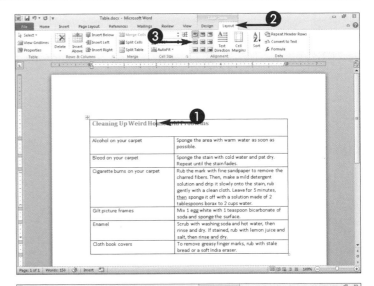

● Word selects the text and aligns it accordingly in the cell.

④ Click anywhere to cancel the selection.

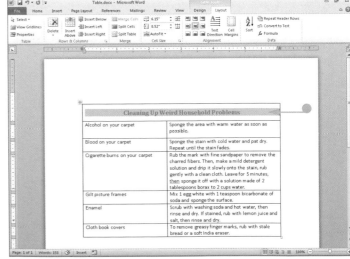

Add Shading to Cells

You can add shading to cells to call attention to them.

Add Shading to Cells

1 Click anywhere in the cell to which you want to add shading.

You can position the mouse pointer over the left edge of any cell (⫿ changes to ➤) and drag to select multiple cells.

2 Click the **Design** tab.

3 Click **Shading**.

The Shading Gallery appears.

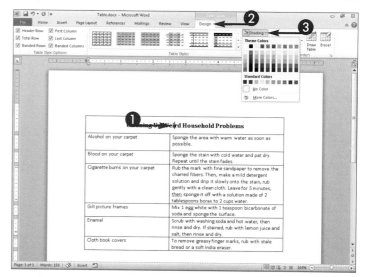

You can position the mouse pointer over a color, and Live Preview displays a sample of the selected cells shaded in the proposed color.

4 Click a color.

● Word applies the shading to the selected cells and closes the Shading Gallery.

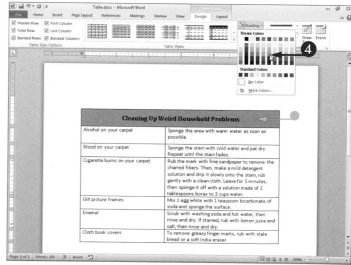

Change Cell Borders

You can change the appearance of cell borders to call attention to them.

① Click anywhere in the cell around which you want to place a border.

You can position the mouse pointer over the left edge of any cell (▯ changes to ◂) and drag to select multiple cells.

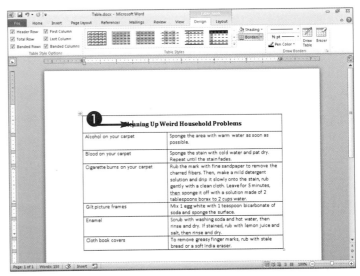

② Click the **Design** tab.

③ Click **Line Style**.

The Line Style Gallery appears.

④ Click the line style you want to apply.

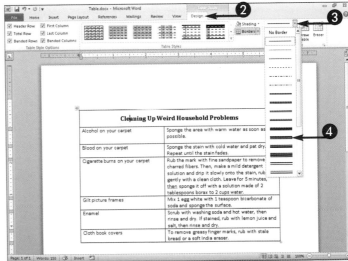

- You can click **Line Weight** and **Pen Color** to select the weight and color of the border line.

⑤ Click the **Borders** ▾.

The Borders Gallery appears.

⑥ Click the type of border to apply.

This example uses Outside Borders.

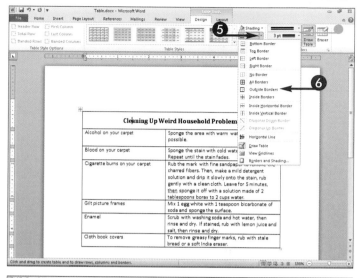

- Word applies the border using the selected line style, weight, and pen color to the selected cells.

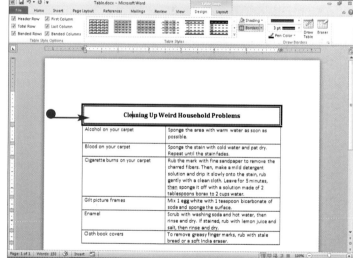

How can I remove borders from table cells?

Follow these steps:

① Complete Steps **1** to **3** in this section.

② Click the **Borders** ▾.

③ Click **No Border**.

Word removes the borders from the table cells.

Dotted blue gridlines appear on-screen, but they do not print.

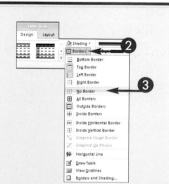

Format
a Table

You can apply any number of predefined table styles to a table to format it.

1. Click anywhere in the table.
2. Click the **Design** tab.
3. Click ☑ in the Table Styles group.

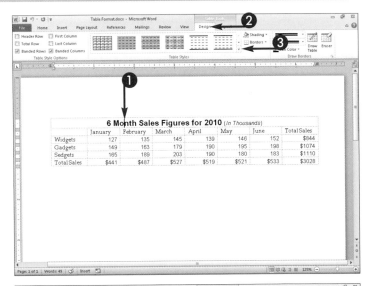

The Table Style Gallery appears.

4. Position the mouse pointer over a table style.

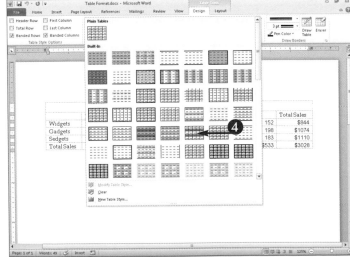

- Live Preview displays the table in the proposed table style.

5 Repeat Step **4** until you find the table style you want to use.

6 Click the table style you want to use.

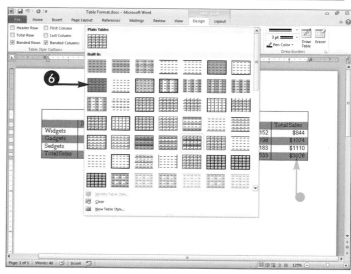

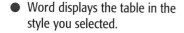

- Word displays the table in the style you selected.

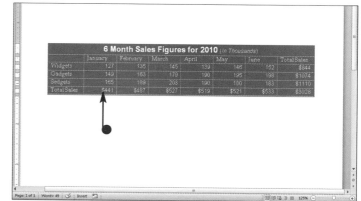

TIP

How can I remove a table formatting design?
You have a few options:

- If you just applied the formatting, you can click the **Undo** button (⌨).

- If you performed other actions since applying the table formatting design, perform Steps **1** to **3** in this section and then click **Clear**.

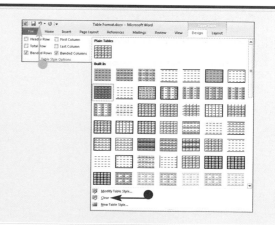

You can chart data from Microsoft Word 2010.
This process uses Microsoft Excel 2010.

Although this example inserts a chart in a document containing a table, the table is independent of the chart. You supply all data for the chart in Excel and you do not need to use table information found in Word.

① Click in the document where you want a chart to appear.

② Click the **Insert** tab.

③ Click **Chart**.

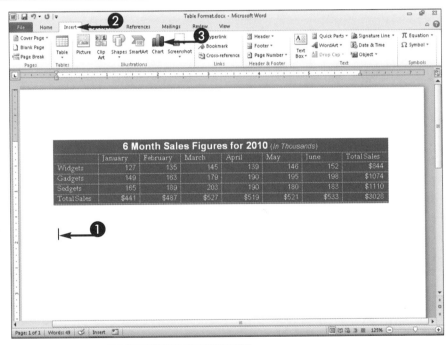

6 Month Sales Figures for 2010 (*In Thousands*)							
	January	February	March	April	May	June	Total Sales
Widgets	127	135	145	139	146	152	$844
Gadgets	149	163	179	190	195	198	$1074
Sedgets	165	189	203	190	180	183	$1110
Total Sales	$441	$487	$527	$519	$521	$533	$3028

The Insert Chart window appears.

④ Click a chart type.

● Categories of chart types appear here.

● Chart types organized by category appear here.

⑤ Click **OK**.

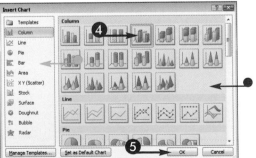

Microsoft Excel opens alongside Microsoft Word.

● A sample chart of the data appears in Word.

● Sample data appears in Excel.

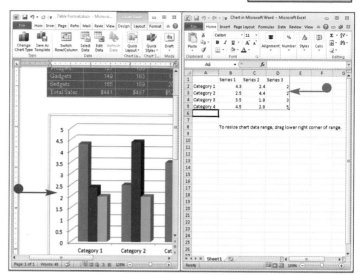

⑥ Change the data in Excel.

● The chart in Word updates to reflect the changes in Excel.

⑦ You can close Excel without saving by clicking the **Close** button (⊠).

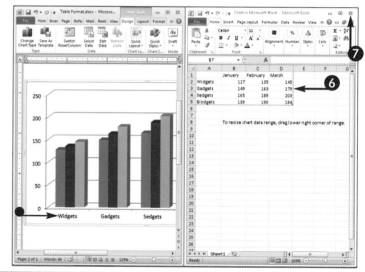

Can I format the chart in Word?

Yes. When you maximize the Word window and select the chart, Word displays Chart Tools on the Ribbon.

● From the Design tab, you can select a layout and style from the Chart Layouts and the Chart Styles Galleries.

● From the Layout tab, you can set up chart and axis titles, add data labels, and modify the legend.

● The Format tab provides options for shape styles and WordArt styles.

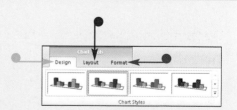

Chart Concepts

When creating a chart, you have a wide variety of choices. You can create column charts, line charts, pie charts, bar charts, area charts, XY charts, stock charts, surface charts, doughnut charts, bubble charts, and radar charts. Each chart type serves a different purpose and communicates different information to the reader. The type of chart you use depends on the information you are trying to convey to your reader. In addition, you are not limited to the first chart type you select; if you discover that you have not selected the optimal chart type, try a different one.

Column Charts

A column chart shows data changes over a period of time and can compare different sets of data. A column chart contains vertically oriented bars.

Line Charts

Line charts help you see trends. A line chart connects many related data points; by connecting the points with a line, you see a general trend.

Pie Charts

Pie charts demonstrate the relationship of a part to the whole. Pie charts are effective when you are trying to show, for example, the percentage of total sales for which the Midwest region is responsible.

Bar Charts

Bar charts typically compare different sets of data and can also show data changes over time. A bar chart closely resembles a column chart, but the bars are horizontally oriented.

Area Charts

Area charts show data over time, but an area chart helps you see data as broad trends, rather than individual data points.

XY Charts

Statisticians often use an XY chart, also called a scatter chart, to determine whether a correlation exists between two variables. Both axes on a scatter chart are numeric, and the axes can be linear or logarithmic.

Stock Charts

Also called High-Low, Open-Close charts, stock charts are used for stock market reports. This chart type is very effective to display data that fluctuates over time.

Surface Charts

Topographic maps are surface charts, using colors and patterns to identify areas in the same range of values. A surface chart is useful when you want to find the best-possible combination between two sets of data.

Doughnut Charts

Like a pie chart, a doughnut chart shows the relationship of parts to a whole. Although a pie chart contains only one data series, a doughnut chart typically contains more than one data series. The doughnut chart is round like a pie chart, but each series in the doughnut chart appears as a separate ring in the circle.

Bubble Charts

A bubble chart is a specific type of XY chart that compares sets of three values. The size of the bubble indicates the value of a third variable. You can arrange data for a bubble chart by placing the X values in one column and entering corresponding Y values and bubble sizes in the adjacent columns.

Radar Charts

You can use a radar chart to compare data series that consist of several variables. Each data series on a radar chart has its own axis that "radiates" from the center of the chart — hence the name radar chart. A line connects each point in the series.

Working with Graphics

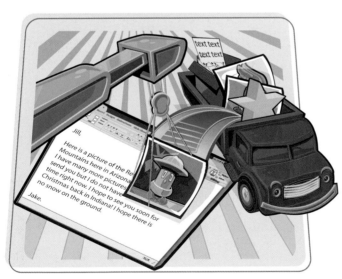

You can spruce up documents by inserting a variety of graphics; the technique to insert graphics varies, depending on the type of graphic.

When you edit, however, some techniques are common to all types of graphics and others vary by graphic type. When a technique applies to all types of graphics, this chapter uses the generic term *graphic*. For editing techniques that apply to pictures, clip art, and screenshots, this chapter calls these graphics *pictures*. Similarly, for editing techniques that apply to WordArt, shapes, and text boxes this chapter calls these graphics *drawings*. Diagrams fall into a category by themselves.

WordArt is decorative text that you can add to a
document as an eye-catching visual effect. You can
create WordArt text as you create a WordArt
graphic, or you can apply a WordArt style to
existing text.

Add WordArt

1 Click in the document where you
want to add WordArt or select
existing text and apply WordArt
to it.

2 Click the **Insert** tab.

3 Click **WordArt**.

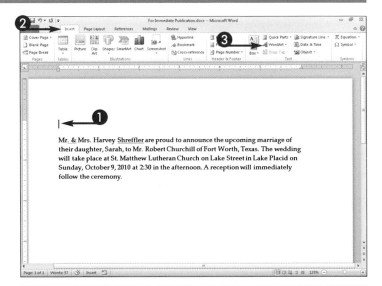

● The WordArt Gallery appears.

4 Click the WordArt style you want
to apply.

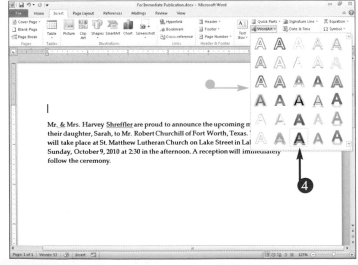

- If you selected text in Step **1**, your text appears selected in the WordArt style you applied; otherwise, the words "Your Text Here" appear selected in the upper-left corner of your document.

- Handles (handle and handle) surround the WordArt graphic.

- Drawing Tools appear on the Ribbon; you can use these tools to format WordArt, shapes, and text boxes.

5 If necessary, type text.

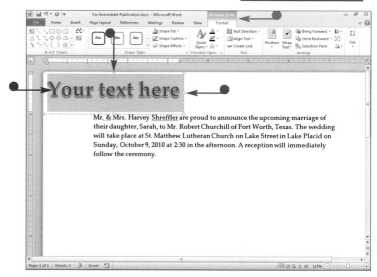

- Word converts the text to a WordArt graphic.

6 Click anywhere to continue working.

Note: You can move the WordArt; see the section, "Move or Resize a Graphic."

Note: You can change the size of the WordArt font by selecting the WordArt text and, on the Home tab, selecting a different font size from the Font list in the Font group.

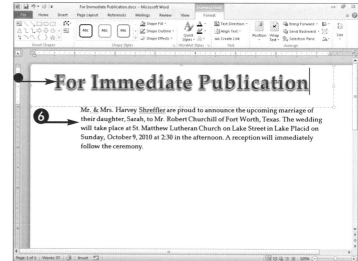

Can I edit the WordArt drawing?
Yes. Click inside the WordArt drawing. Handles (handle and handle) appear around the WordArt. Edit the text the way you would edit any text, deleting and changing as needed.

Can I delete a WordArt drawing?
Yes, but be aware that deleting the drawing also deletes the text. Click near the edge of the drawing or, if you click inside the drawing, click any handle (handle or handle) to select the drawing. Then press Del.

Add a Picture

You can include a picture file graphic stored on your computer in a Word document.

Add a Picture

① Click in your document where you want to add a picture.

② Click the **Insert** tab.

③ Click **Picture**.

The Insert Picture dialog box appears.

● The folder you are viewing appears here.

● You can click here to navigate to commonly used locations where pictures may be stored.

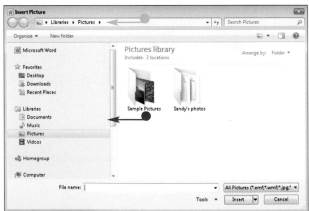

④ Navigate to the folder containing the picture you want to add.

⑤ Click the picture you want to add to your document.

⑥ Click **Insert**.

● The picture appears in your document, selected and surrounded by handles (⬚ and ⬚).

● Picture Tools appear in the Ribbon; you can use these tools to format pictures.

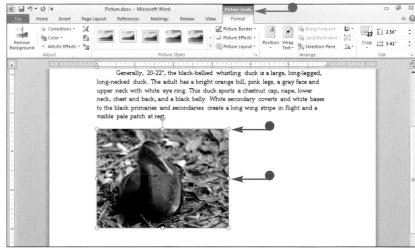

How can I delete a picture?

① Move the mouse pointer over the picture.

● The pointer changes to ⬚.

② Click the picture to select it.

③ Press Del.

Add a Screenshot

You can insert into a Word document an image called a *screenshot* of another document open in Word or of a document open in another program.

❶ Open a document.

● This example shows a chart in Excel.

❷ Open the Word document in which you want to insert a screenshot of the document you opened in Step **1**.

❸ Position the insertion point where you want the screenshot to appear.

④ Click **Insert**.

⑤ Click **Screenshot**.

● The Screenshot Gallery shows open programs and available screenshots of those programs.

Note: *You can open as many programs and documents as your computer permits. In this example, in addition to Excel and Word, the Outlook Calendar is also open.*

⑥ Click the screenshot you want to insert in your Word document.

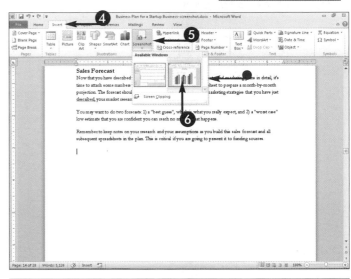

● The screenshot appears selected in your Word document.

Click anywhere outside the screenshot to continue working.

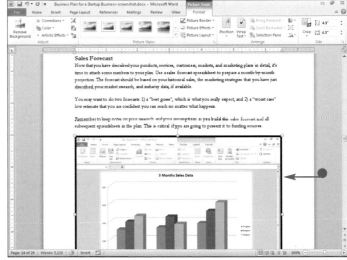

TIPS

Can I use the Screenshot feature to insert a screenshot of the current Word document into the same document?

No, but here is a workaround. Open the document in which you want to insert a screenshot and then open a second, blank document. From the blank document, shoot a screen of the first Word document. The screen appears in the blank document, already selected. Click Copy (📋). Then switch to the Word document, click where the screenshot should appear, and click Paste (📄).

Can I use the Screenshot feature to take a picture of my desktop?

No, but you can take a picture of your desktop and insert it into a Word document. While viewing your desktop, press `Print scrn`. Then switch to Word and position the insertion point where you want the screenshot to appear. Press `Ctrl` + `V` to paste the image into your Word document.

Add a Clip Art Image

You can add clip art images to your document to help get your message across and add graphic interest to your document.

① Click in your document where you want to place an image.

② Click **Insert**.

③ Click **Clip Art**.

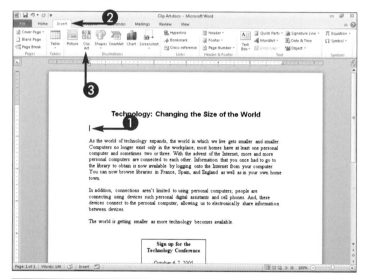

The Clip Art Pane appears on the right side of your screen.

④ Click here and type one or more words to describe the image you want to find.

● You can click here (☐ changes to ☑) to search online at Office.com for additional clip art.

Note: This example does not search online.

⑤ Click **Go**.

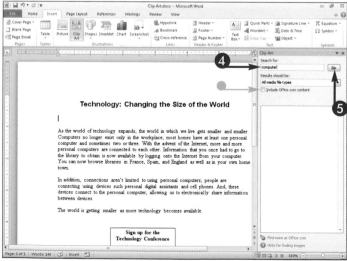

● Images matching the words you typed appear here.

6 Click an image.

● The image appears selected, with handles (and) surrounding it.

● Picture Tools appear on the Ribbon.

7 Click anywhere in the document to continue working.

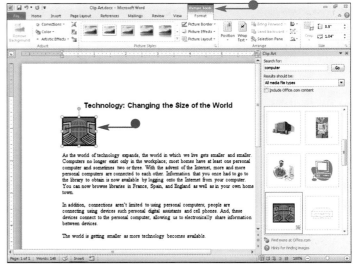

TIPS

What happens if I click the Results should be list box arrow ( )?
You have the opportunity to specify the types of media for which you want to search. Searching takes less time if you limit the search, but the search may not display as many clip art images if you limit it.

What kinds of media types are available for searching?
When you use the default settings, you search for illustrations, photographs, videos, and audio. Using the Results Should Be list, you can limit the search to any one or a combination of those media types.

Add a Shape

To give your Word document pizzazz, you can add graphic shapes such as lines, arrows, stars, and banners.

Shapes are visible in Print Layout, Web Layout, and Reading Layout views.

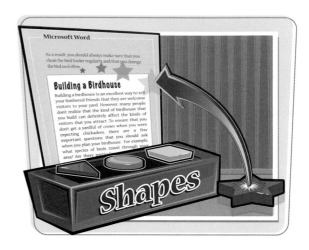

Add a Shape

① Click the **Insert** tab.

② Click **Shapes**.

The Shapes Gallery appears.

③ Click a shape.

The mouse pointer (🖑) changes to ⊞.

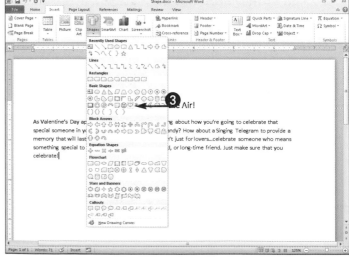

4 Position the mouse pointer at the upper-left corner of the place where you want the shape to appear.

5 Drag the mouse pointer (⊞) down and to the right until the shape is the size you want.

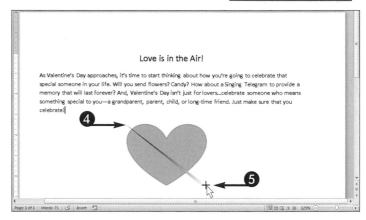

When you release the mouse button, the shape appears.

● The handles (and) that surround the shape indicate that the shape is selected.

● Drawing Tools appear on the Ribbon.

You can press Esc or click anywhere to continue working in your document.

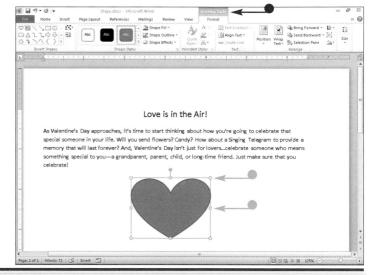

TIP

Can I change the color of a shape?
Yes, you can change the color inside a shape as well as the shape's outline color.

1 Click the shape to select it.

2 On the Ribbon, in the Shape Styles group, click the **Shape Fill** button to display the color gallery.

3 Move the mouse pointer over the Color gallery and Live Preview displays the outline of the shape in the proposed color.

4 Click a color.

5 Repeat these steps, selecting **Shape Outline** in Step 2.

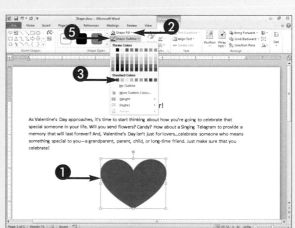

Add a
Text Box

You can add a text box, which is another type of graphic, to your document to control the placement and appearance of the text that appears in the box.

Text boxes are visible only in Print Layout, Web Layout, and Reading Layout views.

Add a Text Box

1 Click the **Insert** tab.

2 Click **Text Box**.

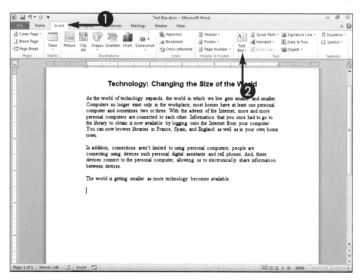

The Text Box Gallery appears.

3 Click a text box style.

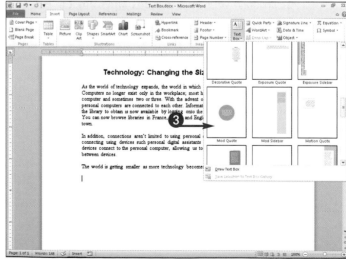

- Word places a text box in your document.

- Existing text flows around the box.

  Sample text appears inside a Pull Quote box, where you can type your text.

4 Position the mouse pointer inside the text box over the sample text and click.

  Word selects the sample text.

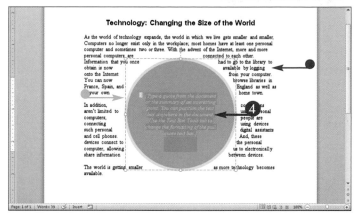

5 Type your text.

6 Click outside the text box.

  Your text appears in the box.

Note: *You can format the text using the techniques described in Chapter 5.*

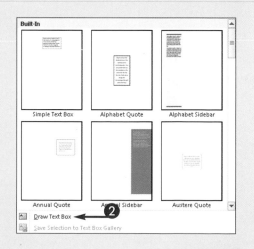

 TIP

What should I do if I do not like any of the predefined text box formats?

You can draw your own text box and format it. Follow these steps:

1 Complete Steps **1** and **2** in this section.

2 Click **Draw Text Box** (☐ changes to ⊞).

3 Drag the mouse pointer (⊞) from the upper-left to lower-right corner of the place where you want the text box to appear.

  The text box appears.

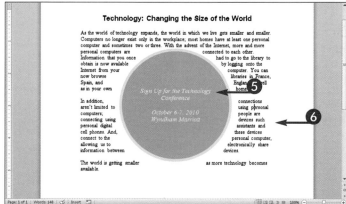

Move or Resize a Graphic

If you find that a graphic — a picture, Clip Art image, shape, text box, or WordArt graphic — is not positioned where you want it or if it is too large or too small, you can move or resize it.

Move a Graphic

1 Click the graphic.

● Handles (,) surround the graphic.

2 Position the mouse pointer over the WordArt image, picture, Clip Art image, or shape, or over the edge of the text box (changes to).

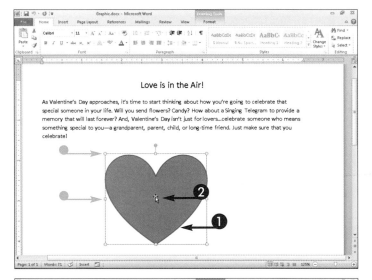

3 Drag the graphic to a new location.

● A lighter-shaded version of the graphic indicates the proposed position of the graphic.

4 Release the mouse button.

The graphic appears in the new location.

5 Click outside the graphic to cancel its selection.

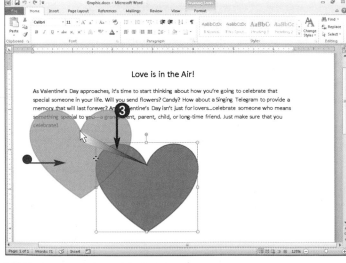

Resize a Graphic

1 Click the graphic.

● Handles (and) surround the graphic.

2 Position the mouse pointer over one of the handles (changes to , , , or).

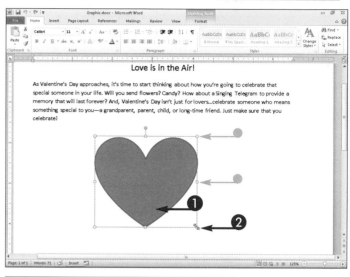

3 Drag the handle until the graphic is the appropriate size (, , , or changes to).

● A lighter-shaded version of the graphic indicates the proposed size of the graphic.

4 Release the mouse button.

The graphic appears in the new size.

5 Click outside the graphic to cancel its selection.

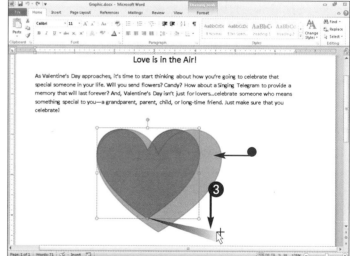

TIPS

Is there an easy way I can make a graphic move only horizontally or vertically but not diagonally?

Yes. Press and hold the Shift key as you drag the graphic. Word allows you to move the graphic horizontally or vertically but not diagonally.

Does it matter which handle I use to resize a graphic?

If you click and drag any of the corner handles, you maintain the proportion of the graphic as you resize it. The square handles on the sides, top, or bottom of the graphic resize the width or the height only of the graphic.

Crop a Picture

You can crop a picture, screenshot, or clip art image to reduce its size or change the focus of the image.

For example, you might want to remove the black border of a screenshot you captured in Word or eliminate the Ribbon from the image.

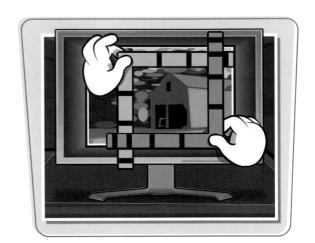

---

① Click the image to select it; handles
(▯ and ◯) surround the image.

② Click **Picture Tools**.

③ Click **Crop**.

● Black crop handles appear at each
corner and in the middle of each side
of the image, framing the portion of the
image that will remain.

④ Slide the mouse pointer over a crop
handle (▯, ▧, or ✛ changes to ⌐,
⌐, ∟, ⌐, ⊥, ⊤, ⊢, or ⊣).

⑤ Click and drag the handle toward
the center of the picture.

● As you drag, the crop handle
changes to ⊞.

● Word displays the area it will
remove shaded in black.

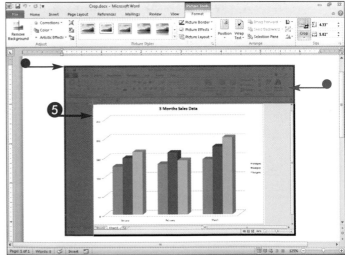

⑥ Repeat Steps **4** and **5** as needed until crop handles frame the portion of the image you want to keep.

● Areas to be removed appear shaded in black.

⑦ Press Enter.

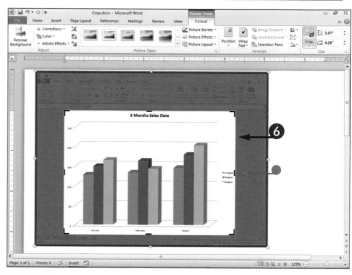

The cropped image appears.

You can press Esc or click outside the image to cancel its selection.

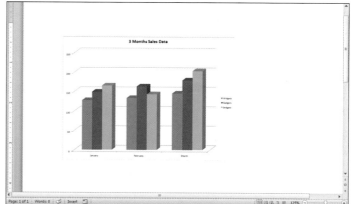

TIP

Is there a way to crop my image using a special shape?

Yes. Follow these steps:

① Complete Steps **1** and **2** above.

② Click the list box arrow (▼) on the **Crop** button.

③ Click **Crop to Shape**.

④ From the Shape gallery that appears, select a shape.

● Word crops the selected image to the shape you choose.

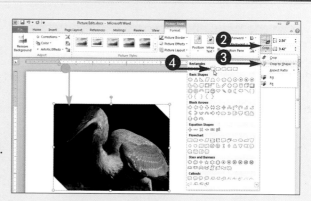

Rotate a Graphic

For dramatic effect, you can rotate pictures, clip art images, and some shapes. You cannot rotate text boxes.

1 Click the image you want to rotate.

● Handles (○ and ○) surround the graphic.

2 Position the mouse pointer over the green handle at the top of the image (○ changes to ○).

3 Drag the mouse in the direction you want to rotate the image (○ changes to ○).

● A lighter-shaded version of the graphic indicates the proposed position of the image.

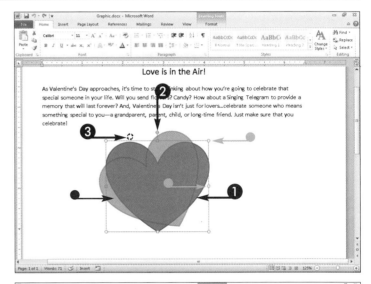

● Word displays the rotated image.

You can press **Esc** or click outside the image to cancel its selection.

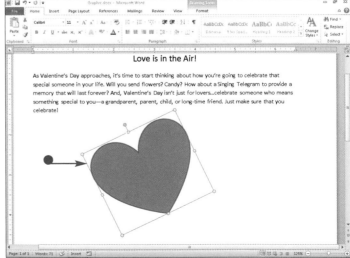

Correct the Brightness or Contrast of a Picture

You can change the brightness and contrast of a picture, clip art, or a screenshot to improve its appearance.

You also can sharpen or soften an image.

Correct the Brightness or Contrast of a Picture

① Click the image to select it.

● Handles (□ and ○) surround the picture.

● Picture Tools appear in the Ribbon.

② Click **Corrections**.

You can slide the mouse pointer over an option in the gallery that appears and Live Preview displays the appearance of the image using that option.

③ Click an option.

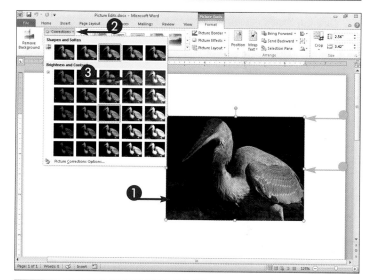

Word applies the correction to the image.

You can press Esc or click outside the image to cancel its selection.

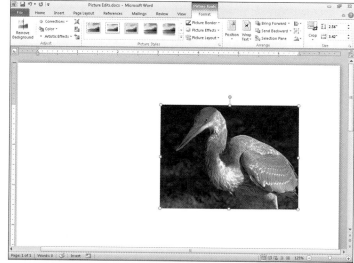

Modify the Color of a Picture

You can adjust the color of a picture or a screenshot by increasing or decreasing color saturation or color tone. You also can recolor a picture, screenshot, or clip art image to create an interesting effect.

Color saturation controls the amount of red and green in a photo, while color tone controls the amount of blue and yellow.

Modify the Color of a Picture

1 Click the image to select it.

● Handles (▯ and ▢) surround the picture.

● Picture Tools appear in the Ribbon.

2 Click **Color**.

You can slide the mouse pointer over an option in the gallery that appears and Live Preview displays the appearance of the image using that option.

3 Click an option.

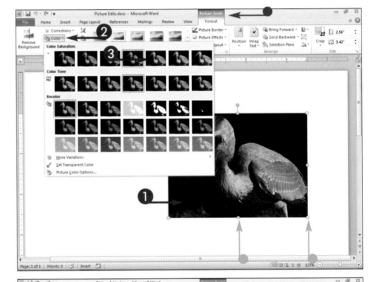

Word applies the option to the image.

You can press Esc or click outside the image to cancel its selection.

You can add to or change the color of a shape, WordArt image, or text box to draw attention to it or to make it more interesting.

Change the Color of a Drawing

① Click the shape or text box to select it.

● Handles (and) appear around the image.

② Click **Drawing Tools**.

③ Click **Shape Fill** to display available colors.

You can slide the mouse pointer over a color in the gallery and Live Preview displays the appearance of the image in that color.

④ Click the color you want to apply.

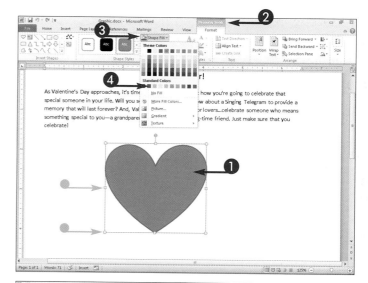

● Word fills the drawing with the selected color.

● To change the color of a drawing outline, you can repeat Steps **1** to **4**, clicking **Shape Outline,** which appears below Shape Fill, in Step **3**.

You can press Esc or click outside the image to cancel its selection.

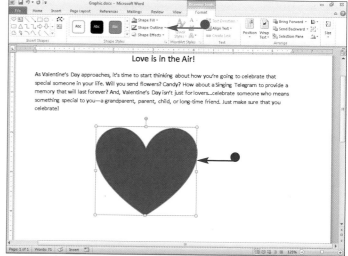

Add a Shadow to a Graphic

You can add depth to any picture or drawing by adding a shadow to it.

① Click a graphic.

● Handles (and) appear around the image.

② Click the **Picture Tools Format** tab.

③ Click **Picture Effects or Shape Effects**.

④ Click **Shadow**.

You can slide the mouse pointer over an option in the gallery and Live Preview displays the appearance of the image using that option.

⑤ Click a shadow effect.

● Word applies the shadow effect to the selected graphic.

To remove a shadow, repeat Steps **1** to **5**, selecting **No Shadow Effect** in Step **5**.

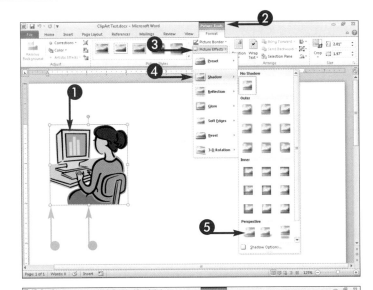

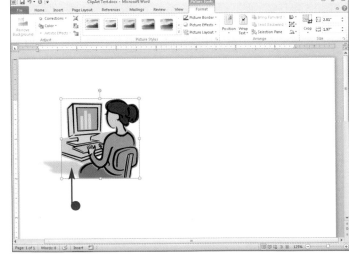

Make a Graphic Three-Dimensional

To create an interesting visual effect, you can make a graphic — a picture, clip art image, WordArt, a text box, or a shape — appear three-dimensional.

Make a Graphic Three-Dimensional

1 Click a graphic.

● Handles (▯ and ▢) appear around the image.

2 Click **Format**.

3 Click **Picture Effects or Shape Effects**.

4 Click **Bevel**.

The Bevel Gallery appears.

You can slide the mouse pointer over an option in the gallery and Live Preview displays the appearance of the image using that option.

5 Click a bevel effect.

Word adds the bevel effect to the graphic, giving it a three-dimensional look.

To remove a three-dimensional effect, repeat Steps **1** to **5**, selecting **No Bevel** in Step **5**.

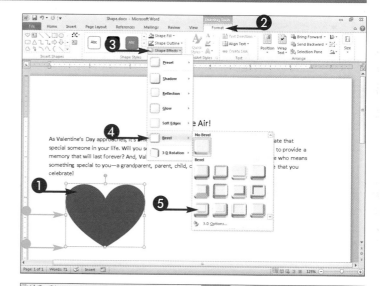

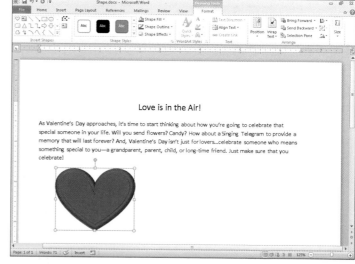

Apply a Style to a Graphic

You can apply a predefined style to a shape, text box, WordArt graphic, picture, or clip art image. Styles contain predefined colors and effects and help you quickly add interest to a graphic.

Applying a style removes other effects you may have applied, such as shadow or bevel effects.

Apply a Style to a Graphic

① Click a graphic.

● Handles (and) appear around the image.

② Click **Format**.

③ Click the **More** button ().

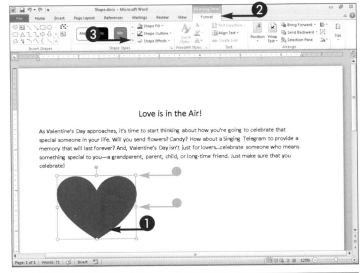

The Styles Gallery for the type of graphic you selected in Step **1** appears.

Note: *This task displays the Shape Styles Gallery.*

You can slide the mouse pointer over an option in the gallery and Live Preview displays the appearance of the image using that option.

④ Click a style.

● Word applies the style to the selected graphic.

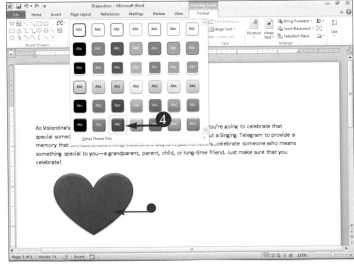

Apply a Color Outline to a Graphic

You can change the color of the outline of a graphic to which you have applied a style.

1. Click a graphic.

   Handles (and) appear around the image.

2. Click the **Picture Tools Format** tab.

3. Click **Picture Border** or **Shape Outline**.

   You can slide the mouse pointer over an option in the gallery and Live Preview displays the appearance of the image using that option.

4. Click **Weight**.

5. Select a line weight for the outline.

   ● Word applies a black outline to the graphic in the weight you selected.

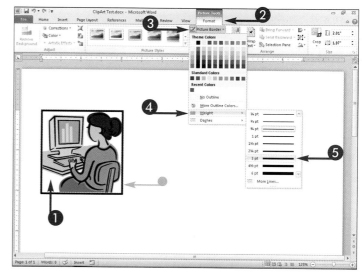

6. Click **Picture Border** or **Shape Outline**.

7. Click a color.

   ● Word applies the color to the outline of the selected graphic.

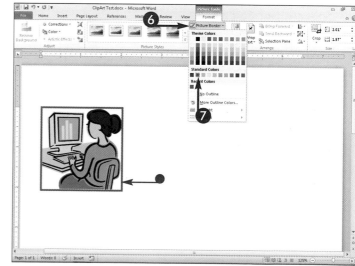

Understanding Text Wrapping and Graphics

When you insert graphics into a Word document, you can control the way that text wraps around the graphic. By default, most graphics you insert have a relatively square boundary, even if the graphic is not a square, and most text wrapping options relate to that relatively square boundary.

By editing a graphic's wrap points, you can change the square boundary to more closely match the graphic's shape and wrap text more closely around the shape.

Square

Wraps text in a square around your graphic regardless of its shape. You can control the amount of space between text and all your graphic's sides.

Tight

Wraps text around the graphic's outside edge. The difference between this and Square is apparent with a nonsquare shape; with Tight, you can control the space between the text and the graphic's right and left sides. Word leaves no space between text and the graphic's top and bottom sides.

Through

With Through, if you edit a graphic's wrap points by dragging them to match the shape of the graphic, you can wrap text to follow the graphic's shape.

Top and Bottom

Wraps text around the graphic's top and bottom, but leaves the space on either side of a graphic blank.

Behind Text

With this, the text runs over the graphic, as if the graphic were not there.

In Front of Text

With this, the graphic blocks the text underneath the graphic's location.

In Line with Text

With this, text does not wrap around the graphic. Word positions the graphic exactly where you placed it. The graphic moves to accommodate added or deleted text, but no text appears on the graphic's right or left.

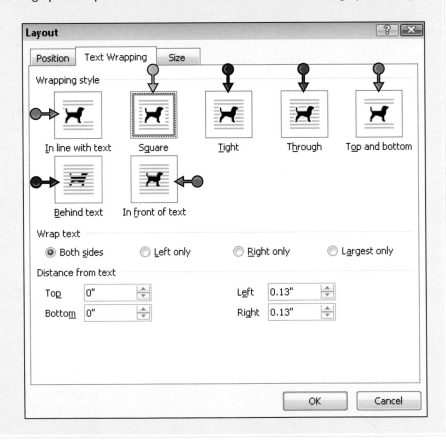

Wrap Text Around a Graphic

You can control the way that Word wraps text around a graphic image in your document. This becomes very important when you want to place graphics in a document where space is at a premium, such as a two-columned newsletter.

The information in this section shows text wrapping for a shape but applies to text wrapping for any kind of graphic.

Wrap Text Around a Graphic

① Click a graphic.

● Handles (and) appear around the image.

② Click **Format**.

③ Click **Wrap Text**.

④ Click the wrapping style you want to apply.

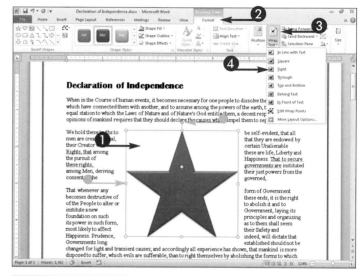

Word wraps text around the graphic using the text wrapping option you selected.

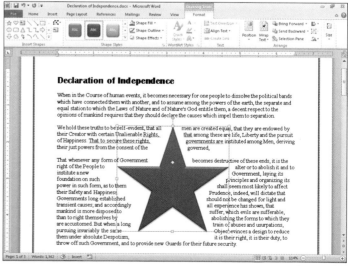

Work with Diagrams

Using SmartArt, you can add any of a variety of diagrams to your document to illustrate a concept. For example, you can create organization charts, process diagrams, diagrams that represent cycles, and diagrams that present list information as well as other types of diagrams.

The example in this section demonstrates adding an organizational chart.

Work with Diagrams

Add a Diagram

① Click in your document where you want the diagram to appear.

② Click the **Insert** tab.

③ Click **SmartArt**.

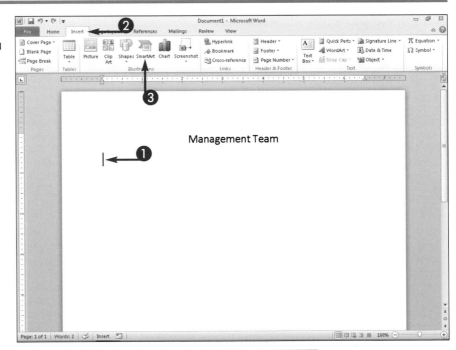

The Choose a SmartArt Graphic dialog box appears.

④ Click a diagram category.

⑤ Click the type of diagram you want to add.

● A description of the selected diagram appears here.

⑥ Click **OK**.

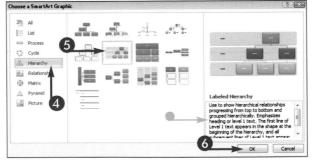

Word adds the diagram to your document.

● The graphic border surrounding the diagram indicates that the diagram is selected; the border will not print.

● SmartArt Tools appear on the Ribbon.

● The Text pane appears here.

● If the Text pane does not appear, click **Text Pane**.

Each object within the diagram is called a *shape*.

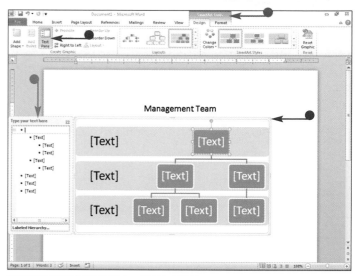

Add Text to the Diagram

⑦ Click next to a bullet in the Text pane.

⑧ Type the text you want to add.

⑨ Repeat Steps **1** to **2** for each shape in the diagram.

Note: You do not need to use the Text pane; you can type directly in a shape.

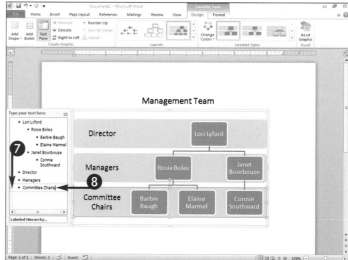

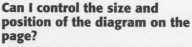

How can I add two lines of text to a shape?

After you type the first line of the text in the Text pane, press **Shift** + **Enter**. Then type the second line, and Word adjusts the font size of the text to fit the shape; for consistency, Word also adjusts the font size of all text in the diagram. Pressing **Enter** alone adds another shape to the diagram and adjusts the size of all shapes in the diagram.

Can I control the size and position of the diagram on the page?

Yes. Click the **Format** tab, click **Size**, and then click the spinner arrows (⬍) to change the height and width. Word sets the default position on the diagram inline with your text. You can use the Position Gallery to place the diagram in one of nine predetermined positions on the page. On the Format tab, click **Arrange** and then click **Position** to display the Position Gallery.

Work with Diagrams
(continued)

To keep your diagrams current and interesting, you can add or delete shapes and apply styles to diagrams.

Work with Diagrams *(continued)*

Add or Delete Shapes

1 Click the **Design** tab.

2 Click the shape above or beside which you want to add a shape.

● Handles (□ and ○) surround the shape.

3 Click the list box arrow (▼) beside Add Shape and select the option that describes where the shape should appear.

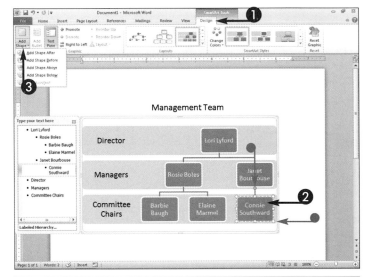

● The new shape appears.

You can add text to the new shape by following the steps in the subsection "Add Text to the Diagram" on the previous page.

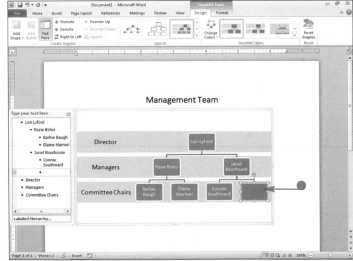

Apply a Diagram Style

① Click the **Design** tab.

② Click the **More** button (⊡) in the SmartArt Styles group to display the Quick Styles Gallery.

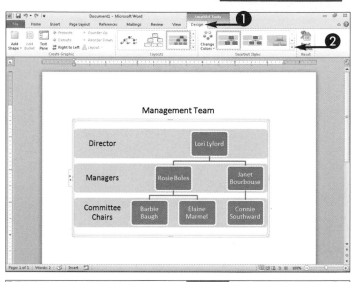

The Quick Styles Gallery appears.

You can slide the mouse pointer over an option in the gallery and Live Preview displays the appearance of the image using that option.

③ Click a style.

● Word applies the selected style to the diagram.

You can click anywhere outside the diagram to continue working.

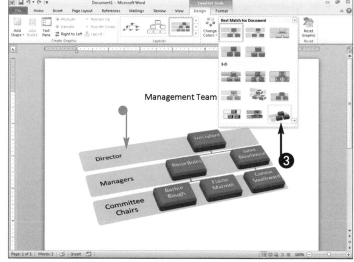

How can I delete a shape?	Can I change the layout of an organization chart diagram after I insert it?
Click the outside border of the shape; handles (▯ and ▭) appear around the shape. Press Del to remove the selected shape from the diagram.	Yes. Click the border of the organization chart to select it. Then click the **Design** tab and, in the Layouts group, click the **More** button ⊡ to display the Layouts Gallery and select a different organization chart structure. You can click **More Layouts** at the bottom of the Layouts Gallery to reopen the Choose a SmartArt Graphic dialog box shown earlier in this task.

CHAPTER 11

Customizing Word

Do you like the default Word settings? If not, you can easily customize portions of the Word program to make it perform more in line with the way you work.

Control the Display of Formatting Marks

Although you can display all formatting marks, you also can limit the formatting marks that Word displays to view just the ones that interest you.

Using the Show/Hide button displays all formatting marks.

Control the Display of Formatting Marks

1 Click the **File** tab.

The Backstage view appears.

2 Click **Options**.

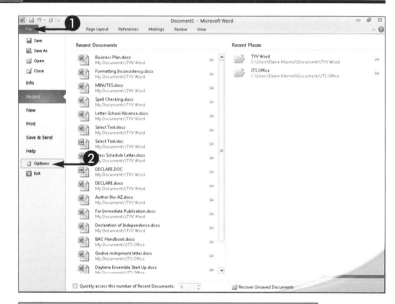

The Word Options dialog box appears.

3 Click **Display**.

● You can select the **Show all formatting marks** option (☐ changes to ☑) to display all formatting marks.

4 Select the check boxes of the formatting marks you want to display (☐ changes to ☑).

5 Click **OK**.

Word displays only the selected formatting marks in your document.

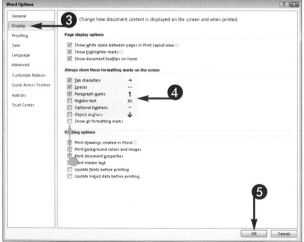

Customize the Status Bar

You can customize the status bar to display information you want visible while you work, such as page numbers and the position of the insertion point.

Customize the Status Bar

1. Right-click the status bar.

● Word displays the Customize Status Bar menu.

2. Click the option you want to display on the status bar.

3. Repeat Step **2** for each option you want to display.

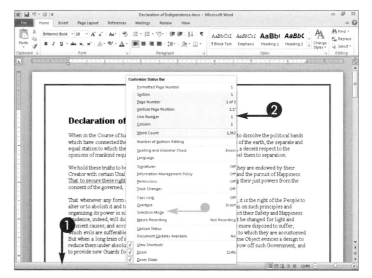

● Word displays the option(s) you selected on the status bar.

You can click anywhere outside the menu to close it.

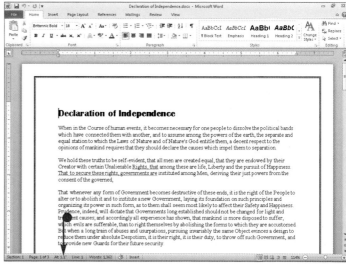

Hide or Display Ribbon Buttons

You can hide the Ribbon while you work and then redisplay it when you need it. Hiding the Ribbon can make your screen appear less crowded.

When you hide the Ribbon, you hide the buttons on each tab, but the tab names continue to appear.

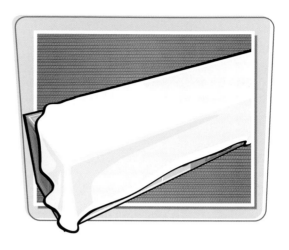

Hide or Display Ribbon Buttons

● By default, Word displays the Ribbon.

① Click the **Minimize the Ribbon** button (⌃).

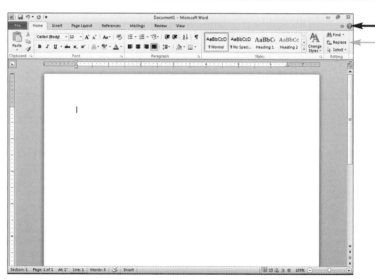

● Word hides the buttons on the Ribbon but continues to display the tabs.

● The Quick Access Toolbar continues to appear.

② Type in your document as usual.

③ When you need a Ribbon button, click that Ribbon tab.

Note: You can click any Ribbon tab, but you will save time if you click the tab containing the button you need.

274

● Word redisplays the Ribbon buttons.

④ Click the button you need.

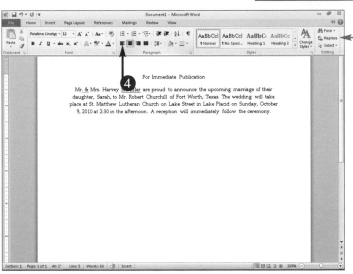

● Word applies the command.

● Word hides the Ribbon buttons again.

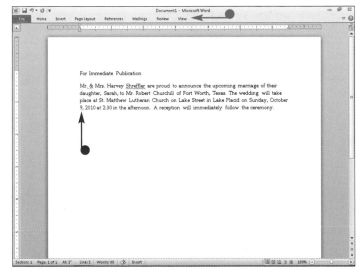

TIPS

How can I redisplay the Ribbon buttons permanently?
Repeat Step **1**.

Is there another way to hide the Ribbon buttons?

Yes, you can right-click the bottom edge of any group on the Ribbon and, from the menu that appears, click **Minimize the Ribbon**. When the Ribbon buttons are hidden, you can right-click a Ribbon tab to see that a check mark appears beside the Minimize the Ribbon command. You can click the **Minimize the Ribbon** command to redisplay the Ribbon buttons.

Add a Predefined Group to a Ribbon Tab

You can set up Word so that you can work more efficiently if you customize the Ribbon to place the groups of buttons that you use most often on a single tab.

For example, suppose that most of the buttons you need appear on the Home tab, but you often use the Page Setup group on the Page Layout tab to change document margins and set up columns. You can add the Page Setup group to the Home tab.

Add a Predefined Group to a Ribbon Tab

1 Click the **File** tab.

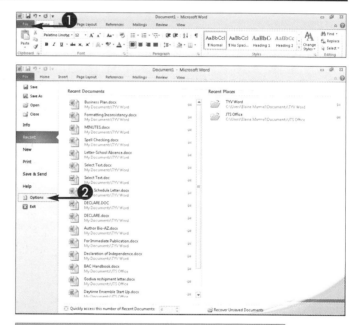

The Backstage view appears.

2 Click **Options**.

3 In the Word Options dialog box, click **Customize Ribbon**.

4 Click the list box arrow (▼) and select **Main Tabs**.

5 Click the plus sign (⊞) beside the tab containing the group you want to add (⊞ changes to ⊟).

6 Click the group you want to add.

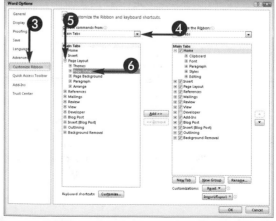

7 Click ⊞ beside the tab where you want to place the group you selected in Step **6** (⊞ changes to ⊟).

8 Click the group you want to appear on the Ribbon to the left of the new group.

9 Click **Add**.

● Word adds the group you selected in Step **6** below the group you selected in Step **8**.

10 Repeat Steps **5** to **9** as needed.

11 Click OK.

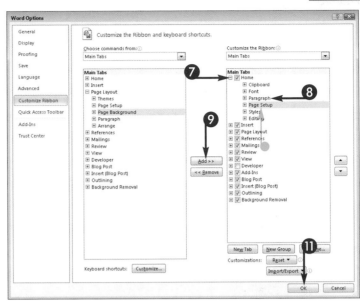

● Word adds the group you selected to the appropriate Ribbon tab.

Note: Word might collapse other groups to fit the new group on the tab. In this example, Word collapsed the Quick Styles gallery.

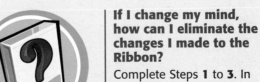

TIPS

How do I add a single button – instead of a group – to one of the existing groups on the Ribbon?

You cannot add or delete a button to one of the default groups on the Ribbon. But, you can create your own group that contains only those buttons you want to use and then hide the default group Word displays. See the section "Create Your Own Ribbon Group" later in this chapter.

If I change my mind, how can I eliminate the changes I made to the Ribbon?

Complete Steps **1** to **3**. In the column on the right, select the Ribbon tab and group you added. Just above the OK button, click **Restore Defaults**, and from the menu that appears, click **Restore only selected Ribbon tab**. Then click **OK**.

Create Your Own Ribbon Group

You cannot add or remove buttons from predefined groups on a Ribbon tab, but you can create your own group and place the buttons you want in the group.

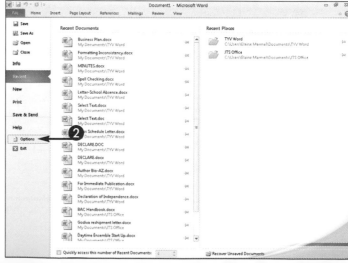

Make a Group

1 Click the **File** tab.

The Backstage view appears.

2 Click **Options**.

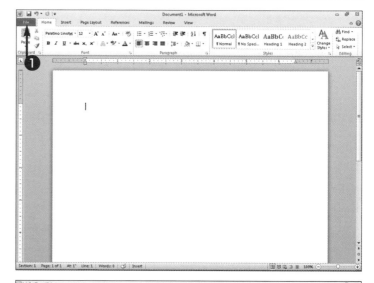

The Word Options dialog box appears.

③ Click **Customize Ribbon**.

④ Click ⊞ beside the tab to which you want to add a group (⊞ changes to ⊟).

⑤ Click the group you want to appear on the Ribbon to the left of the new group.

⑥ Click **New Group**.

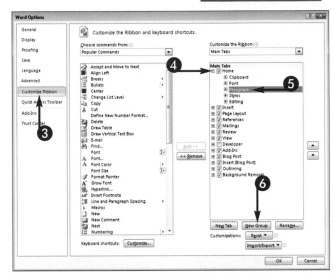

● Word adds a new group to the tab below the group you selected in Step **5** and selects the new group.

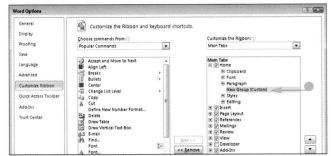

Can I move the location of my group to another tab?

Yes. Complete Steps **1** to **3**. Then follow these steps:

① Click ⊞ beside the tab containing the group you want to move and the tab to which you want to move the group to display all groups on both tabs.

② Click the group you want to move.

③ Click the **Move Up** button (▲) or the **Move Down** button (▼) repeatedly to position the group.

④ Click **OK** to save your changes.

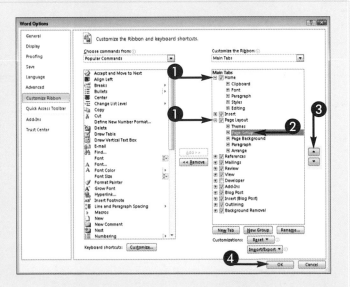

Create Your Own Ribbon Group *(continued)*

When you add a group to a tab, you can assign a name to it that you find meaningful and then you can add whatever buttons you need to the group.

Assign a Name to the Group

① Click **Rename**.

The Rename dialog box appears.

② Type a name for your group.

③ Click **OK**.

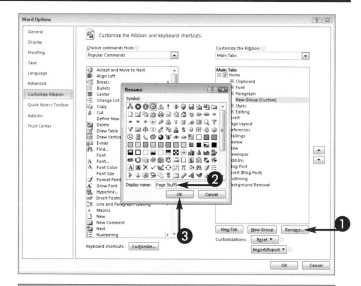

● Word assigns the name to your group.

Add Buttons to Your Group

1 Click the group you created.

2 Click a command.

● If the command you want does not appear in the list, click the list box arrow (▼) and select **All Commands**.

3 Click **Add**.

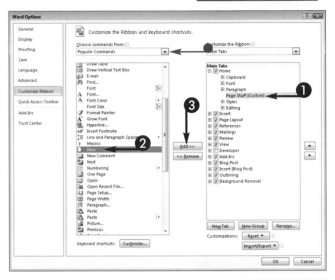

● The command appears below the group you created.

4 Repeat Steps **2** and **3** for each button you want to add to your group.

5 Click **OK** to save your changes.

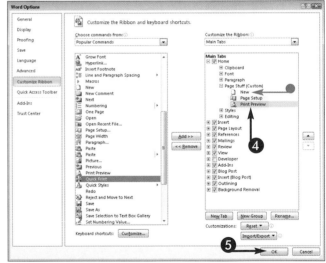

TIPS

Are there any restrictions for the names I assign to groups I create?

No. In fact, you can even use a name that already appears on the Ribbon, such as Font, and you can place that custom group on the Home tab, where the predefined group already exists, or on another tab.

How do I assign keyboard shortcuts to the buttons I add to my group?

You do not need to assign keyboard shortcuts; Word assigns them for you, based on the keys already assigned to commands appearing on the tab where you placed your group. Be aware that you can place the same button on two different tabs, and if you do, Word assigns different keyboard shortcuts to that button on each tab. You cannot change the key Word assigns to buttons in your group, but you can change the key assigned to a command that appears on the default Ribbon; see the section "Add Keyboard Shortcuts" later in this chapter.

Create Your Own Ribbon Tab

You can create your own tab on the Ribbon to store all of the buttons you use most frequently. Then you can leave the Ribbon positioned on your tab, saving you the time of locating the buttons you need on the various Ribbon tabs.

Create Your Own Ribbon Tab

Make a Tab

① Click the **File** tab.

The Backstage view appears.

② Click **Options**.

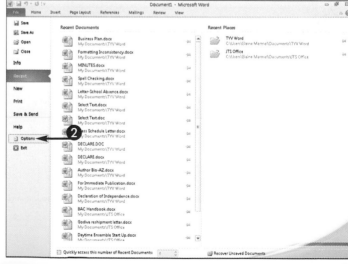

The Word Options dialog box appears.

③ Click **Customize Ribbon**.

④ Click the tab you want to appear to the left of the new tab.

⑤ Click **New Tab**.

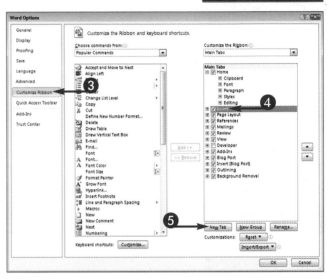

● Word creates a new tab below the tab you selected in Step **4**, along with a new group on that tab.

TIPS

Can I reposition a tab?

Yes. You reposition tabs the same way you reposition groups. Complete Steps **1** to **3** to open the Word Options dialog box to the Customize Ribbon pane. In the list on the right, click the tab and then click ⬆ or ⬇; these buttons appear on the right edge of the Word Options dialog box.

What is on the Developer tab and why does no check mark appear beside it?

The Developer tab contains tools used by those who write programs to make Word perform actions automatically. When no check mark appears beside a tab, Word does not display that tab on the Ribbon; in the case of the Developer tab, most users do not need the tools on that tab, so Word does not display it by default.

continued

When you create a custom tab, Word automatically creates one group for you so that you can quickly and easily add buttons to the new tab.

You can add other groups to the tab; see the section "Create Your Own Ribbon Group" earlier in this chapter.

Create Your Own Ribbon Tab *(continued)*

Assign Names

① Click **New Group (Custom)**.

② Click **Rename**.

The Rename dialog box appears.

③ Type a name for your group.

④ Click **OK**.

⑤ Click **New Tab (Custom)**.

⑥ Repeat Steps **2** to **4**.

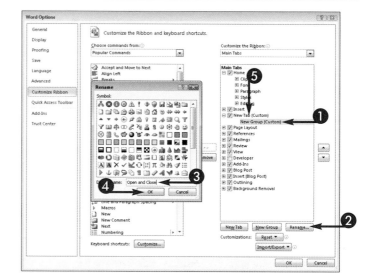

● Word assigns names to your tab and your group.

Add Buttons to Your Group

① Click the group on the tab you created.

② Click a command.

● If the command you want does not appear in the list, click the list box arrow (▼) and select **All Commands**.

③ Click **Add**.

● The command appears below the group you created.

④ Repeat Steps **2** and **3** for each button you want to add to the group.

⑤ Click **OK**.

● The new tab appears on the Ribbon, along with the group containing the buttons you added.

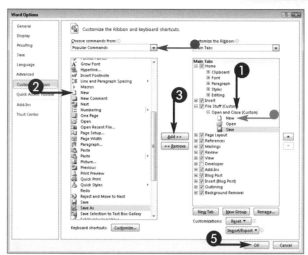

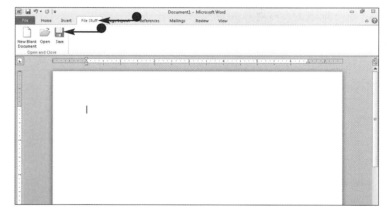

TIP

What can I do if I decide I do not want a custom tab on the Ribbon?

You can hide the tab, which makes it invisible without deleting it.

① Complete Steps **1** to **3** in the subsection "Make a Tab."

② Click the check box beside the tab you want to hide (☑ changes to ☐).

③ Click **OK**.

Word redisplays the Ribbon without your custom tab.

Work with the Quick Access Toolbar

You can customize the Quick Access Toolbar (QAT) in Word 2010 by changing both its appearance and its content.

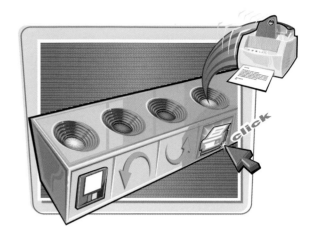

Work with the Quick Access Toolbar

Change Placement

① Click the **Customize Quick Access Toolbar** button (▾).

Word displays a menu of choices.

② Click **Show Below the Ribbon**.

● The Quick Access Toolbar (QAT) appears below the Ribbon instead of above it.

You can repeat these steps to move the QAT back above the Ribbon.

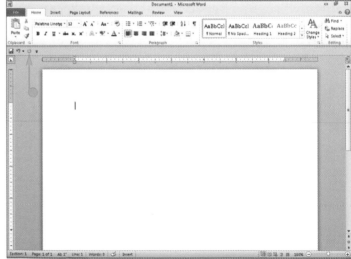

Add Buttons to the QAT

① Click 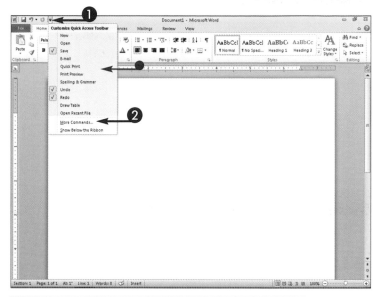.

Word displays a menu of choices.

● You can click any command on the menu to add it to the QAT.

② Click **More Commands**.

The Word Options dialog box appears, showing the Quick Access Toolbar customization options.

● You can add any of these commands to the QAT.

● If the command you want to add does not appear in the list, click the list box arrow (▾) and select **All Commands**.

● Commands already on the QAT appear here.

● You can use this list to customize the QAT for all documents or just the current document.

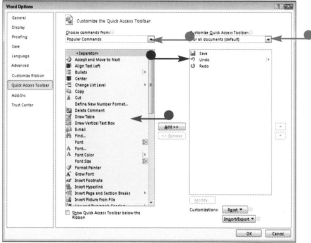

TIP

Is there an easy way to get rid of changes I made to the Toolbar?

Yes. You can reset it by following these steps:

① Perform Steps **1** and **2** above.

② In the Word Options dialog box, click **Reset** and select **Reset only Quick Access Toolbar**.

The Reset Customizations dialog box appears, asking if you are sure of your action.

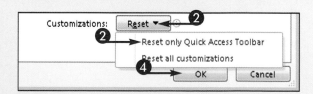

③ Click **Yes** and Word resets the QAT.

④ Click **OK**.

You can add commands to the Quick Access Toolbar and reorganize the order in which commands appear on the QAT.

Work with the Quick Access Toolbar *(continued)*

③ Click the list box arrow (▼) to display the various categories of commands.

You can select **All Commands** to view all commands in alphabetical order regardless of category.

④ Click a category of commands.

This example uses the Commands Not in the Ribbon category.

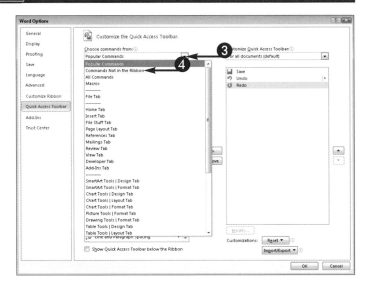

⑤ Click the command you want to add to the Toolbar.

⑥ Click **Add**.

● Word moves the command from the list on the left to the list on the right.

⑦ Repeat Steps **3** to **6** for each command you want to add to the Quick Access Toolbar.

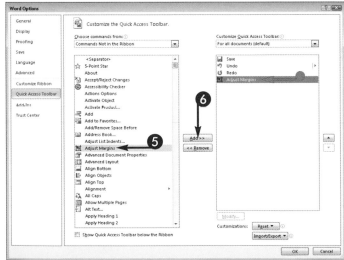

Reorder QAT Buttons

1 While viewing QAT customization options in the Word Options dialog box, click a command in the right-hand column.

2 Click the **Move Up** button (⬜) or the **Move Down** button (⬜) to change a command's placement on the Quick Access Toolbar.

3 Click **OK**.

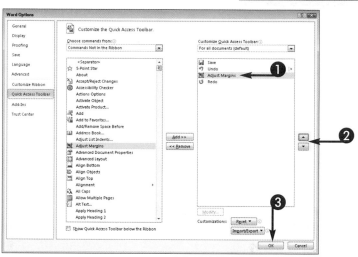

● The updated Quick Access Toolbar appears.

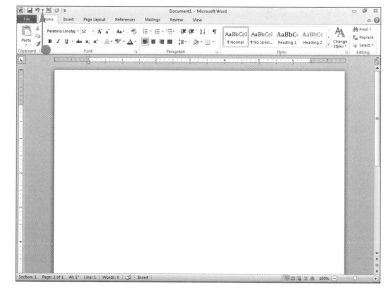

TIP

How do I add a button from the Ribbon to the Quick Access Toolbar?
To add buttons from the Ribbon to the Quick Access Toolbar follow these steps:

1 Right-click the button.

2 Click **Add to Quick Access Toolbar**.

Word adds the button to the QAT.

Add Keyboard Shortcuts

You can add keyboard shortcuts for commands you use frequently. Using a keyboard shortcut can be faster and more efficient than clicking a button on the Ribbon or the QAT.

The appearance of the command as a button on the Ribbon is not relevant; you can create keyboard shortcuts for any command.

Add Keyboard Shortcuts

1 Click the **File** tab.

The Backstage view appears.

2 Click **Options**.

The Word Options dialog box appears.

3 Click **Customize Ribbon**.

4 Click **Customize**.

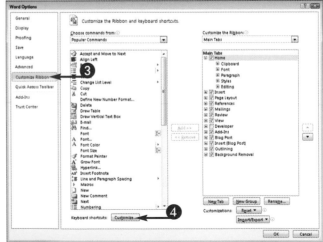

The Customize Keyboard dialog box appears.

● Categories of commands appear here.

● Commands within a category appear here.

5 Click the category containing the command to which you want to assign a keyboard shortcut.

6 Click the command.

● Any existing shortcut keys for the selected command appear here.

7 Click here and press a keyboard combination.

● The keys you press appear here.

● The command to which the shortcut is currently assigned appears here.

8 Click **Assign**.

9 Click **Close**.

10 Click **OK**.

Word saves the shortcut.

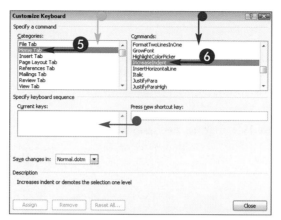

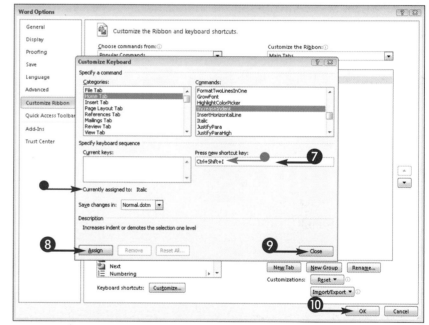

How can I test my shortcut to make sure it works?

You can press the keys you assigned. You also can position the mouse pointer over the tool on the Ribbon; assigned keyboard shortcuts appear in the ToolTip.

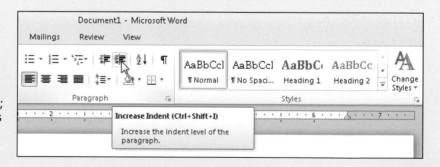

Create a Macro

You can create a macro to save time. A macro combines a series of actions into a single command. For example, you can store repetitive text that you type frequently in a macro so that you can insert it quickly and easily.

Most people find it easiest to create a macro by recording the keystrokes that used to take the action they want to store in the macro.

Create a Macro

① Click the **View** tab.

② Click the arrow (▼) under **Macros**.

③ Click **Record Macro**.

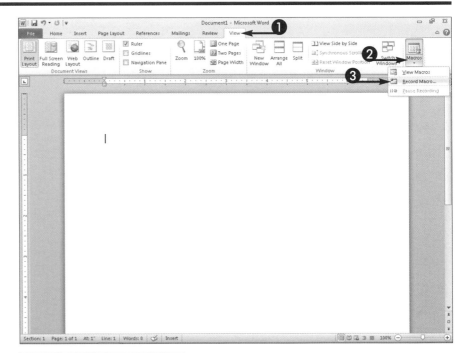

The Record Macro dialog box appears.

④ Type a name for the macro.

Note: Macro names must begin with a letter and contain no spaces.

⑤ Type a description for the macro here.

⑥ Click **OK**.

● Stop Recording and Pause Recording buttons appear when you click **Macros**.

The mouse pointer changes to 🔲.

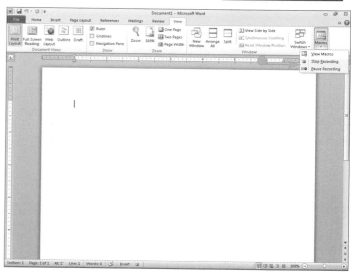

7 Perform the actions you want included in the macro.

Note: Macros can include typing, formatting, and commands. You cannot use the mouse to position the insertion point.

8 When you have taken all the actions you want to include in the macro, click 🔽 under **Macros**.

9 Click **Stop Recording**.

Word saves the macro.

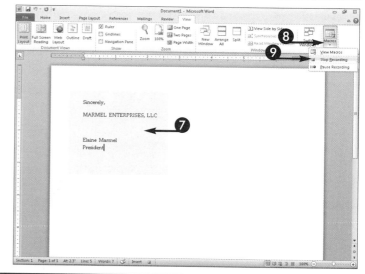

 TIPS

In the Record Macro dialog box, what do the Button and Keyboard buttons do?

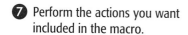

They enable you to assign a macro to a button on the QAT or to a keyboard shortcut at the same time that you create the macro. You can always assign a macro to a QAT button or a keyboard shortcut after you create it. See the section "Run a Macro" later in this chapter.

Do I need to re-create my macros from Word 2003 or Word 2007?

No. If you upgrade from Word 2003 or Word 2007, Word 2010 converts the Normal template you used in those versions. The converted Normal template contains all your macros, and they should appear in the Macros dialog box and work in Word 2010.

You can save time by running a macro you created because Word performs whatever actions you stored in the macro. The method you choose to run a macro depends primarily on how often you need to run it. If you use the macro only occasionally, you can run it from the Macros window. If you use it often, you can assign a macro to a keyboard shortcut or a Quick Access Toolbar button.

To record a macro, see the section "Create a Macro" earlier in this chapter.

Run a Macro

Use the Macros Dialog Box

1 Position the insertion point in your document where you want the results of the macro to appear.

2 Click the **View** tab.

3 Click **Macros**.

The Macros dialog box appears.

● Available macros appear here.

4 Click the macro you want to run.

● The macro's description appears here.

5 Click **Run**.

Word performs the actions stored in the macro.

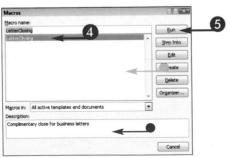

Assign and Use a QAT Button

1 Click the **File** tab.

The Backstage view appears.

2 Click **Options**.

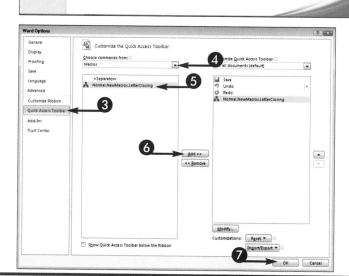

The Word Options dialog box appears.

3 Click **Quick Access Toolbar**.

4 Click ▾ and select **Macros**.

5 Click the macro to add to the QAT.

6 Click **Add**.

7 Click **OK**.

8 Click the **QAT** button to perform the actions stored in the macro.

TIPS

How do I assign a keyboard shortcut to a macro?

You use the same method you use to assign a keyboard shortcut to any command, as described in the section "Add Keyboard Shortcuts" earlier in this chapter. Complete Steps **1** to **4** as described. In Step **5**, scroll to the bottom of the list and select Macros. In Step **6**, select the macro. Then complete Steps **7** to **10**.

Can I create a Screen Tip for my QAT button that contains a name I recognize when I point the mouse at the QAT button?

Yes, you can rename the QAT button. Complete Steps **1** to **6** in the section "Assign a QAT Button." Then, in the list on the right, click the macro, and below the list, click **Modify**. In the Modify Button dialog box that appears, you can select a button image to assign — this image appears on the QAT — and in the Display Name text box below the button symbols, type the new name for your macro.

Work with Mass Mailing Tools

Why do the work yourself? You can use Word's mass mailing tools to create and mail form letters.

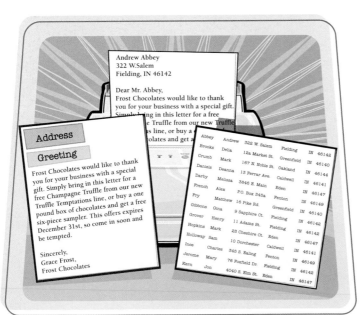

Create Letters to Mass Mail

Using a form letter and a mailing list, you can quickly and easily create a mass mailing that merges the addresses from the mailing list into the form letter.

Typically, the only information that changes in the form letter is the addressee information. You can create the mailing list as you create the mass mailing, or you can use a mailing list that exists in another Word document, an Excel file, or your Outlook Contact List. This example uses an Excel file.

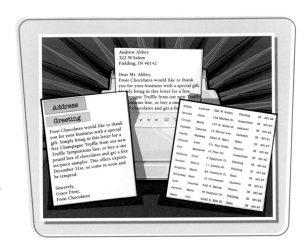

Create Letters to Mass Mail

Set Up for a Mail Merge

① Open the Word document that you want to use as the form letter.

Note: *The letter should not contain any information that will change from letter to letter, such as the inside address.*

② Click the **Mailings** tab.

③ Click **Start Mail Merge**.

④ Click **Letters**.

Nothing visible happens on-screen, but Word sets up for a mail merge.

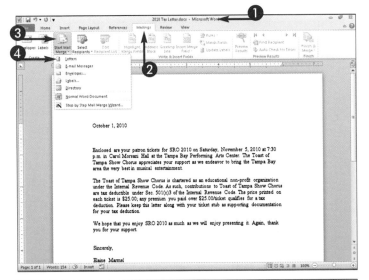

Identify Recipients

① Click **Select Recipients**.

② Click to identify the type of recipient list you plan to use.

This example uses an existing list in an Excel file.

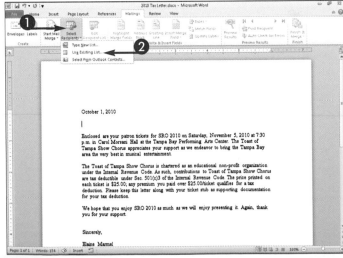

The Select Data Source dialog box appears.

3 Click here to navigate to the folder containing the mailing list file.

4 Click the file containing the mailing list.

5 Click **Open**.

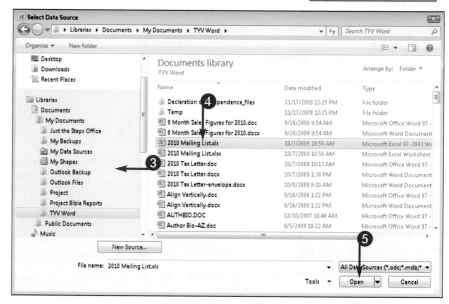

Word links with Excel and the Select Table dialog box appears.

Note: _If the Excel notebook contains multiple sheets, you can select a specific sheet in the Select Table dialog box._

6 If necessary, select a sheet.

7 Click **OK**.

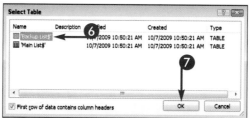

How do I create a mailing list?

To create a mailing list, follow these steps:

1 In Step **2** in "Identify Recipients," click **Type New List**.

2 In the New Address List dialog box, type recipient information for each addressee.

3 Click **OK**.

4 Save the file in the Save Address List dialog box that appears.

5 Skip to the subsection "Create the Address Block" to finish the steps.

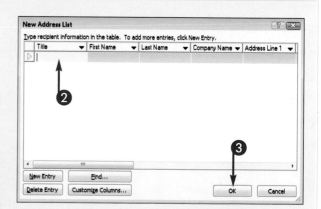

You can select specific recipients from the mailing list to receive the form letter, and you use merge fields to specify the place in your document where the recipient's address and greeting should appear.

8 Click **Edit Recipient List**.

The Mail Merge Recipients window appears.

● A check box (☑) appears beside each person's name, identifying the recipients of the form letter.

9 Click beside any addressee for whom you do not want to prepare a form letter (☑ changes to ☐).

10 Click **OK**.

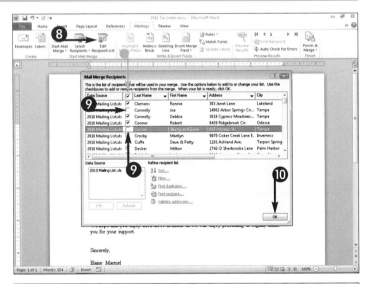

Create the Address Block

1 Click the location where you want the inside address to appear in the form letter.

2 Click **Address Block**.

The Insert Address Block dialog box appears.

3 Click a format for each recipient's name.

● You can preview the format here.

4 Click **OK**.

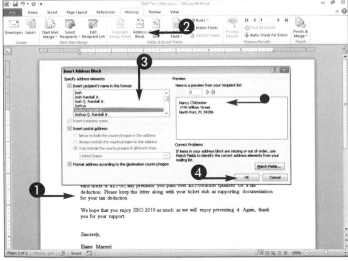

- The <<Address Block>> merge field appears in the letter.

Create a Greeting

1 Click at the location where you want the greeting to appear.

2 Click **Greeting Line**.

The Insert Greeting Line dialog box appears.

3 Click these list box arrows (▼) to select the greeting format.

- A preview of the greeting appears here.

4 Click **OK**.

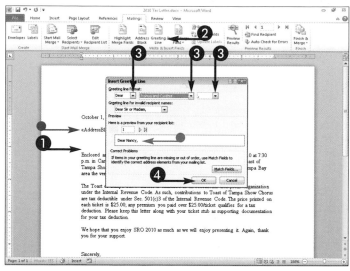

- The <<Greeting Line>> merge field appears in the letter.

Note: When you complete the merge, Word replaces the merge field with greeting information.

- You can click **Preview Results** to preview and merge your results.

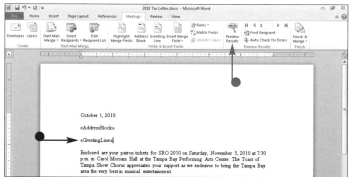

TIP

What should I do if the preview in the Insert Address Block dialog box is blank or incorrect?
Follow these steps:

1 After you complete Step **3** in "Create the Address Block," subsection click **Match Fields**.

The Match Fields dialog box appears.

2 Beside each field you use in your merge, click the list box arrow (▼) and select the corresponding field name in your mailing list file.

3 Click **OK** and continue with Step **4** in "Create the Address Block."

Word matches your fields.

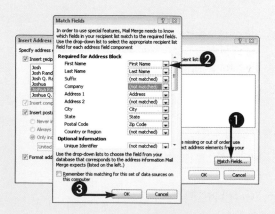

continued

After you finish adding merge fields, you can preview the letters, select specific recipients, and then create individual letters for each person in the mailing list file.

You also can merge the letters directly to your printer by creating an electronic file of letters. And you can send the letters as e-mail messages.

Create Letters to Mass Mail *(continued)*

● Word displays a preview of the merged letter, using the unchanging content of the letter and information from the address file.

● You can click the **Next Record** button (◀) to preview the next letter and the **Previous Record** button (▶) to move back and preview the previous letter.

● You can click **Preview Results** to redisplay merge fields.

⑤ Click **Finish & Merge**.

⑥ Click **Edit Individual Documents**.

The Merge to New Document dialog box appears.

⑦ Select an option to identify the recipients of the letter (◯ changes to ◉).

The **All** option creates a letter for all entries on the mailing list; the **Current record** option creates only one letter for the recipient whose letter you are previewing; and the **From** and **To** option creates letters for recipients you by their numeric position in the address list, not by their names.

⑧ Click **OK**.

● Word merges the form letter information with the mailing list information, placing the results in a new document named Letters1.

● The new document contains individual letters for each mailing list recipient.

⑨ Click the **Customize Quick Access Toolbar** button (▾).

⑩ Click **Quick Print**.

● You can click the **Save** button (◻) on the QAT and assign a new name to save the merged letters.

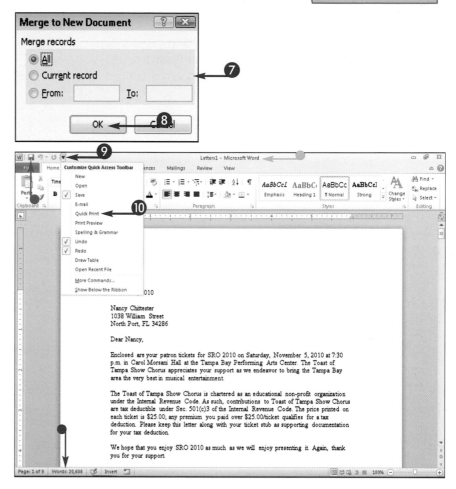

What should I do differently if I want to send letters to Outlook Contacts?

The process is very much the same as described in these steps. In Step **2** of "Identify Recipients," click **Select from Outlook Contacts**. If you have more than one Outlook profile, you are prompted to select a profile. Then the Select Contacts window appears. Select a contact folder and click **OK**. The Mail Merge Recipients window, shown in Step **6** of "Identify Recipients," appears and you can select contacts to receive the letter.

Add Envelopes to Mass Mailing Letters

You can add addressed envelopes for letters you create using the Mail Merge feature in Word.

1 Create letters for the envelopes.

Note: *See the section "Create Letters to Mass Mail" for more on creating letters.*

2 On the Windows taskbar, click the form letter you used to create the merged letters.

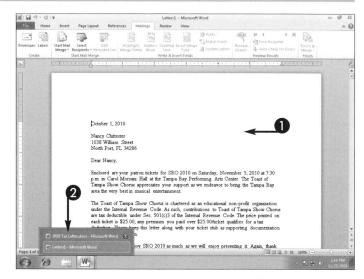

● Word displays the letter you set up to create the mail merge.

Note: *This example shows merge fields; click **Preview Results** to switch between merge fields and final text.*

3 Click **Envelopes**.

The Envelopes and Labels dialog box appears.

4 Click **Add to Document**.

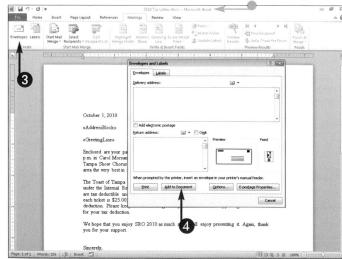

An envelope appears in your document.

● You can type a return address.

5 Click in the lower center of the envelope to locate the address box.

● Dotted lines surround the address box.

6 Click **Address Block**.

The Insert Address Block dialog box appears.

7 Click an address format.

8 Click **OK**.

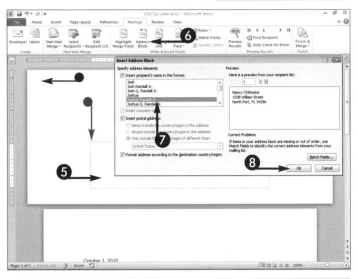

● The <<Address Block>> merge field appears on the envelope.

9 You can follow the steps in "Preview and Merge" in the preceding section "Create Letters to Mass Mail" to preview envelopes, merge address information on envelopes, and print envelopes along with your letters.

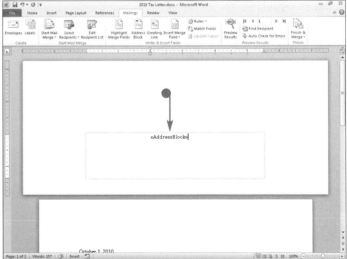

TIP

My printer does not have two trays, so I cannot print two paper sizes at the same time, which the technique in this section requires. Can I still create envelopes for my letters?

Yes. You can create your envelopes in a separate merge document. Start in a blank document and follow the steps in the section "Create Letters to Mass Mail," but in Step **4**, click **Envelopes** instead of **Letters**. The Envelope Options dialog box appears. Select your envelope size and click **OK**. Then complete the rest of the steps in the section "Create Letters to Mass Mail."

Create Labels for a Mass Mailing

In addition to creating personalized form letters for a mass mailing, you can use the merge feature to create mailing labels for mass mailing recipients.

This example uses addresses stored in an Excel file.

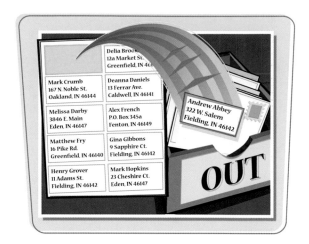

Create Labels for a Mass Mailing

Select a Label Format

1 Start a new blank document.

Note: See Chapter 2 for details starting a new document.

2 Click the **Mailings** tab.

3 Click **Start Mail Merge**.

4 Click **Labels**.

The Label Options dialog box appears.

5 Select a printer option (○ changes to ◉).

6 Click ▾ to select a label vendor.

7 Use the scroll arrows (▲ and ▼) to find and click the label's product number.

● Information about the label dimensions appears here.

8 Click **OK**.

Word sets up the document for the labels you selected.

*Note: If gridlines identifying individual labels do not appear, click the **Layout** tab and then click **View Gridlines**.*

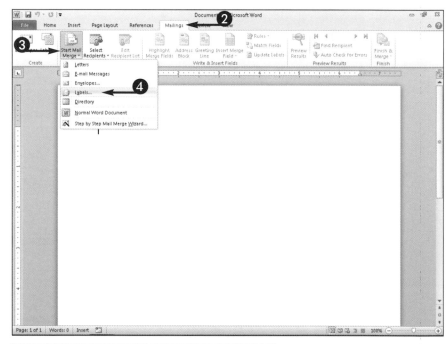

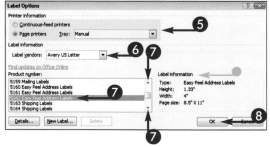

Identify Recipients

① Click **Select Recipients**.

② Click to identify the type of recipient list you plan to use.

This example uses an existing list in an Excel file.

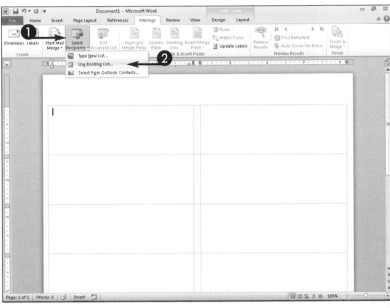

The Select Data Source dialog box appears.

③ Click here to navigate to the folder containing the mailing list file.

④ Click the file containing the mailing list.

⑤ Click **Open**.

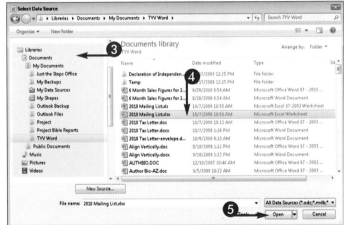

 TIPS

What happens if I click Details in the Label Options dialog box?

A dialog box appears, displaying the margins and dimensions of each label, the number of labels per row, and the number of rows of labels, along with the page size. Although you can change these dimensions, you run the risk of having label information print incorrectly if you do.

What happens if I click New Label in the Label Options dialog box?

A dialog box appears that you can use to create your own custom label. Word bases the appearance of this dialog box on the settings selected in the Label Options dialog box. Type a name for the label and then adjust the margins, height and width, number across or down, vertical or horizontal pitch, and page size as needed.

Create Labels for a Mass Mailing *(continued)*

Using the label options you specify, Word sets up a document of labels to which you attach a file containing recipient information and then add merge information.

You can create an address file as you create labels, or you can use addresses stored in an Excel file or contacts stored in Outlook.

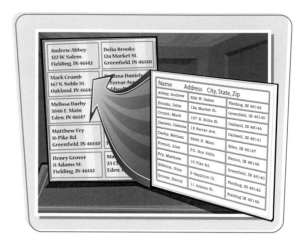

Create Labels for a Mass Mailing *(continued)*

Word links with Excel and the Select Table dialog box appears.

Note: *If the Excel notebook contains multiple sheets, you can select a specific sheet in the Select Table dialog box.*

⑥ If necessary, select a sheet.

⑦ Click **OK**.

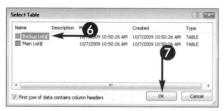

Word inserts a <<Next Record>> field in each label but the first one.

Add Merge Fields

① Click the first label to place the insertion point in it.

② Click **Address Block**.

The Insert Address Block dialog box appears.

③ Click a format for each recipient's name.

● You can preview the format here.

④ Click **OK**.

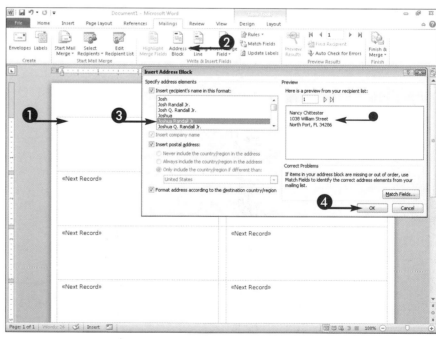

- Word adds the <<Address Block>> merge field to the first label.

Note: *When you merge the information, Word replaces the merge field with information from the mailing address file.*

⑤ Click **Update Labels**.

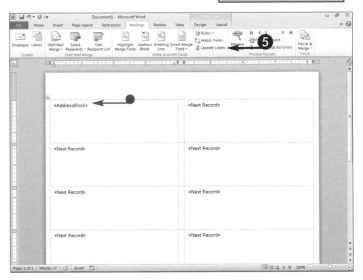

- Word adds the <<Address Block>> merge field to every label.

- You can click **Preview Results** to preview and merge your results.

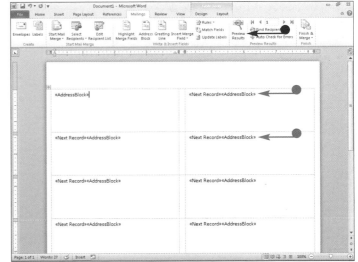

Can I selectively create labels using an existing file?
Yes. Follow these steps:

① Click **Edit Recipient List**.

The Mail Merge Recipients dialog box appears.

② Click beside any addressee for whom you do not want to create a mailing label (☑ changes to ☐).

③ Click **OK**.

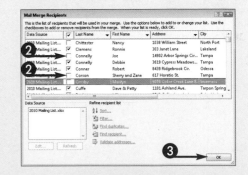

continued

You can preview the labels before you print them. When you complete the merge, you can merge all records in the mailing list file or only those you select.

Word displays a preview of your labels, replacing the merge field with information from the mailing list file.

● You can click ◀ to preview the next label and ▶ to move back and preview the previous label.

6 Click **Preview Results** to redisplay merge fields.

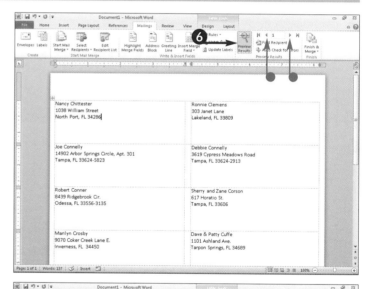

7 Click **Finish & Merge**.

8 Click **Edit Individual Documents**.

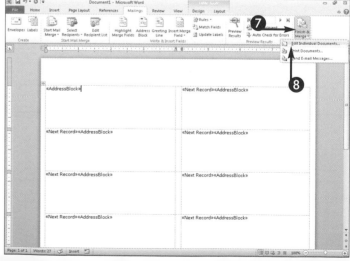

The Merge to New Document dialog box appears.

9 Select an option to identify the recipients of the letter (⊙ changes to ⊙).

The **All** option creates a label for all entries on the mailing list; the **Current record** option creates only one label for the recipient you are previewing; and the **From** option creates labels for recipients you specify.

10 Click **OK**.

● Word creates the labels in a new Word document named Labels1.

The new document contains individual labels for each mailing list recipient.

11 Click ⊟.

12 Click **Quick Print**.

The labels print.

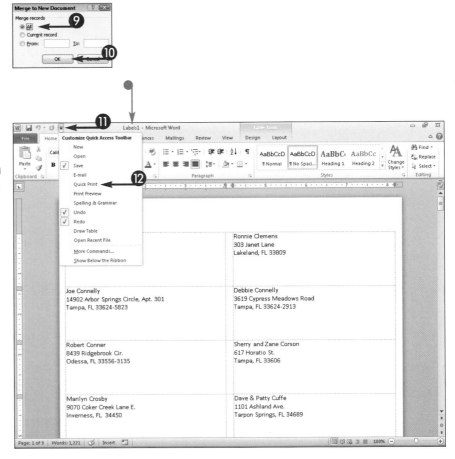

What does the Auto Check for Errors button on the Ribbon do?

When you click this button, Word gives you the opportunity to determine whether you have correctly set up the merge. The Checking and Reporting Errors dialog box appears; select an option (⊙ changes to ⊙) and click **OK**. Depending on the option you choose, Word reports errors as they occur or in a new document.

CHAPTER 13

Using Word to Interact Over the Internet

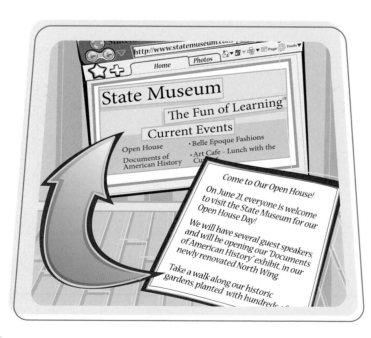

Using Word, you can interact with others over the Internet. You can e-mail a document, create a hyperlink in a document that opens a Web page or another document at your own site, save a document as a Web page, use Word to post to your blog, and more.

E-mail a Document

You can e-mail a Word document while you work in Word; you do not need to open your e-mail program and send the document from there. Word sends the document as an attachment.

Although you do not need to send the document from your e-mail program, your e-mail program must be set up on your computer.

E-mail a Document

1. Open the document you want to send by e-mail.

2. Click the **File** tab.

   The Backstage view appears.

3. Click **Save & Send**.

4. Click **Send Using E-Mail**.

5. Click a method to send the document.

   This example sends the document as an attachment.

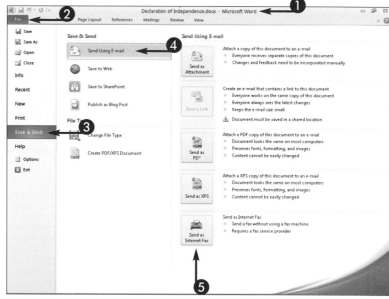

An e-mail message window appears.

● The e-mail attachment appears here; in this example, the attachment is the Word document.

6. Click here to type the e-mail address of the recipient.

● You can also type the e-mail address of someone to whom you want to send a copy of the message.

Note: To send to multiple recipients, separate each e-mail address with a semicolon (;) and a space.

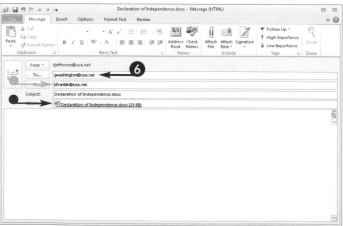

7 Click here to type a subject for the e-mail message.

Note: *Subjects are not required but including one is considerate. Word automatically supplies the document name for the subject; you can replace the document name with anything you want.*

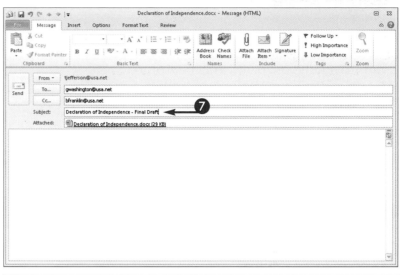

● You can type a message here.

8 Click **Send**.

Word places the message in your e-mail program's Outbox and closes the e-mail message window.

Note: *You must open your e-mail program, and, if your e-mail program does not automatically send and receive periodically, send the message.*

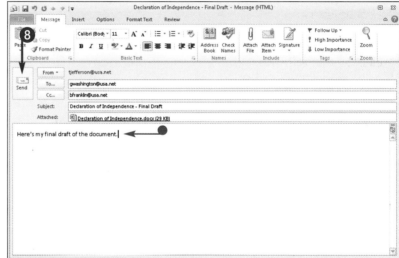

TIPS

What should I do if I change my mind about sending the e-mail message while viewing the e-mail message window?

Click ⊠ in the e-mail message window. A message appears, asking if you want to save the message. Click **No**.

What happens if I choose Send as PDF in Step 5?

Word creates a PDF version of the document and attaches the PDF version to the e-mail message instead of attaching the Word file. The recipient cannot edit the PDF file with Word; to edit the document, the recipient would need special software.

Create a Hyperlink

Using a hyperlink, you can connect a word, phrase, or graphic image in a Word document to another document on your computer or in your company's network, or to a Web page on the Internet.

Create a Hyperlink

1 Select the text or graphic you want to use to create a hyperlink.

2 Click the **Insert** tab.

3 Click **Hyperlink**.

You can right-click the selection and click **Hyperlink** instead of performing Steps **2** and **3**.

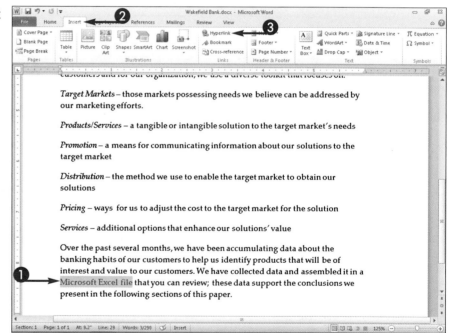

The Insert Hyperlink dialog box appears.

4 Click **Existing File or Web Page**.

● Files in the current folder appear here.

5 Click here and navigate to the folder containing the document to which you want to link.

6 Click the file to select it.

7 Click **ScreenTip**.

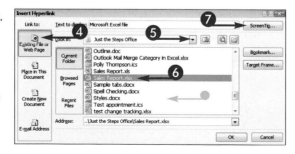

The Set Hyperlink ScreenTip dialog box appears.

8 Type text that should appear when a user positions the mouse pointer over the hyperlink.

9 Click **OK**.

The Insert Hyperlink dialog box reappears.

10 Click **OK**.

● Word creates a hyperlink shown as blue, underlined text in your document.

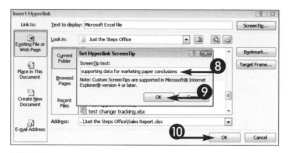

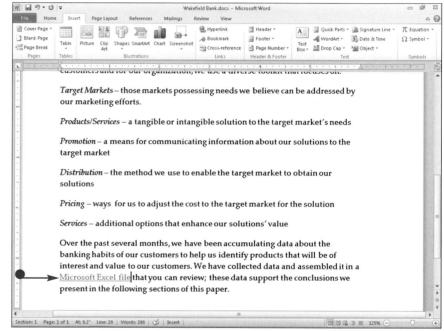

If I do not create a ScreenTip for the hyperlink, what appears when I position the mouse pointer over the hyperlink?

Word displays the location on your computer's hard drive or in your network, or if you linked to a Web page, Word displays the Web address.

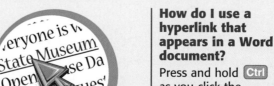

How do I use a hyperlink that appears in a Word document?

Press and hold Ctrl as you click the hyperlink. The linked document or Web page will appear.

Save a Document as a Web Page

You can save any Word document as a Web page that you can then upload to the Internet.

① Open the document you want to save as a Web page.

② Click the **File** tab.

The Backstage view appears.

③ Click **Save As**.

The Save As dialog box appears.

● The location where Word will save the file appears here.

● You can click here to navigate to a different location.

④ Click here.

⑤ Select **Web Page**.

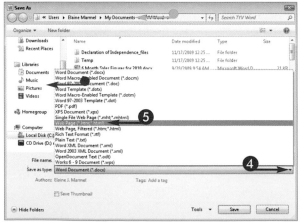

6 Type a name for the Web page here.

7 Click **Change Title**.

The Enter Text dialog box appears; use this dialog box to assign a title to the Web page.

8 Type the title that you want to appear at the top of the screen when the page is displayed in a Web browser.

9 Click **OK**.

The Save As dialog box reappears.

10 Click **Save**.

● Word saves the document as a Web page and displays the document in Web Layout view, showing the document as it will appear in a Web browser.

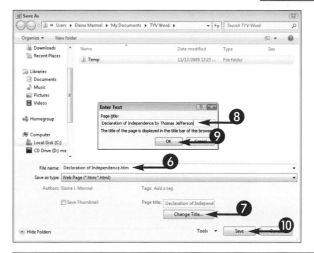

After I close the Web page, what should I do if I want to reopen it?

Follow these steps:

1 Click the **File** tab, and from the Backstage view, click **Open**.

2 Click here and navigate to the folder where you saved the Web page.

3 Click the Web page document.

4 Click **Open**.

Word reopens the Web page.

Post to Your Blog

If you already have a blog space, you can use Word to post entries to your blog. If you do not have a space, you can sign up using any of several free blog service providers, or you can use other providers that charge a fee.

Post to Your Blog

① Click the **File** tab.

The Backstage view appears.

② Click **Save & Send**.

③ Click **Publish as Blog Post**.

④ Click **Publish to Blog**.

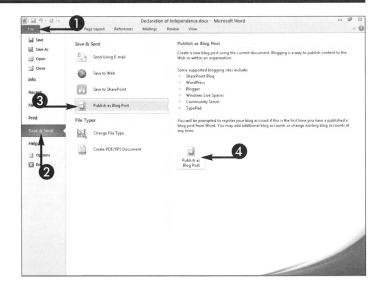

Word opens a new document designed to post blog entries.

● You can use these buttons to manage blog entries. For example, you can click Manage Accounts to set up blog accounts.

● You can use these tools to format text as you type.

⑤ Click the **Insert** tab.

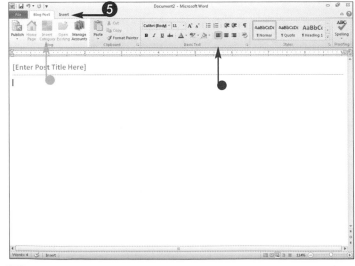

● Use these buttons to incorporate tables, pictures, clip art, shapes, graphics, screenshots, WordArt, symbols, and hyperlinks in a blog entry.

6 Click here and type a title for your blog entry.

7 Click here and type your entry.

8 Click the **Blog Post** tab.

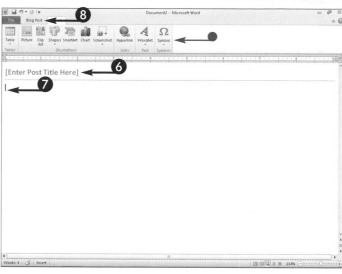

Note: *You can save your blog entry on your hard drive the same way you save any document.*

9 Click **Publish**.

Word connects to the Internet and posts your entry.

● A message like this one appears, identifying when the entry was posted.

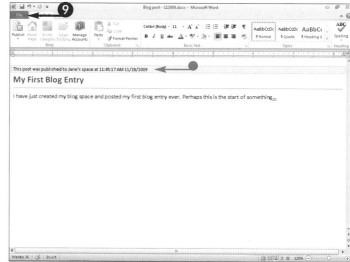

 TIPS

If I already have a blog account, how do I make Word use it?

Word prompts you to register your blog account after you complete Step **4** for the first time. Click **Register Now**. The Blog Registration wizard appears; in the New Blog Account dialog box that appears, select your blog provider and click **Next**. In the New Account dialog box that appears, provide the identification information requested; the information varies from provider to provider. Click **OK**, and Word registers your blog account. Click **Manage Accounts** to set up additional blog accounts.

Can I post entries as drafts to review them before making them visible to the public?

Yes. Click ▼ on the bottom of the **Publish** button and click **Publish as Draft**. When you are ready to let the public review your entry, open it in Word and click **Publish**.

Explore New Ways to Work

Office 2010 introduces new ways to collaborate while creating Office documents. In addition to using desktop editions of Office products, you can collaborate over the Internet using Office Web Apps.

Introducing Web Apps

The Office Web Apps give you a familiar Microsoft Office experience when you are away from your Microsoft Office applications on your computer. The Office Web Apps are browser based and enable you to perform lightweight editing of Word 2010, Excel 2010, PowerPoint 2010, and OneNote 2010 files. The Office Web Apps also make sharing documents easier, because friends and colleagues do not need to worry about the version of Office they use.

Coauthor a Word Document

Using the Word Web App, multiple authors can edit a Word document simultaneously regardless of geographic location. An icon displaying each person's name appears in the section that person is editing. You can block other authors from editing the sections of the document on which you are working. Saving makes changes available and visible; when you save, changes you made become available to others, and you see changes made and saved by others. Other authors see changes you save when they save.

Communicate as You Work

As you work, you can communicate with others working on the document. In Backstage view, while viewing properties for a document, you can hover the mouse pointer over an author's name. Buttons appear that enable you to e-mail or instant message the author. While working online, the Presence button indicates whether a coauthor is online and you can initiate communication without leaving Word.

Work from Anywhere

Because of the browser-based Office Web Apps, you can work from any location containing a computer connected to the Internet. The computer can be a PC or a Mac, using Windows or the Macintosh operating system. And, using Office Mobile, you can create, edit, and save Microsoft Office documents from your Smartphone. Office Mobile enables you to use your Smartphone to view charts, graphs, and images as you see them on your main computer. You also can copy and paste across programs and send documents via e-mail or save them directly back to SharePoint 2010 or Windows Live.

Corporate Users: Share Your Desktop

If your organization uses Office Communicator 2007 R2 and Office Communications Server 2007 R2, you can use Backstage view to start a sharing session that shares your computer's desktop, not Word. Those connected to your shared session can watch you make changes to the document. You also can send documents via instant messaging.

Requirements for Corporate Users

To coauthor a document, corporate users need SharePoint 2010. To communicate with others while collaborating, corporate users need Office Communicator 2007 R2 and Office Communications Server 2007 R2.

Requirements for Individuals

Individuals can also use Office Web Apps to collaborate and communicate even though they have no access to SharePoint 2010. Individuals can use Office Web Apps instead by signing up for a Windows Live ID and logging in to Windows Live services offerings.

Index

Index

Index

Index

Index

Index